AF479067

# LAURIE LEWIS
# PORTRAITS

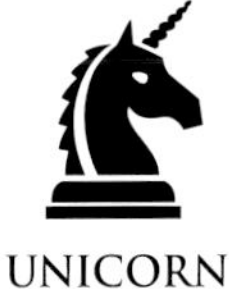

UNICORN

Published in 2018 by
Unicorn, an imprint of Unicorn Publishing Group LLP
101 Wardour Street
London
W1F 0UG
www.unicornpublishing.org

Text & Images © Laurie Lewis

All rights reserved. No part of the contents of this book may be reproduced, stored in or introduced into a retrieval system, or transmitted, in any form or by any means (electronic, mechanical, photocopying, recording or otherwise), without the prior written permission of the copyright holder and the above publisherof this book.

Every effort has been made to trace copyright holders and to obtain their permission for the use of copyrighted material. The publisher apologises for any errors or omissions and would be grateful to be notified of any corrections that should be incorporated in future reprints or editions of this book.

ISBN 978-1-911604-08-2

10 9 8 7 6 5 4 3 2 1

Designed by Jonathan Christie
Printed in China on behalf of Latitude Press

# CONTENTS

# FOREWORD

**Zelda Cheatle**

A strong portrait cannot be summed up through style or aesthetic judgement, nor by light, shadow or even emotion. A great portrait can only be defined by something deeper. The success of these portraits by Laurie Lewis is a complexity of language and his use of it. I would compare him to the great 19th-century portrait photographer Félix Nadar, who claimed 'the portrait I do best is of the person I know best'.

Laurie often has to make portraits within minutes of meeting his subjects, commissioned by the good and the great to make images for publication in papers and magazines internationally. Despite being granted only minutes to shoot, Laurie makes a connection … during an extraordinary session in Oxford with Isaiah Berlin, restricted to ten minutes, he was still in conversation five hours later. I believe a good portrait is the result of a collaboration between the photographer and the subject. If an emotional bridge is crossed, as is clearly evident in much of Laurie's work, it enables the viewer, in turn, to develop a relationship with the subject. There is a shared moment of exchange.

In some situations, portraits can become more about the photographer, the subject becoming secondary. Diane Arbus or Martin Parr are two examples of how the subject is used for the photographer's narrative and language; it fulfils an objective quite separate to the subject. The portrait then becomes an act of glorious fiction and although the subject dominates the scene, reality and real emotion become less important.

Laurie Lewis connects with his sitters, so their world, their reality, is reflected back to the viewer through the image.

*"The poetry creeps through the mistakes."*

—JEAN COCTEAU

# PORTRAITS

# DAVID BOWIE

The strongest memory from the 'Serious Moonlight Tour' was of squashed girls being lifted by willing hands over the barrier, through the scaffolding into a makeshift casualty ward while Bowie, immaculately dressed, performed above their heads. A curious sight to see the White Duke on an improvised stage in a field outside Milton Keynes ... a circus tent might have been more appropriate, most certainly for Lindsay Kemp, a mentor for Bowie and Kate Bush, as was Marcel Marceau for Michael Jackson.

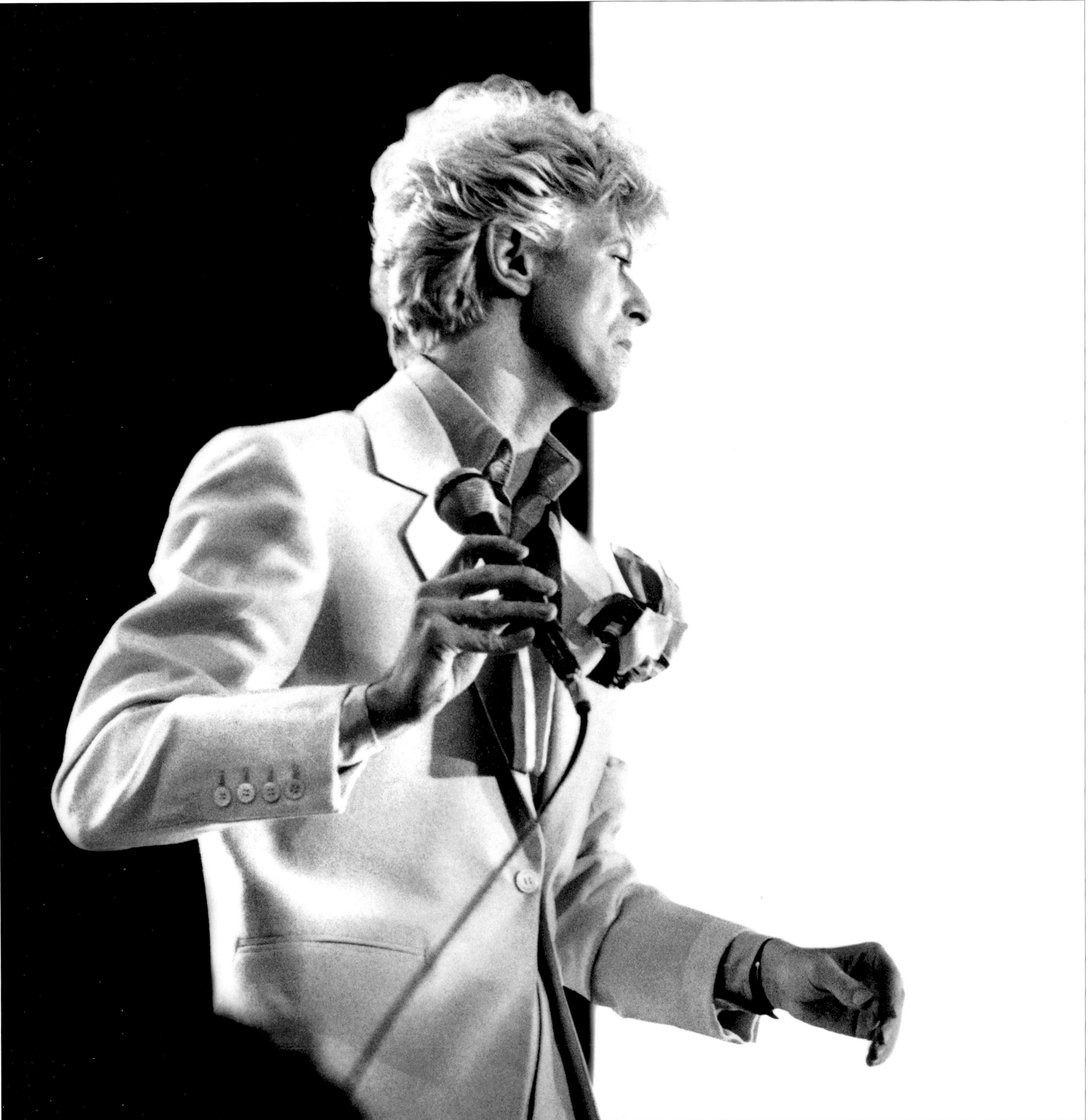

# NATALIA MAKAROVA

In a Park Lane apartment she sits down, putting both legs up on another chair, declaring 'I sew these decorations myself.' She is promoting a BBC series *Ballerina*, as author and presenter, following fellow defectors Nureyev and Baryshnikov ... 'I am a selector, not a defector' ... As her dress falls revealing her upper thigh, I reach over and cover her leg; unconcerned about losing her dignity she smacks my hand ... I leave it and retouch the print later. Next time we meet the occasion is for a 'How We Met' article with Brian Masters ... no mention of the changing hemline.

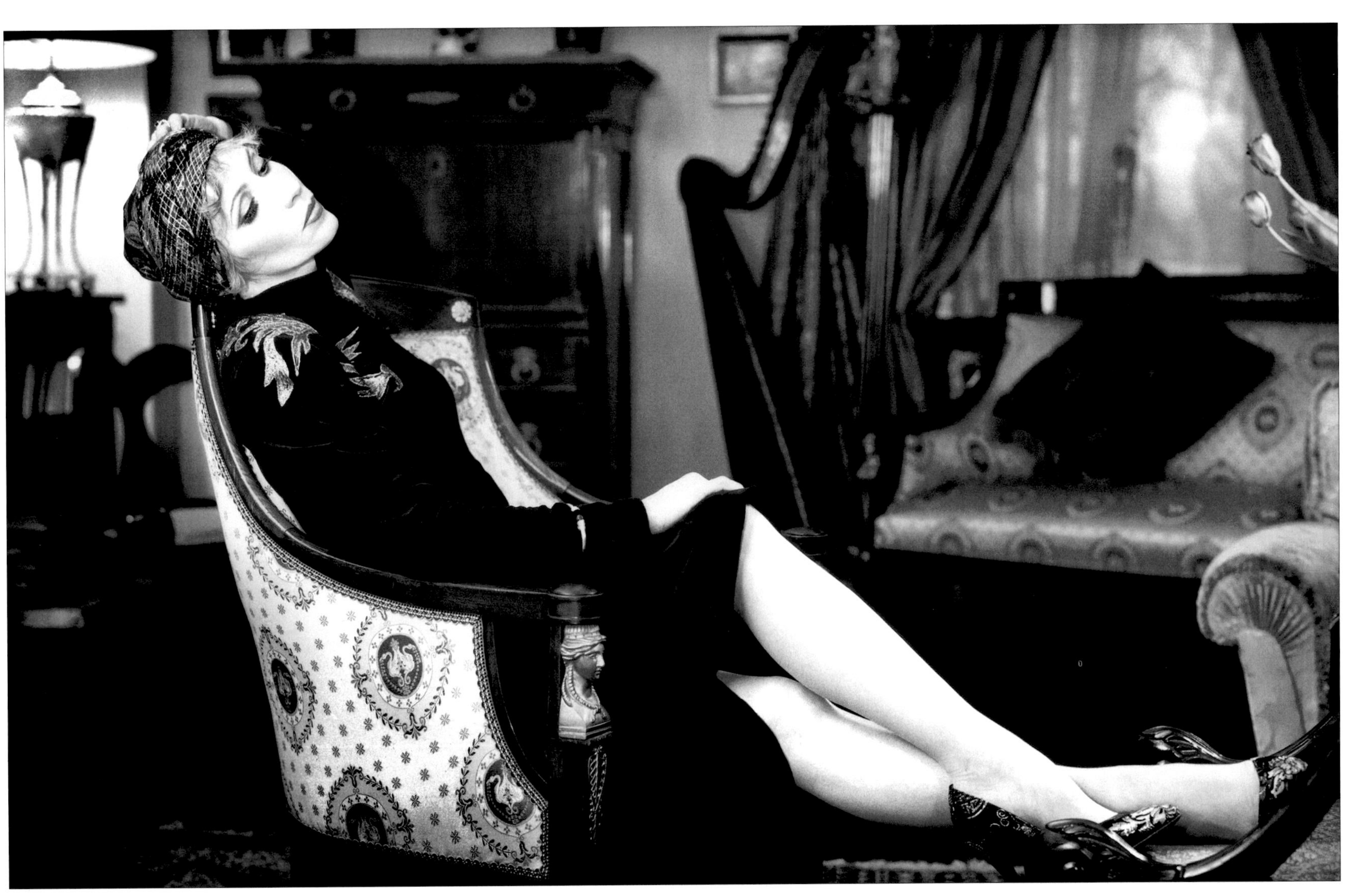

# YURI GRIGOROVICH

The Albert Hall isn't ideal for traditional ballet. There is no proscenium, there are no wings nor facilities for shifting scenery but, despite this, the Bolshoi was booked for a six-week run at the venue. Grigorovich had been the Artistic Director for twenty-seven years and was now being persuaded to abridge the company repertoire into 'suites' by a rock'n'roll promoter. The idea was to stage selections from *Swan Lake*, *Les Sylphides*, *Giselle* and others, aiming at a different audience. The promoter hired an orchestra, improvised a proscenium and extended the stage to work in the round. The enterprise was a commercial success but the purists stayed away.

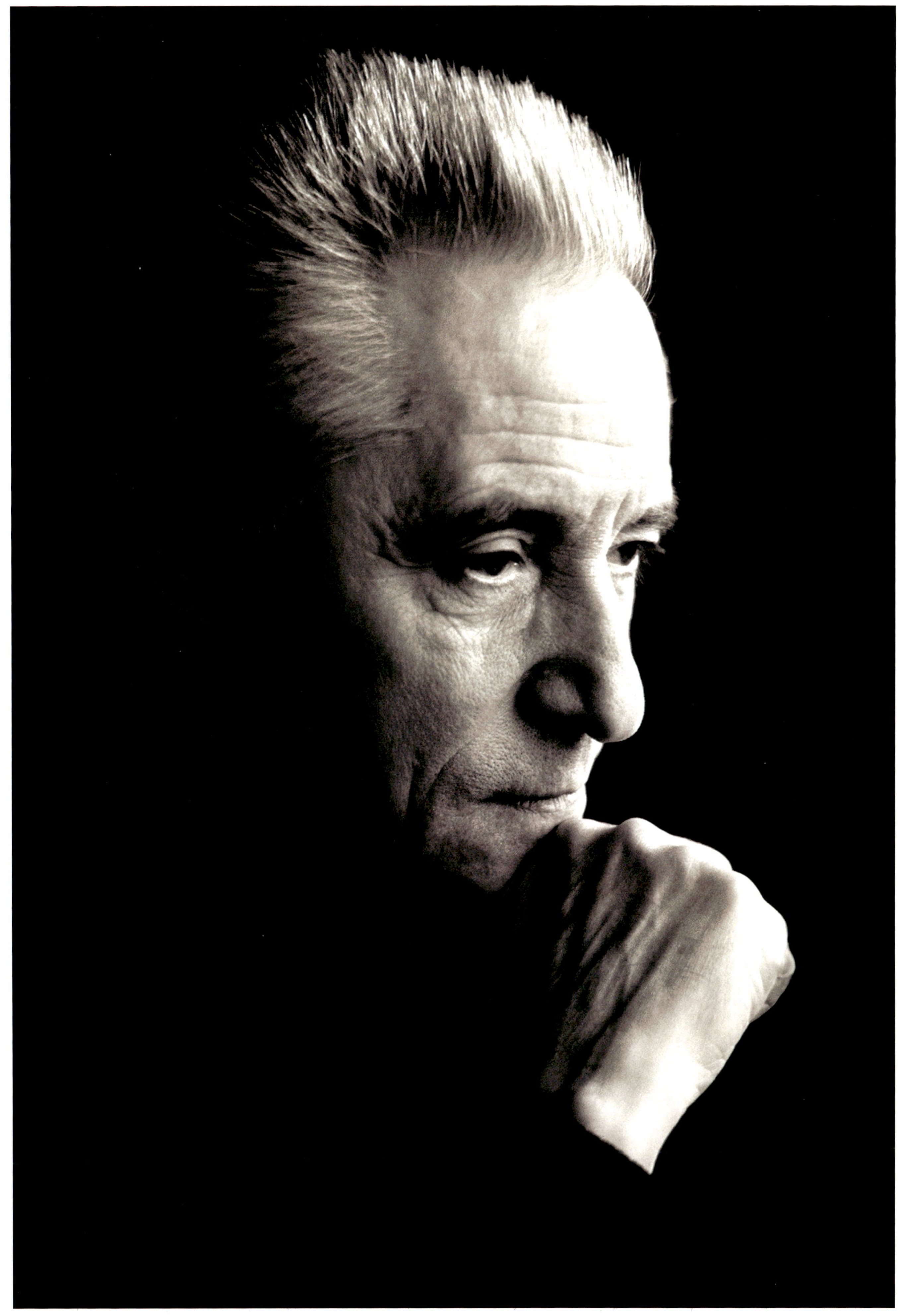

## CORNELIA PARKER

The artist cites *Tom & Jerry* and *The Bible* as inspiration for her installation *Thirty Pieces of Silver* ... 'These objects will have their identities transformed by being burned, shot, squashed, stretched, exploded or simply dropped off a cliff' ... The portrait was made in her studio before the items were to meet their symbolic doom, steamrollered flat and suspended at The Tate Gallery in rows of thirty silver cartoon circles.

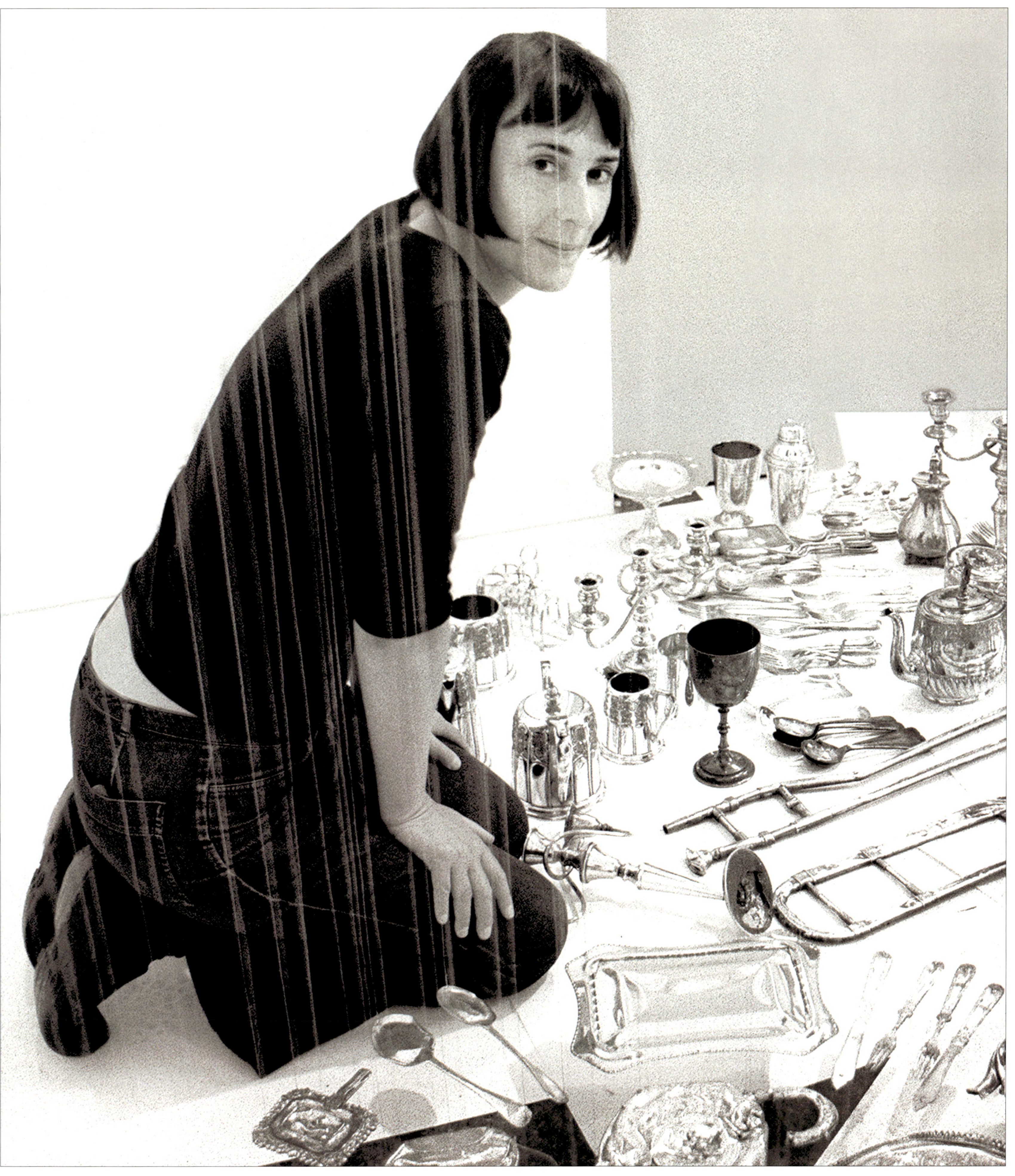

# ANDRE & TOMAS

Andrezej Piechota and Tomasz Wlezien were appearing in Cirque du Soleil's Saltimbanco at the Royal Albert Hall and the press was invited to the dress rehearsal. The telephoto lens used was a little too long for action photography but the tight crop made the shot. The production was designed around the antics of Commedia dell'arte but there was no trickery about these athletes, just strength and grace performed with an air of self-deprecating panache.

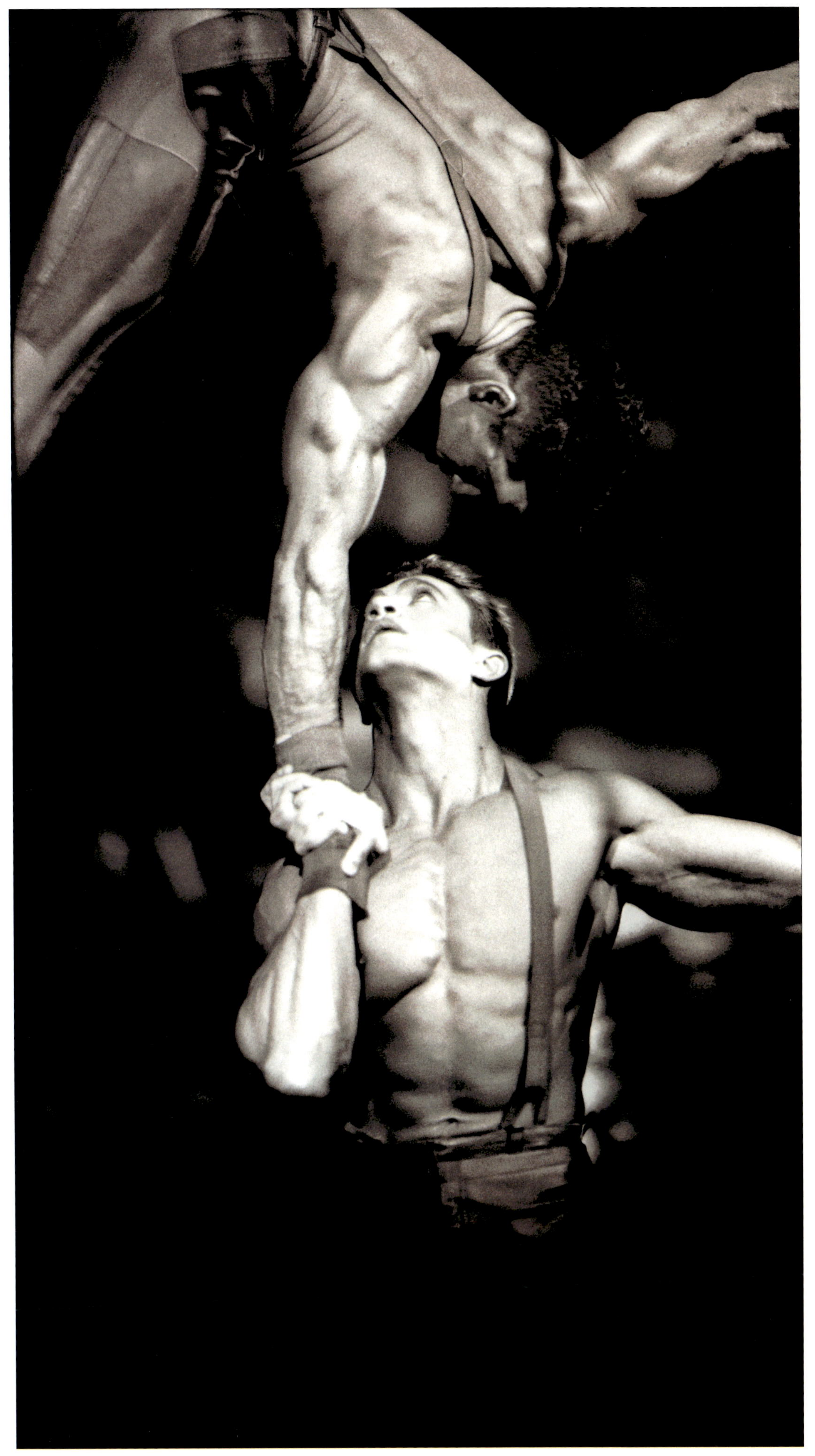

# BRENDA BLETHYN

All day shoots in a studio with an assistant, make-up and a hairdresser are common enough in advertising but rare in editorial, and this shoot was for a magazine not known for its profligacy. The actress arrived on time, accompanied by a young dresser and with enough clothes for a year abroad. We laughed a lot working through most of the outfits, as long as the daylight lasted. Thespians are used to taking direction which makes for a more productive session, which this was ... Ms Blethyn is a true professional.

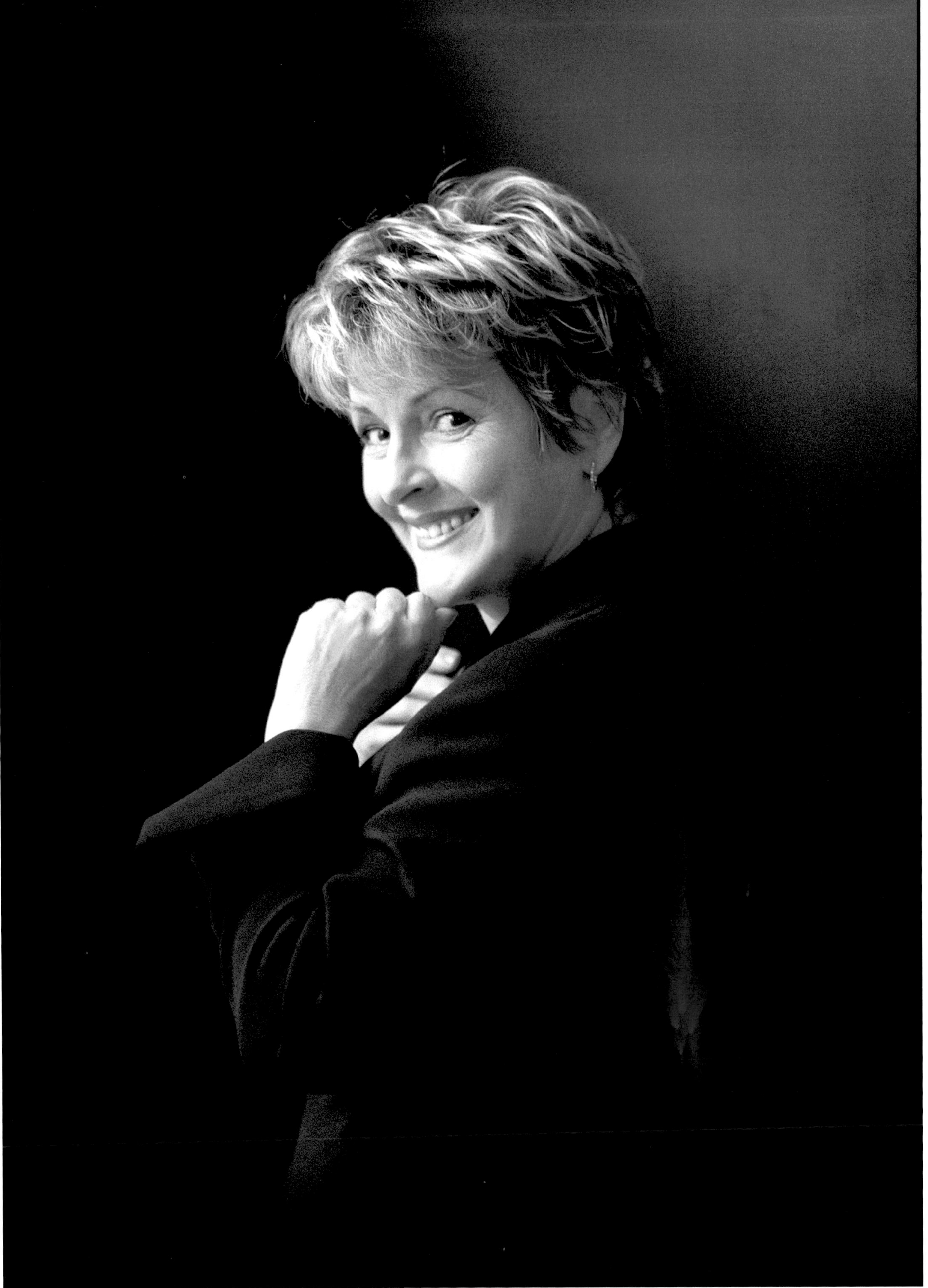

## SIMON RATTLE

I suspect there is some magical continuity in a percussionist waving a stick, and turning into a conductor, such was Rattle's early experience in an orchestra. Studying several instruments, piano and viola stood the maestro in good stead for joining the illustrious Berlin Philharmonic. During his tenure with them he found time to conduct a seminar with students at the Guildhall School of Music in London.

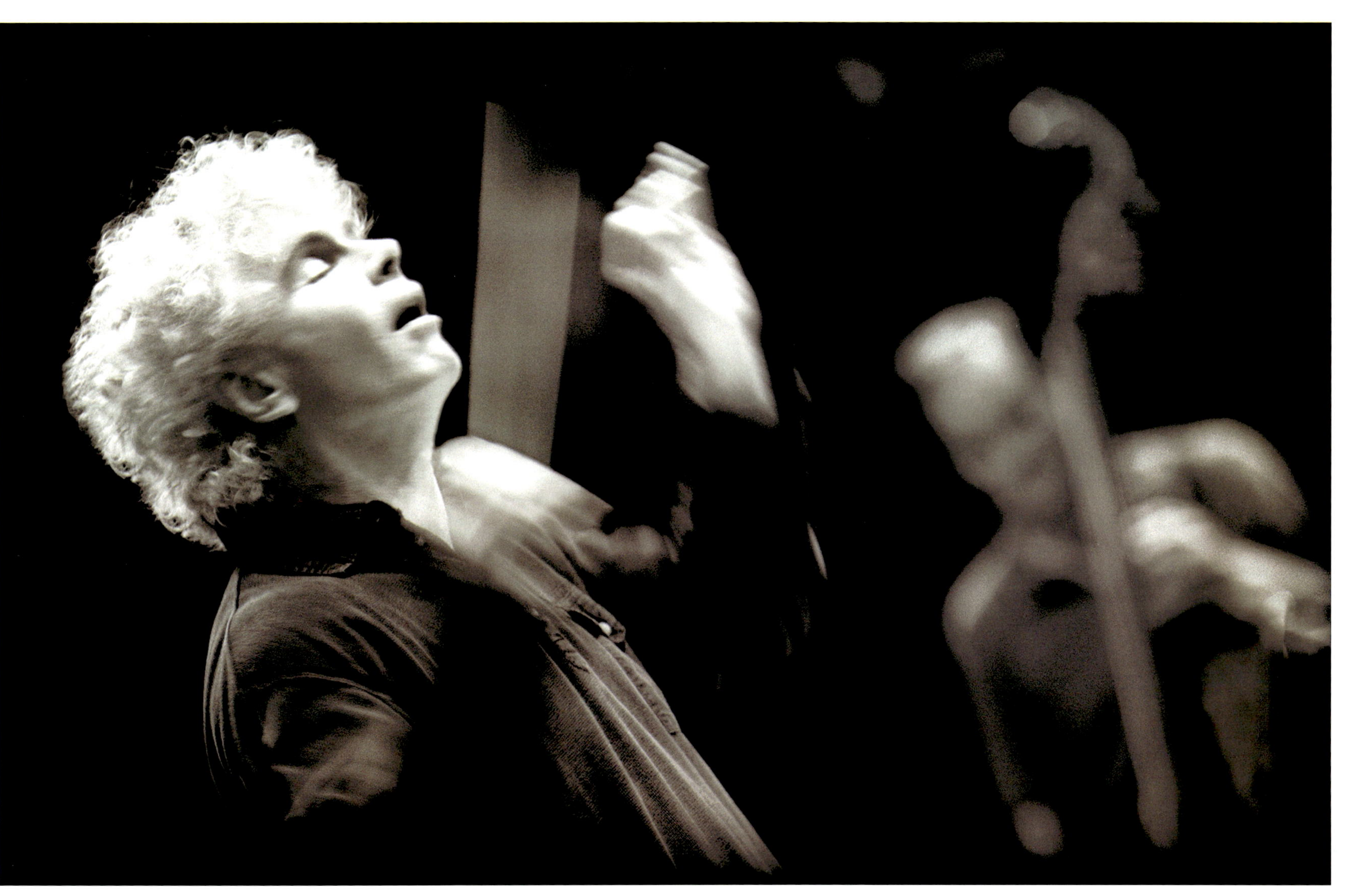

# JENNY AGUTTER

The actress agreed to model a series of Andrea Gayler designs, choosing Ernő Goldfinger's 1939 Modernist home for the setting. The shoot was improvised on the day, against the clock, relying on natural light. It went surprisingly well, Jenny Agutter uncomplaining and professional despite the quick changes and cramped location.

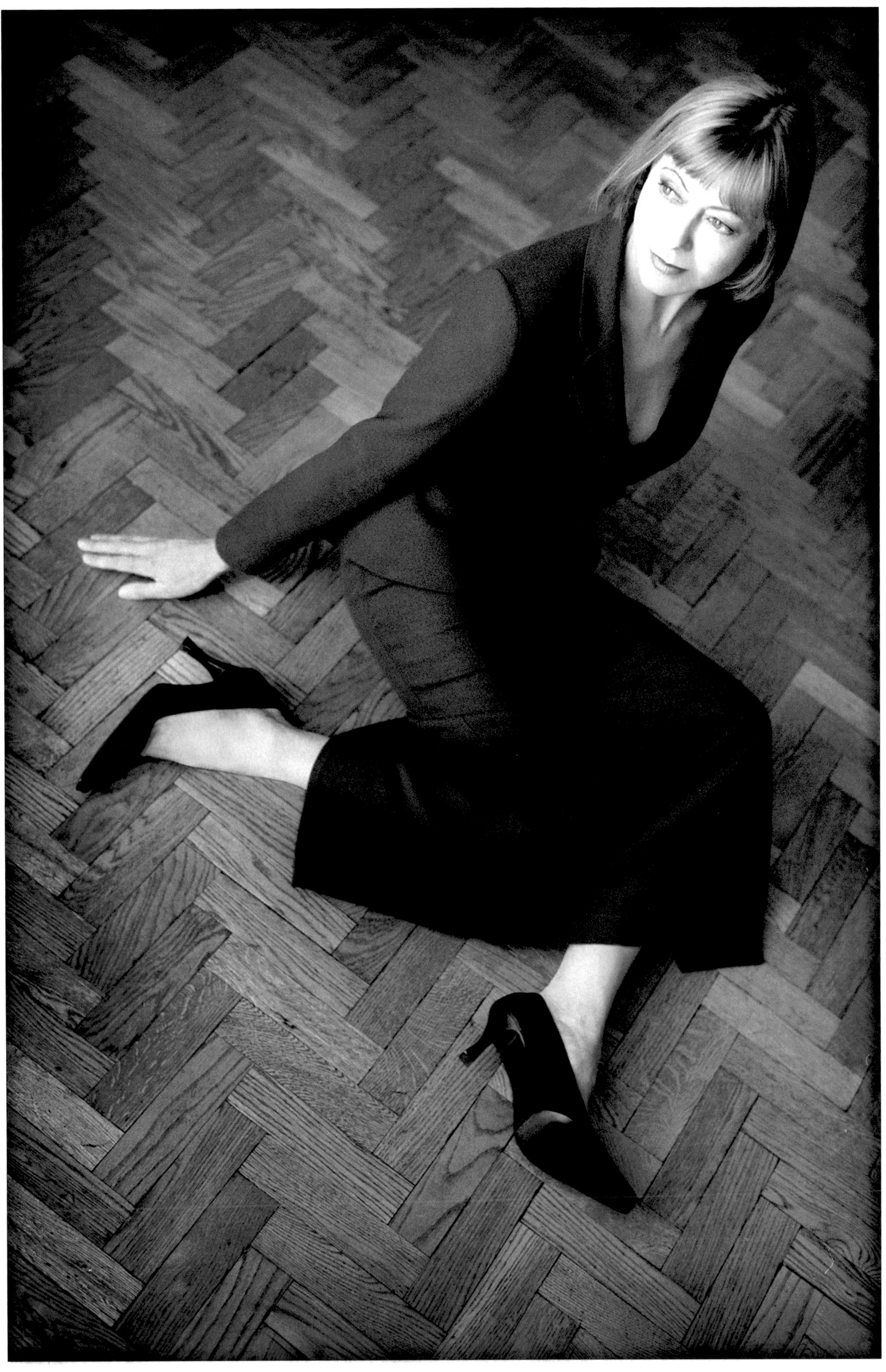

# THE EVERLY BROTHERS

*Rolling Stone* editor Jan Wenner, noticing that more was happening in the UK than in San Francisco, opened a London office to put a supplement in the magazine. First assignment was in a cabaret club on the east coast; the Everlys were back on the road. The dance floor surrounded by tables was empty, nowhere to hide or be discreet, so deep breath, mid-performance stepped into the empty space feeling very conspicuous and vulnerable. The wide lens necessitated standing close, about 5 ft from the performers. Mid-song Don Everly stopped singing and politely asked ...

'What are you doing?' ...

'A close-up.' ...

'With that?' ...

'Yes, it's a panoramic camera.' ...

'How does it work?' ...

'Well, it would be easier to show you than explain.'

In the middle of a song, in the middle of a set, surrounded by diners and chuckling musicians, we held an impromptu photo session, which produced this double portrait, and from the stage, a reverse angle against the follow-spot.

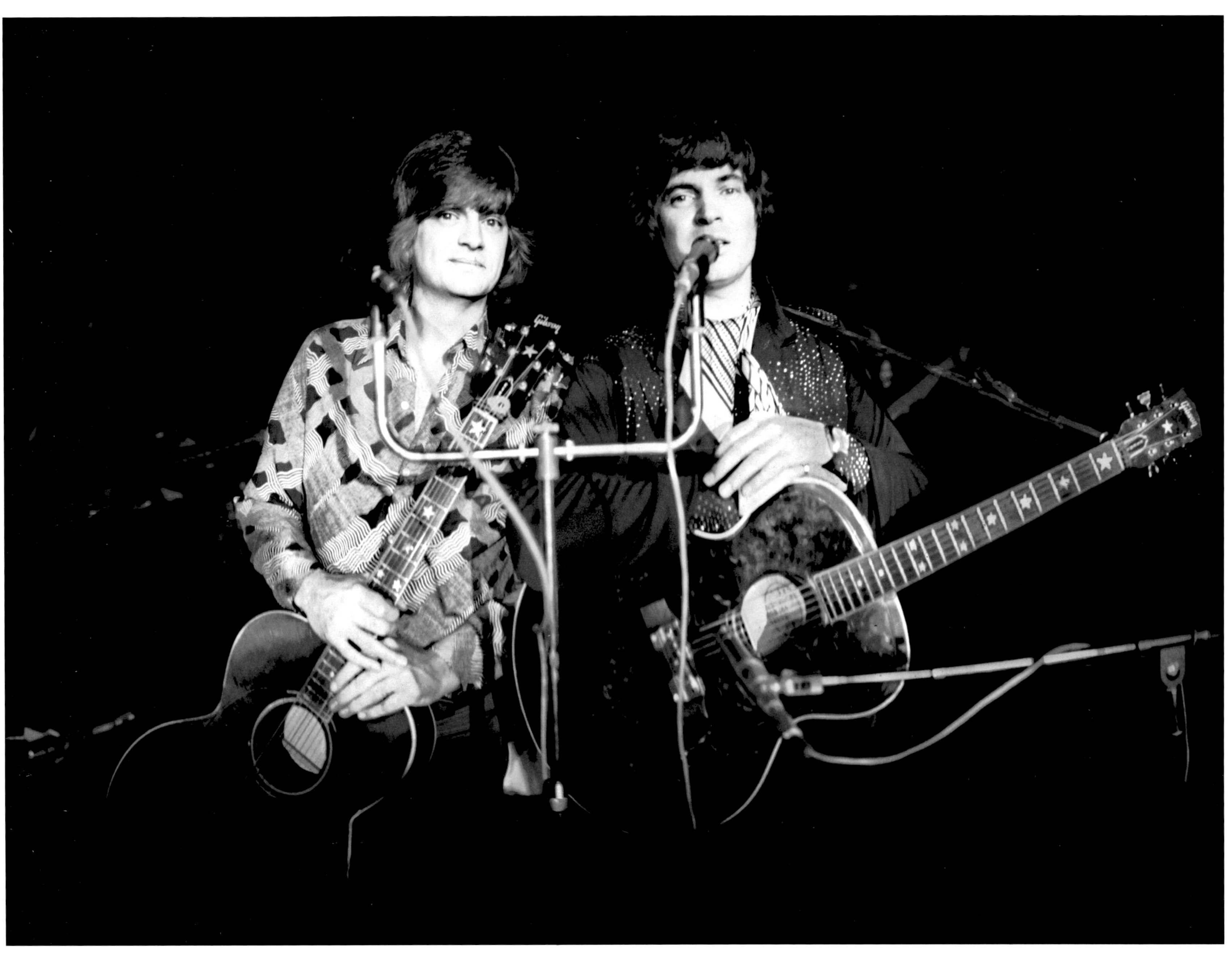

# MARGARET DRABBLE

The author invited us into her kitchen to conduct the interview in her Hampstead home ... 'I'm rather pushed for time, you won't mind if I cook while we talk?' Fielding questions she danced merrily around the stove, occasionally waving a wooden spoon to emphasise a point.

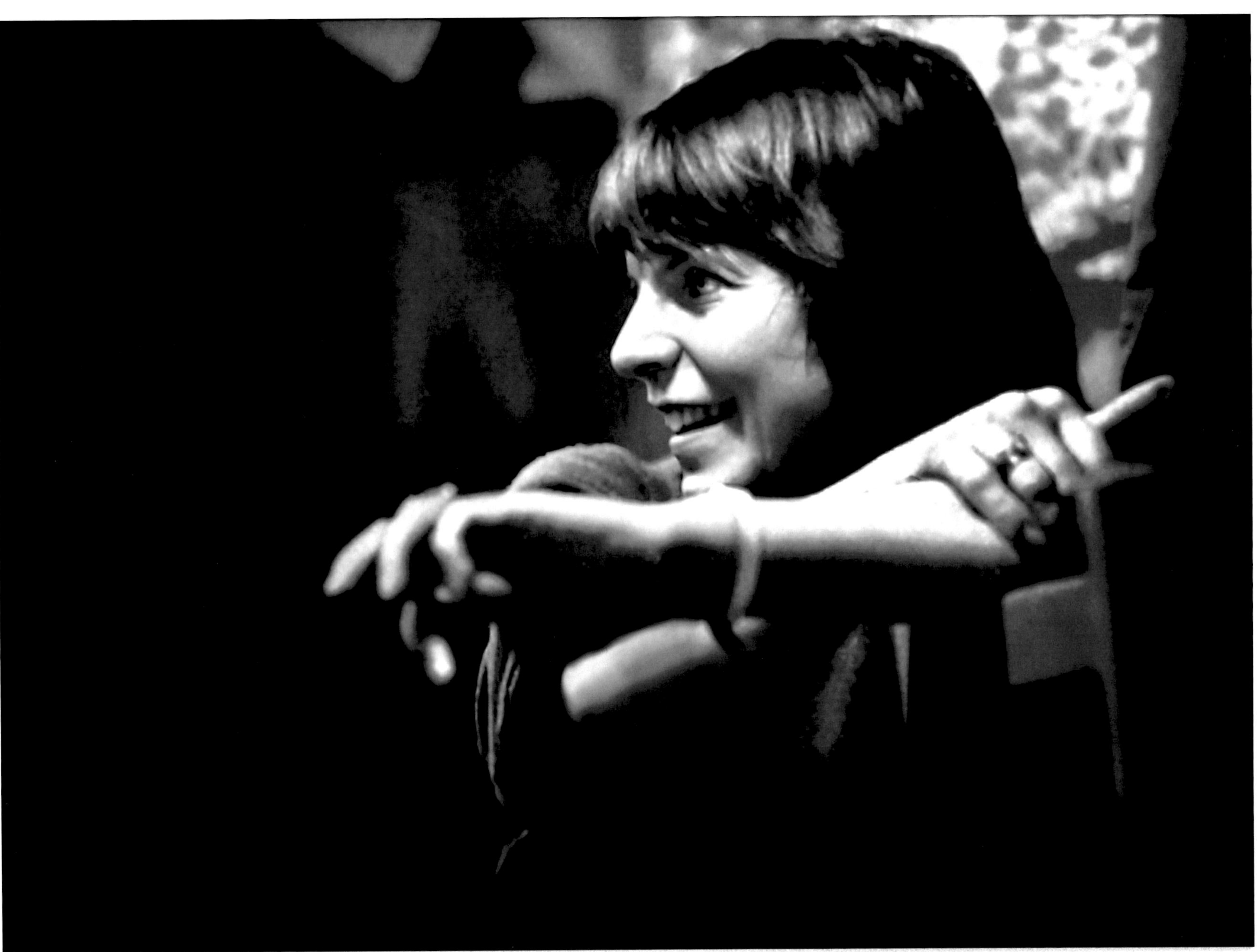

# BO DIDDLEY

I'd read that Colonel Parker had sent Elvis to watch Bo Diddley's stage show which now, fifteen years later, was about to commence. The pass permitted working from the stage but it was the camera that gave me the few extra seconds in the wings for the portrait. The bulky panoramic with clockwork motor and moving lens resembled a piece of Victoriana ... which made him smile. Then he was bouncing across the stage to his signature bom da bom bom, da bom bom ... Elvis would have seen him flying through the air with rectangular guitar and landing in the splits; now a little heavier, he remained grounded but the music lifted the stadium crowd to its feet and they danced.

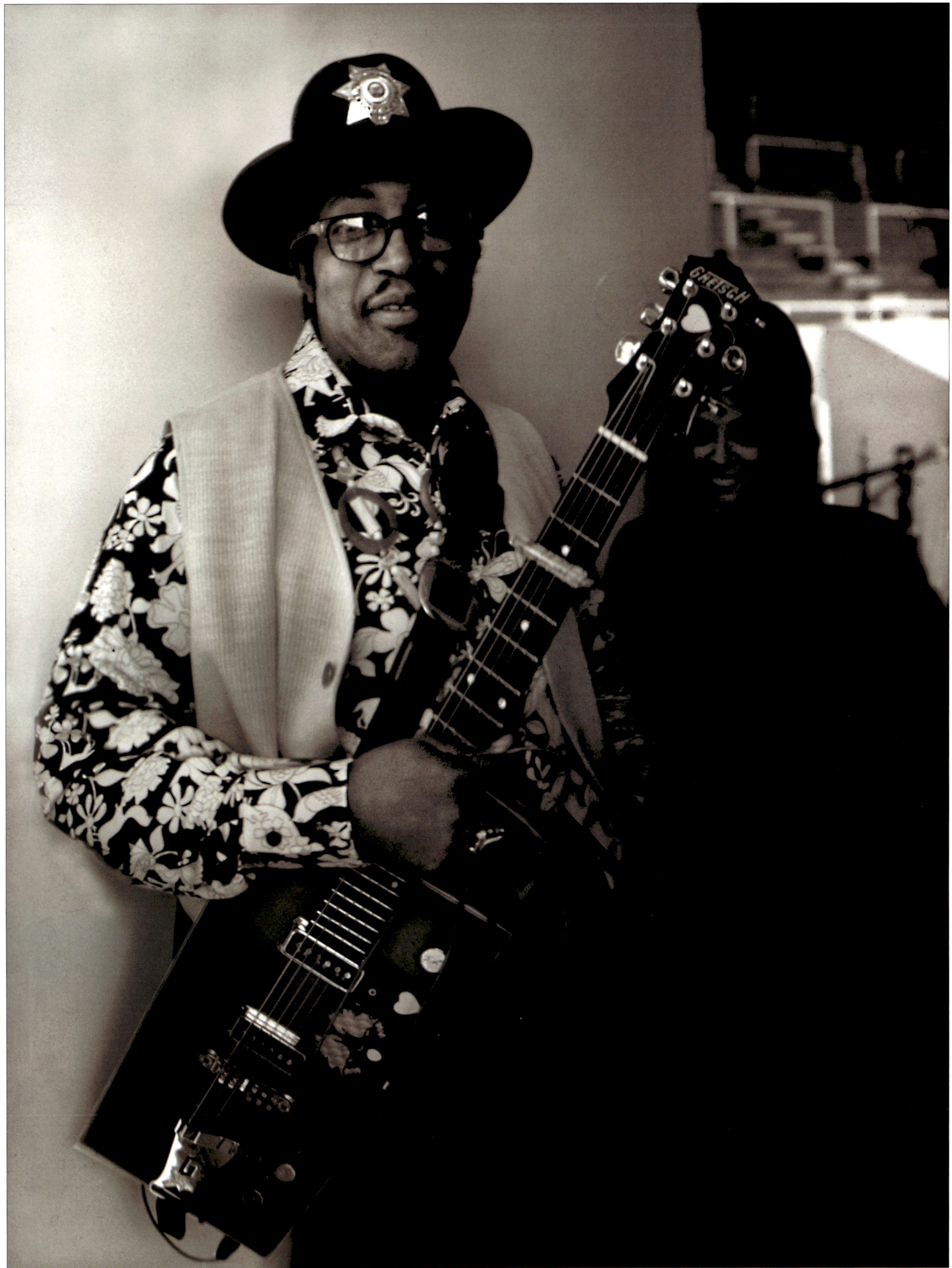
GRETSCH

# UTE LEMPER

Before the theatre's reconstruction, the singer-songwriter permitted a shot in Margot Fonteyn's former dressing room at Sadler's Wells. She was preparing for a programme of music from the Weimar Republic with songs by Kurt Weill and Bertolt Brecht, and more by Marlene Dietrich and Edith Piaf.

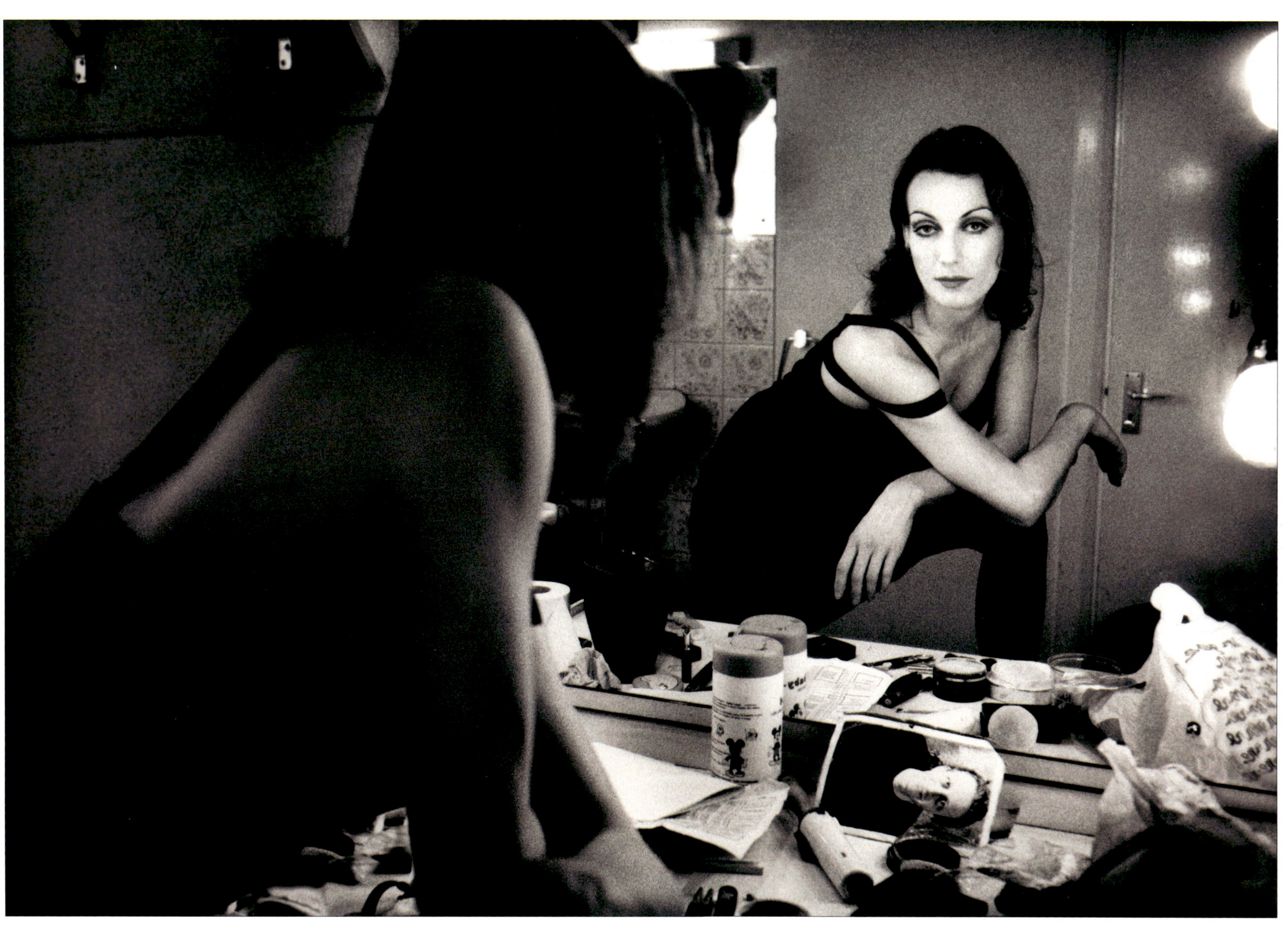

# ABDUL KURESHI

Mr Kureshi, a Kashmiri farmer, waits patiently on a mountain track for relief supplies three months after the 2005 earthquake as the snows arrive. He has taken responsibility for two families who have lost their breadwinners; their homes at 8,000 ft are too high for the aid agencies to reach. Two thousand feet below is what remains of Balakot, the nearest town. A VSO volunteer, Commander Lane, describes the scene ... 'It looks as if it has been carpet-bombed, almost nothing left standing.' It is hard to grasp the scale of the unfolding tragedy... over 78,000 killed outright, more dying from the cold, disease and starvation. Sometimes journalists can make a difference; on this occasion *The Independent on Sunday* raised almost £200,000 towards the relief effort ... I can only hope that some of it reached the survivors.

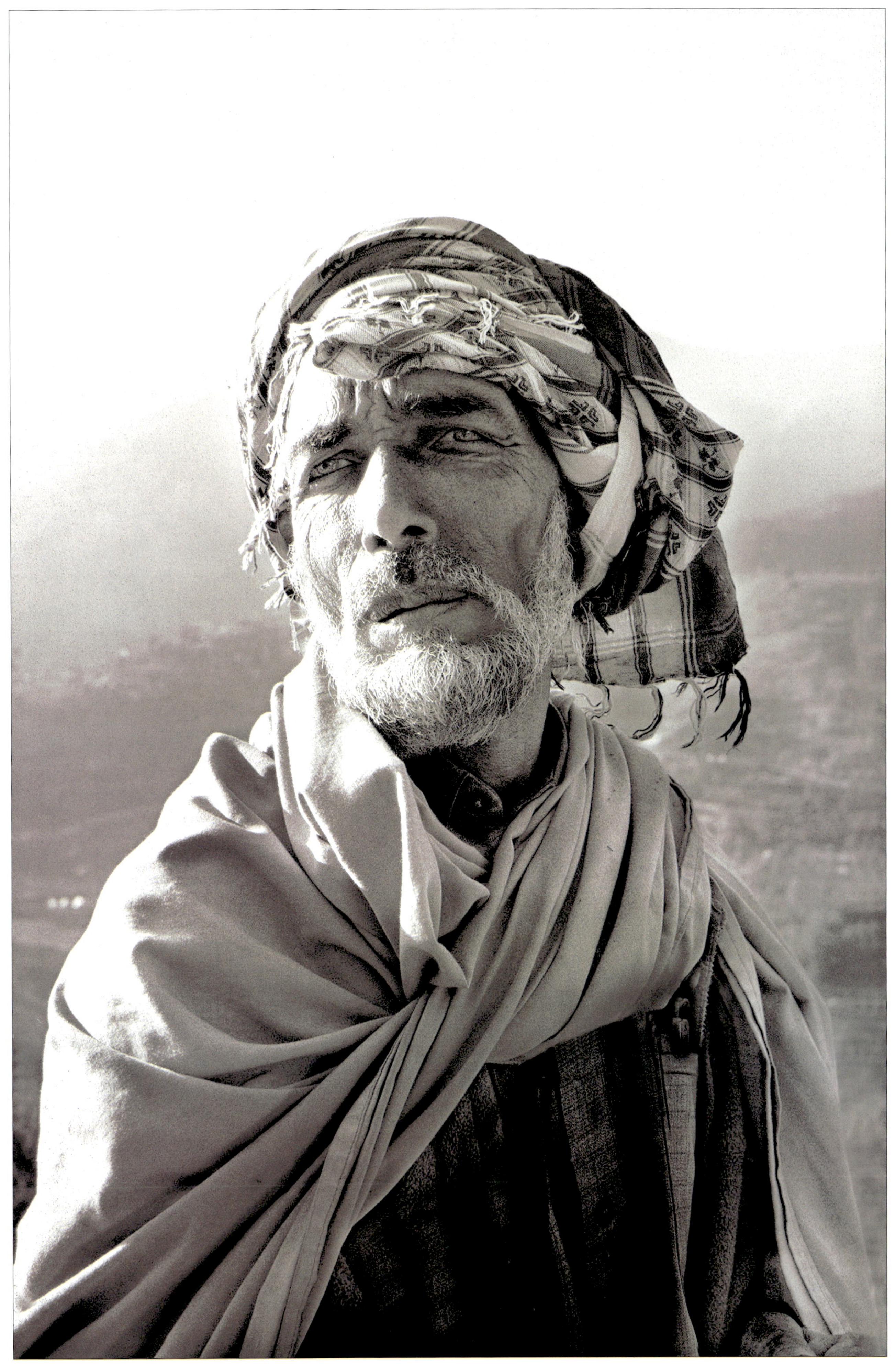

## IKE & TINA TURNER

It was a full-tilt high-energy gig with the band and the three dancing Ikettes, resembling a James Brown concert, using some of his routines and choreography. Ike and Tina looked cool and relaxed in a dingy dressing room for the interview ...

'Aren't you exhausted?' ...

'Honey I was back on stage three days after my last child was born.' ...

A seriously impressive woman. This turned out to be her last performance with Ike, at Wembley Arena, before going solo.

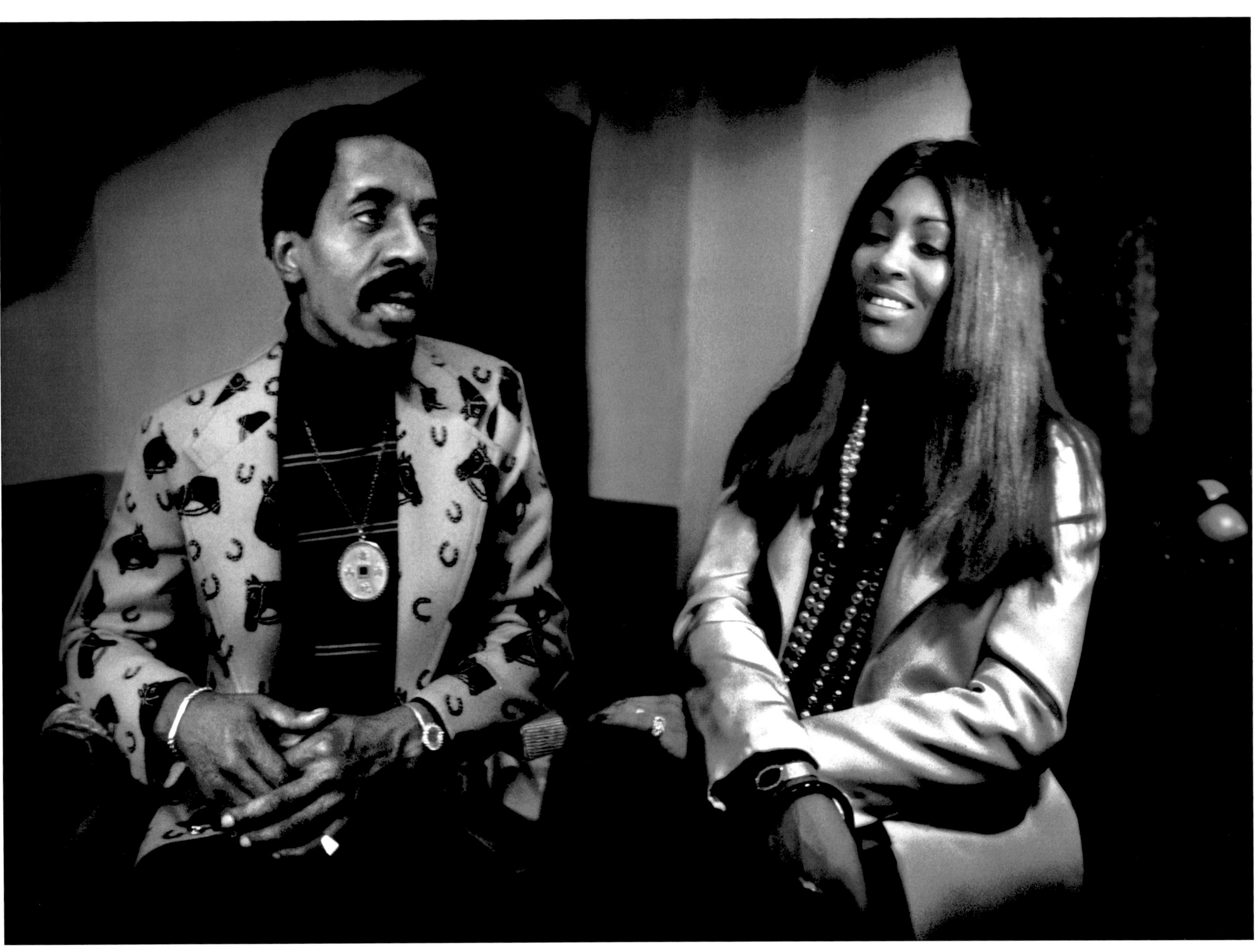

## CHRIS BLACKWELL

'It wasn't Bob Marley that put the label on the map, it was Millie Small's *My Boy Lollipop*,' he replied after I mentioned I'd shot the Marley sleeve *Babylon By Bus* ... He continued, 'she sold six million copies'. Blackwell founded Island Records when he was twenty-four, having grown up in a wealthy Jamaican family with Nöel Coward and Ian Fleming for neighbours. He probably didn't need the money, having proved he could make the company profitable. He sat obligingly in front of the Island logo to celebrate the label's first twenty-five years.

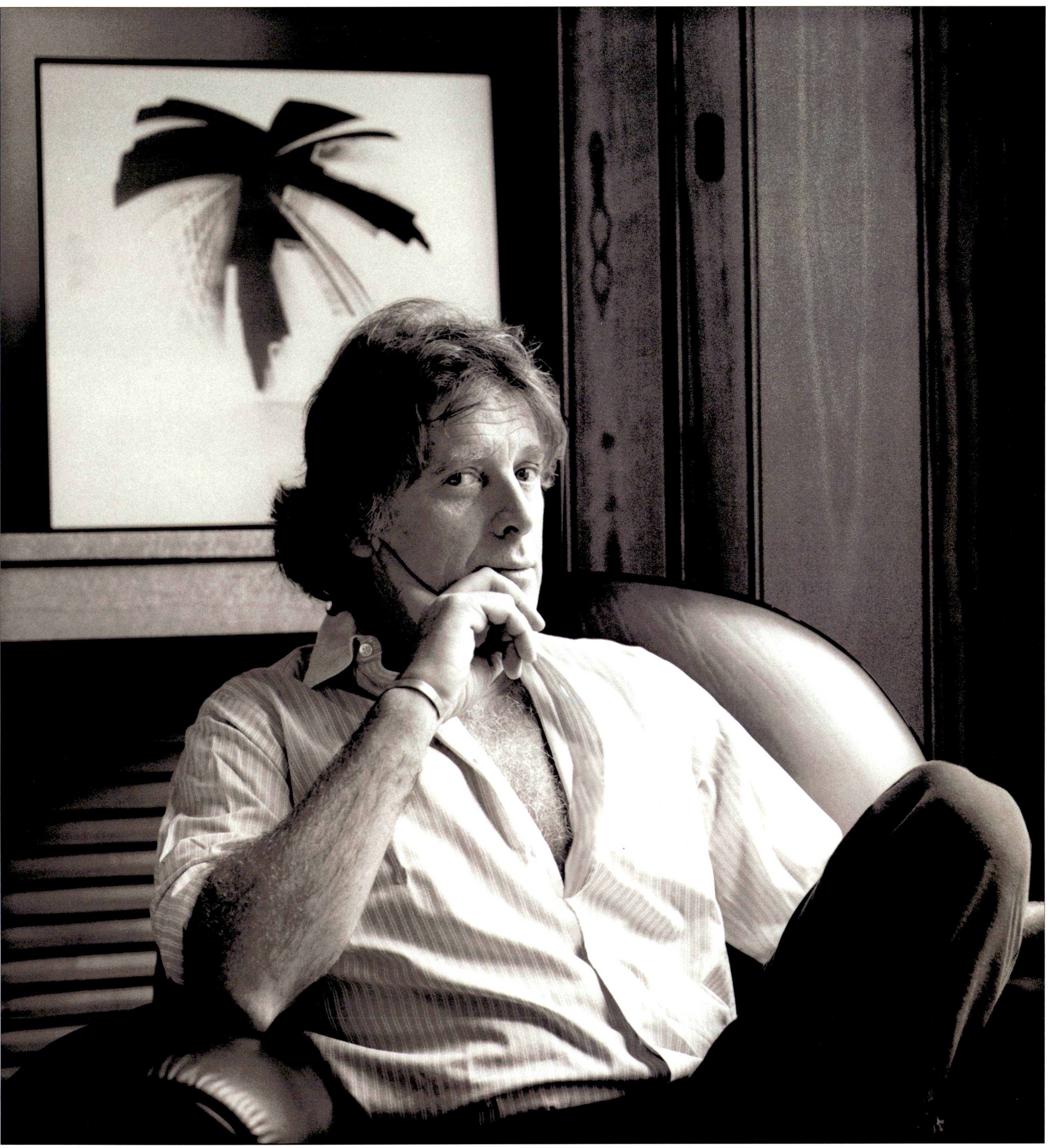

# DARCEY BUSSELL

The Albert Memorial was having a facelift. The bright spark at English Heritage charged with promoting the £17m makeover came up with the idea ... 'it coincides with London Fashion Week and the new Royal Ballet season.' So, a ballerina in a designer frock atop the Memorial ... simple. Wearing a Neil Cunningham creation, Darcey looked unhappy with the hard-hat she was expected to wear as a lift took us up the scaffolding. I'd misjudged how high it was, the view across London was impressive and so were the newly gilded angels surrounding the cross at the summit. Left alone it was a swift if vertiginous shoot, hard-hats abandoned, the ballerina lying gallantly in the arms of a golden angel, nearly 200 ft above the ground.

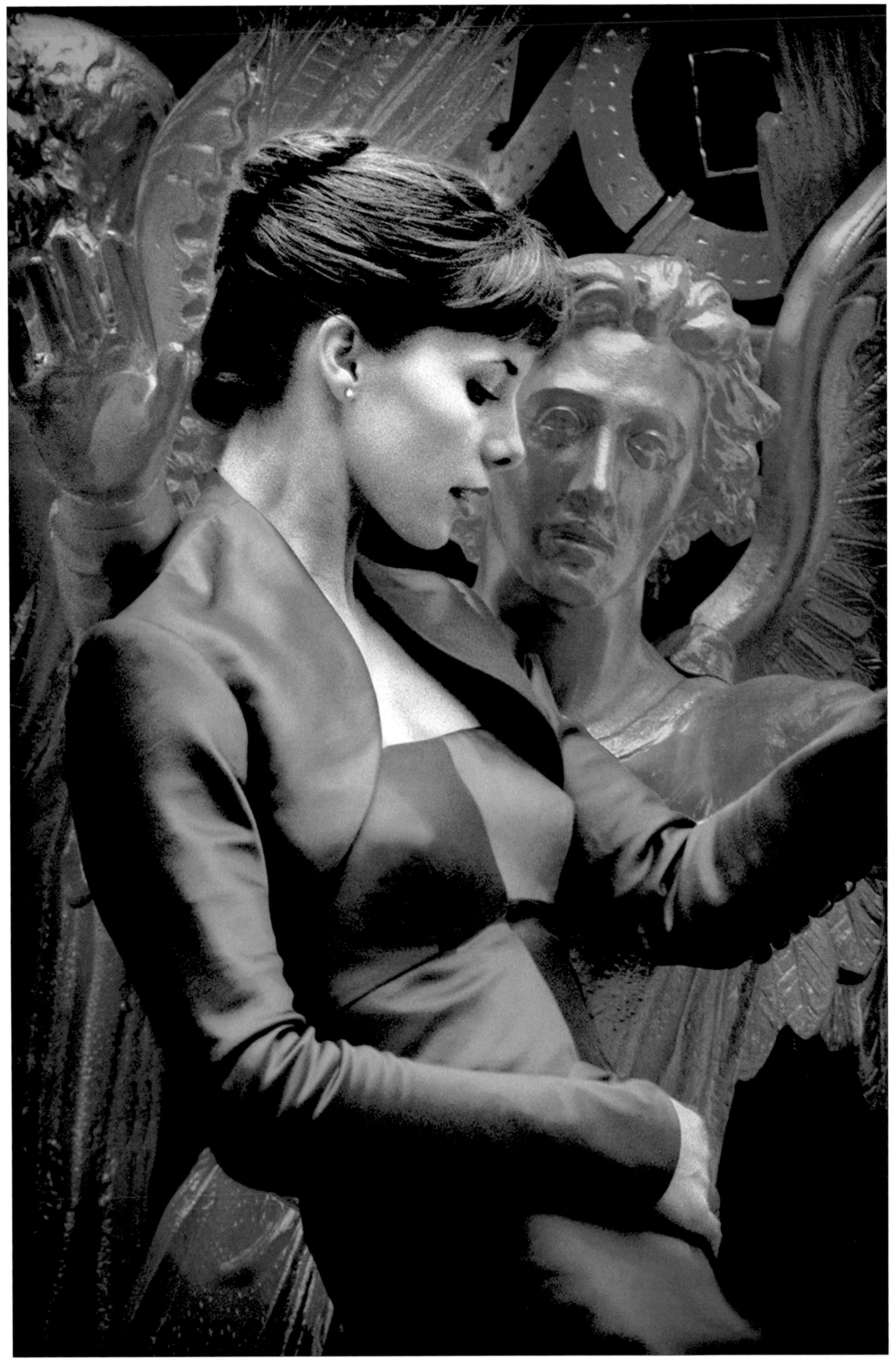

# JOHN McENROE

He may be remembered for his on-court tantrums but he should more properly be remembered as one of the last great touch players in the wake of Rod Laver and Ken Rosewall, subsequently overtaken by contemporary power play. I covered Wimbledon on successive occasions, here concentrating on the action, the other on the 'colour' surrounding it; however this image was chosen over the graceful versatility of McEnroe's play.

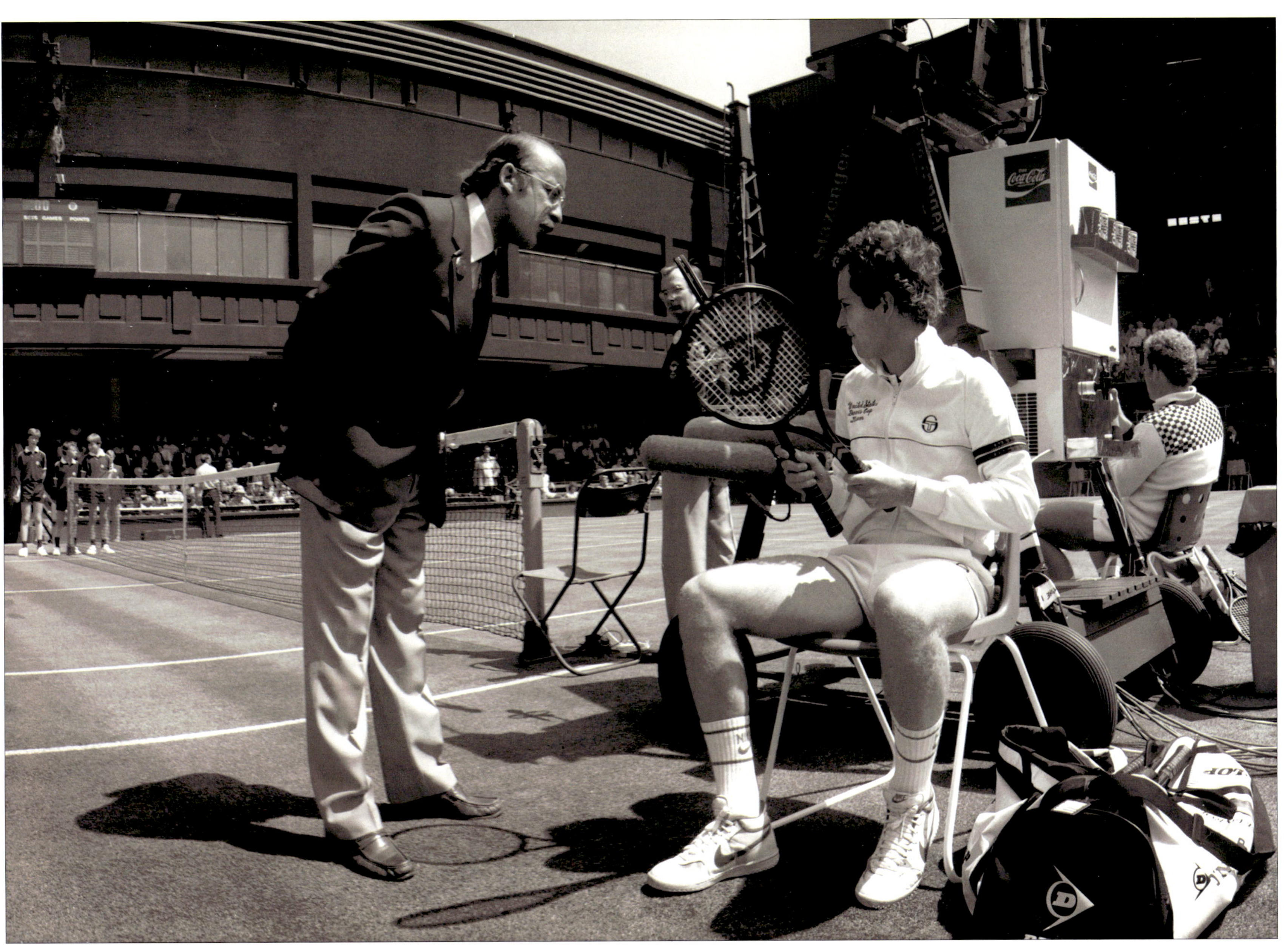
Coca-Cola

# IRENE THOMAS

I'd heard her on the radio often but had never seen her. A tall, willowy, elegantly dressed woman opened the door and said … 'You're very punctual, please enter.' She had enormous vitality and those blue twinkling eyes concealed a Mensa rating of 160. With John Julius Norwich she made *Round Britain Quiz* seem easy and waltzed through *Brain of Britain* enough times to hold the title 'Brain of Brains'.

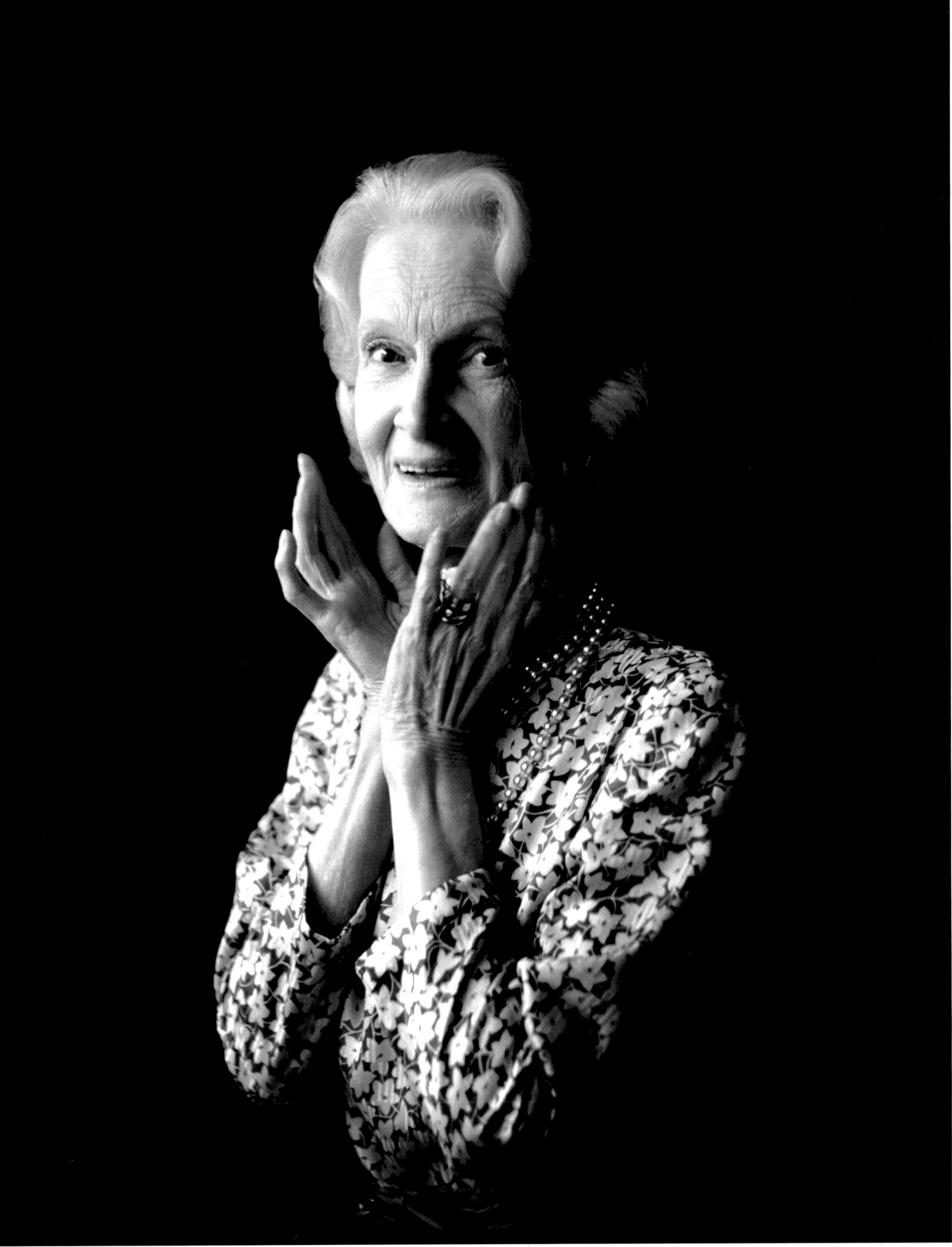

## ROBERT WYATT

When Soft Machine was playing at Ronnie Scott's Jazz Club, I witnessed this gentle charming, self-deprecating musician kick his drum-kit into the laps of the punters that had the temerity to chatter through his set. At home with his wife Alfie, I reminded him of this, and he replied ... 'I can't really blame my younger self for being young.' On considering my own youthful misdemeanours, I wished I'd thought of that.

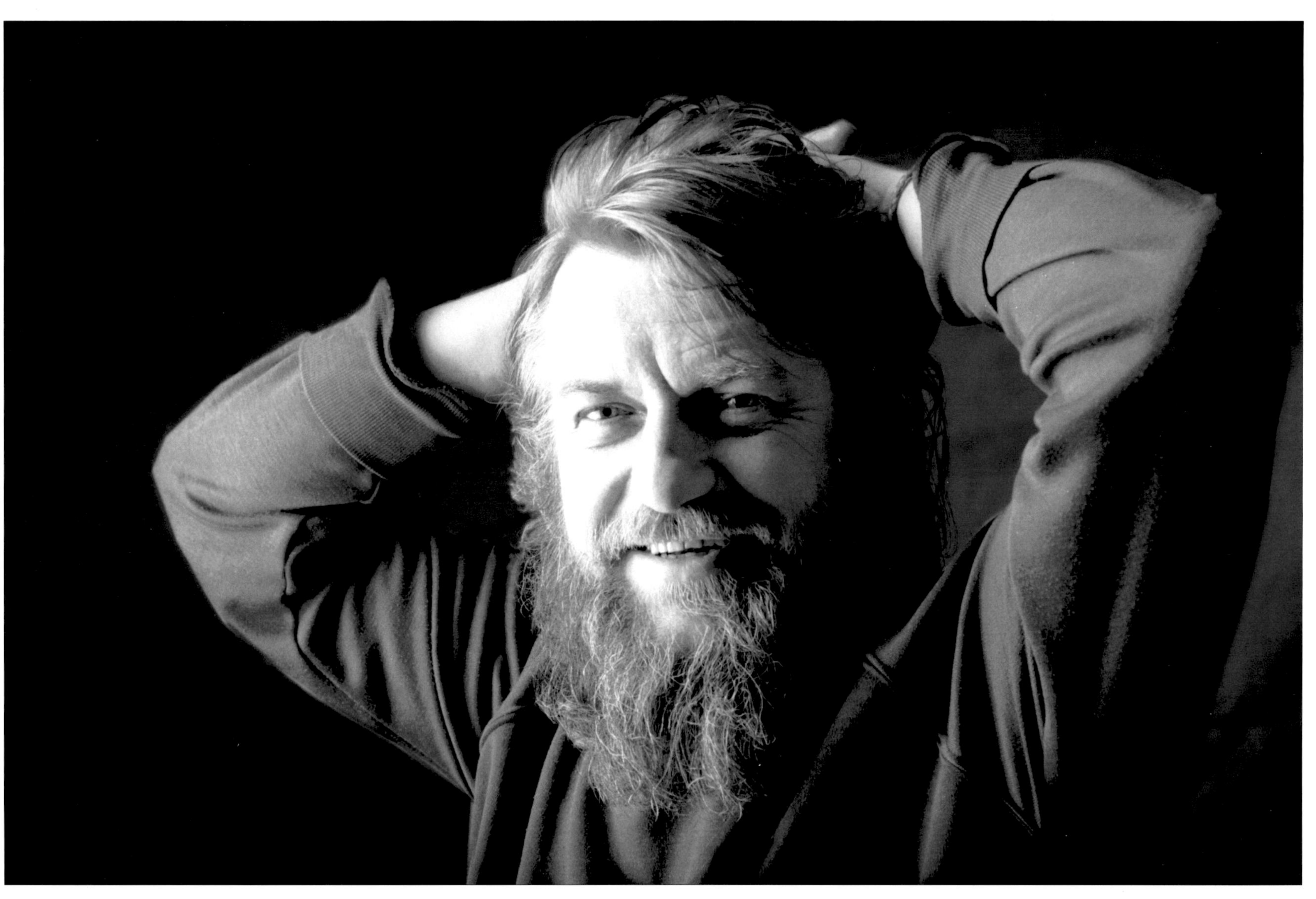

## LIZ SMITH

Mary Cavanagh introduced us to Liz Smith who was opening a jumble sale at Camden School for Girls, soon after a portrait was commissioned at her home near to Parliament Hill Fields ...

'May I look upstairs?' ...

'Go ahead.' ...

'Who did these?'

'Why, they are mine' ...

Several self-portraits were stacked against the wall. The light was good, a double portrait, no argument.

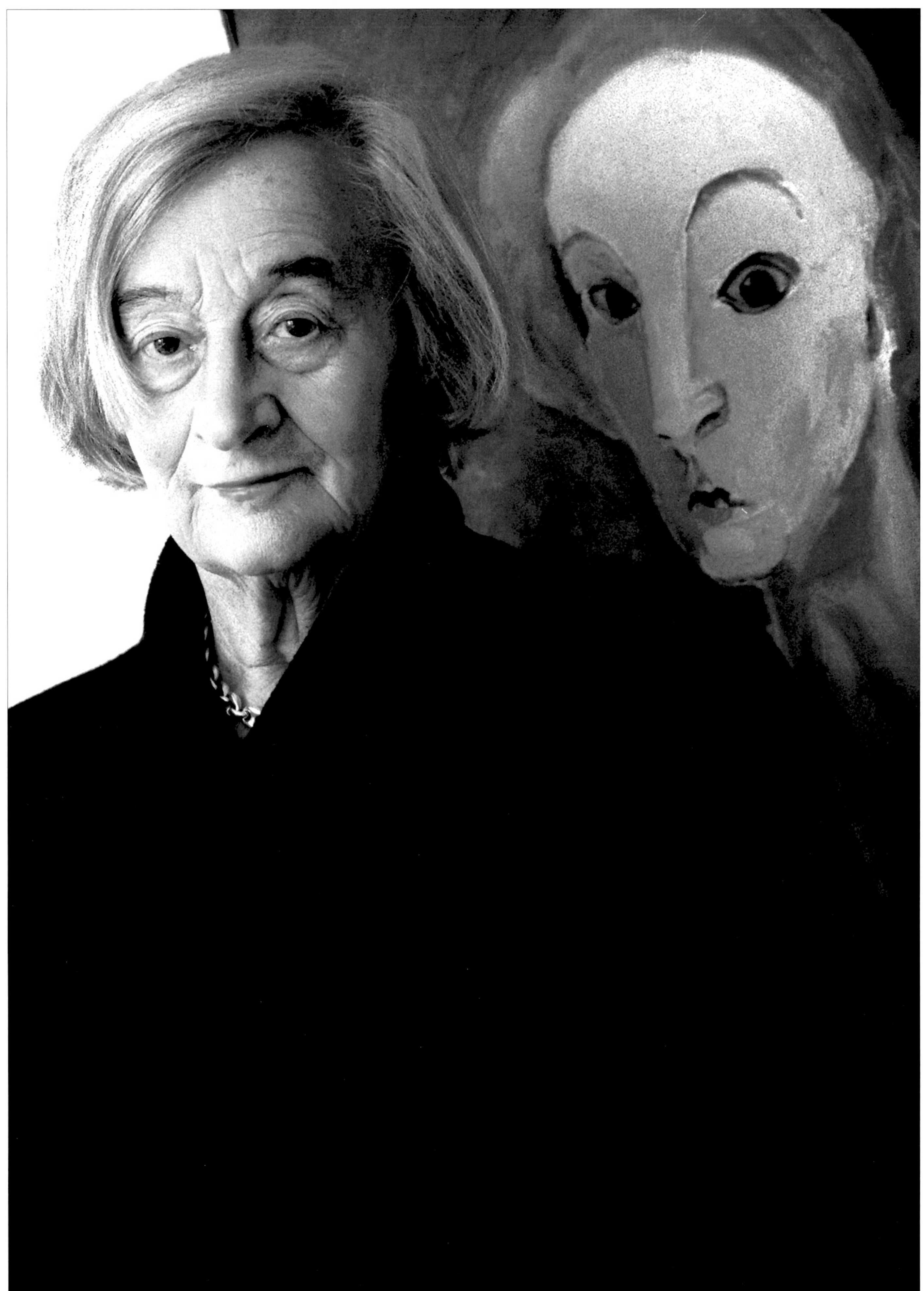

## MICHAEL KAUFFMANN

The Director of the Courtauld succeeded Anthony Blunt when the Institute was rehoused in the Strand, at Somerset House. As art students we visited the earlier premises in Portman Square, ascending a flight or two in a rickety industrial lift to attend drawing classes. For the portrait it seemed natural to pose him in front of a painting …

'Any preference?' …

'*Te Rerioa*, the Gauguin.'

It was interesting to learn the bust was of Mette-Sophie Gad, the artist's Danish wife.

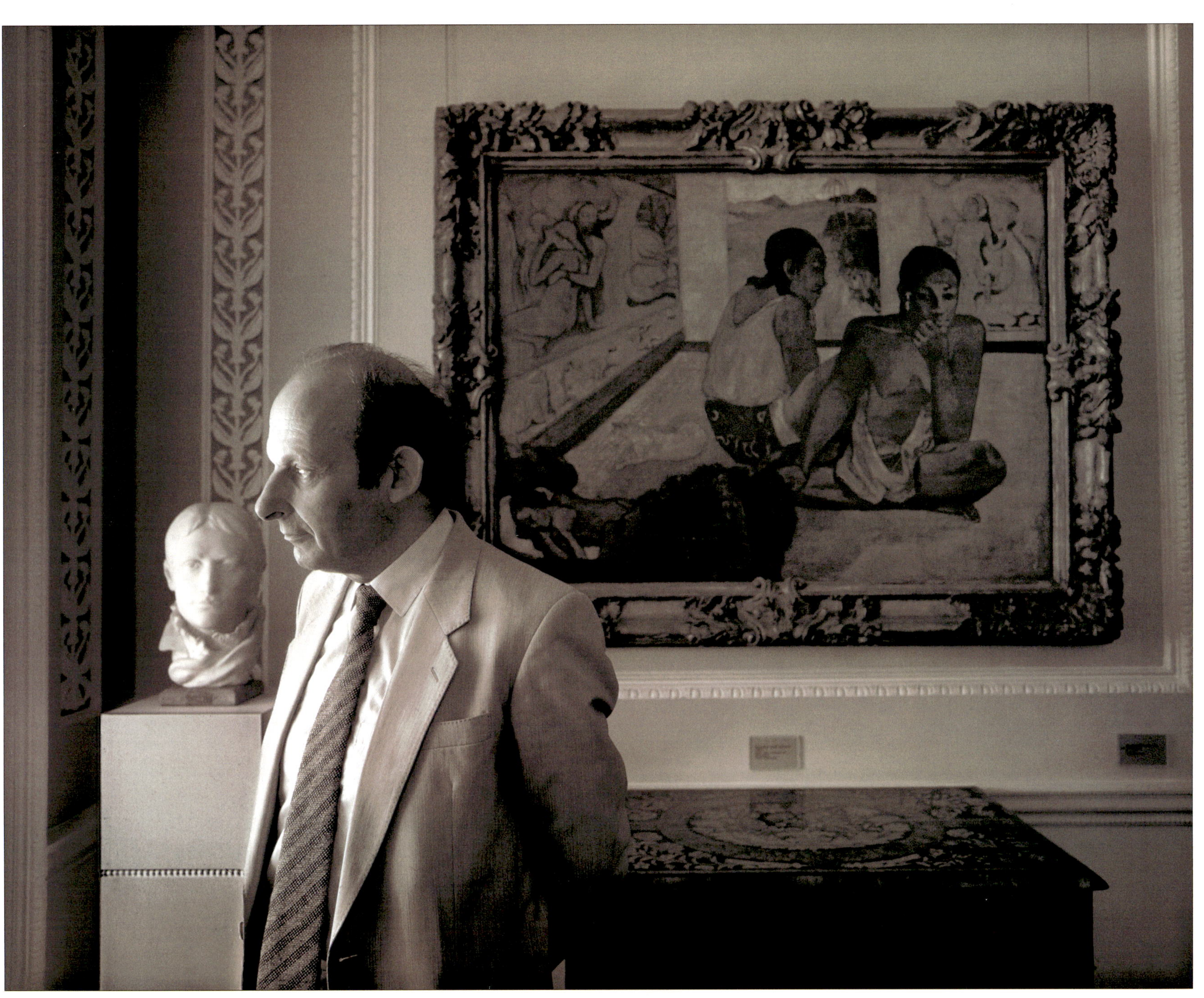

# ROXY BEAUJOLAIS

The Seven Stars was given a new lease of life when Ms Beaujolais gave it a facelift and opened its doors on weekends, attracting friends from her days working in Ronnie Scott's Jazz Club. During the week she plays host to lawyers and felons, from the Royal Courts of Justice opposite, celebrating or seeking solace in the building that escaped the Great Fire of London in 1666. In some ways the clientele of the club and the pub has hardly changed since Roxy was dreaming of running her own salon, with the underworld equitably rubbing shoulders with the establishment.

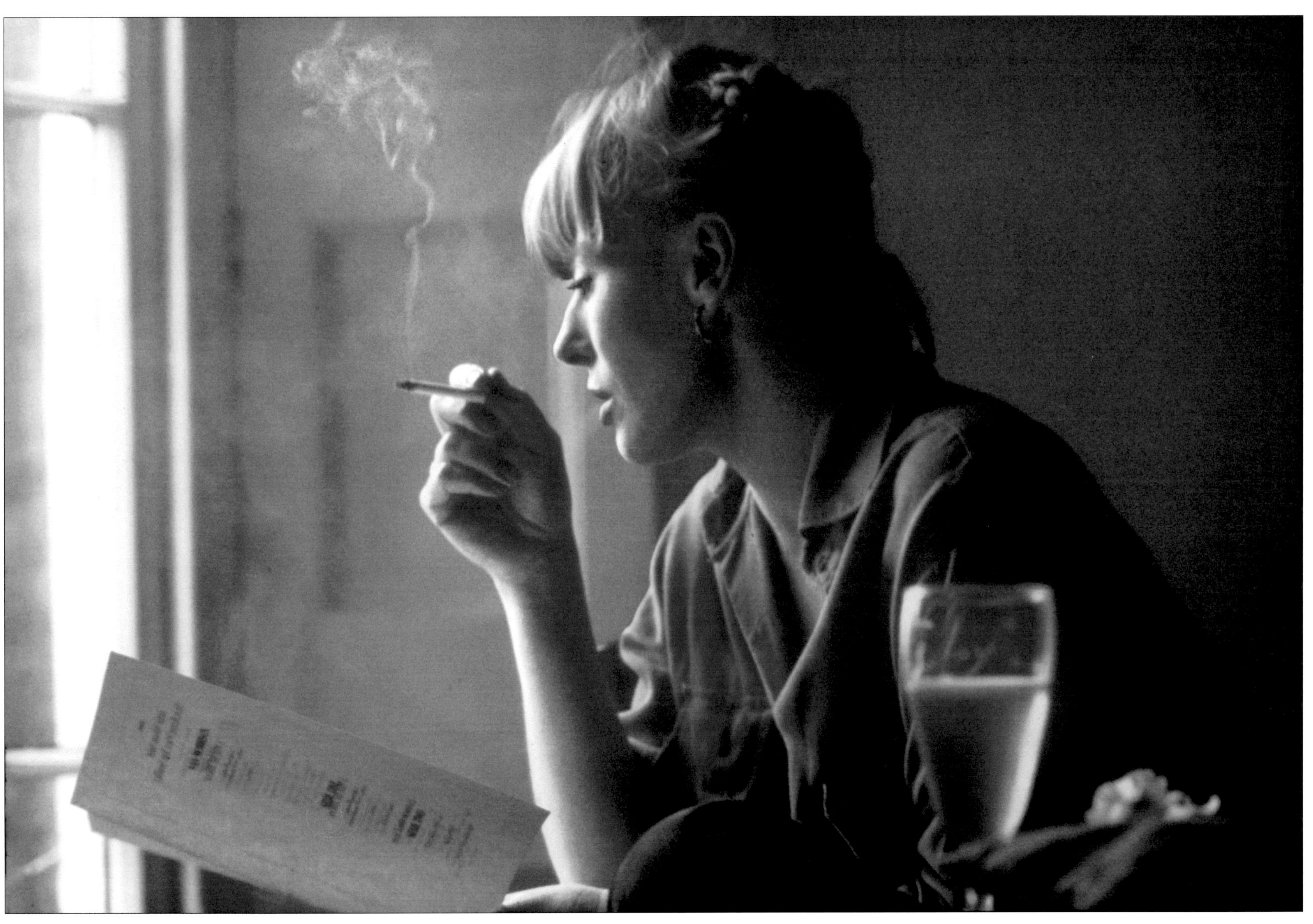

## SPIKE MILLIGAN

A red mini skidded into the parking place ahead of us, 'Swine!' ... out jumped Milligan shouting '... race you inside!' ... We got to our seats as he emerged on stage ... 'a dead heat!' This was before curtain up for the play *The Bed-Sitting Room*. Charlie Mingus, Miles Davis. Picasso and Matisse all came later, at school it was Presley and Milligan that broke the rules, especially Spike, the arch role model of unrestrained anarchy. I bumped into him a few more times, at Ronnie Scott's, at Heathrow off to see his mother in Woy Woy, and in Kensington Gardens restoring the Elfin Oak carved with elves and fairies. It was Milligan's lunacy that kept me sane during the tribulations of adolescence.

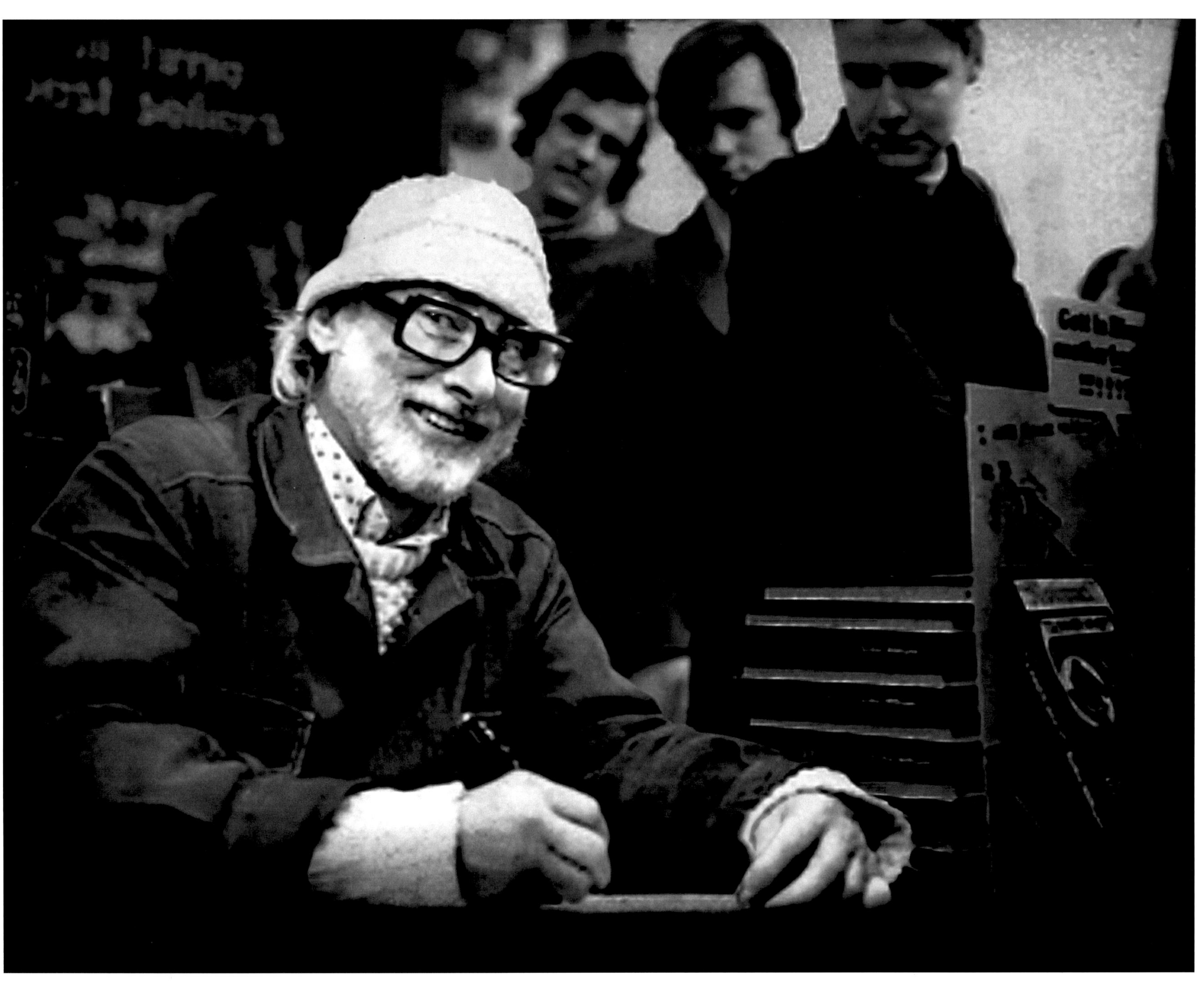

## ANTONIA FRANCESCHI

Former New York City ballerina Antonia Franceschi breezed through a short Wayne McGregor piece wearing a skimpy Julien McDonald item, first for the camera and again for an enthusiastic crowd of fashionistas. *Cut & Thrust*, a site-specific event at the Saatchi Gallery showed professional dancers in designer clothes negotiating the flat white concrete space between exhibits, as a one-off fundraiser for the contemporary dance centre The Place.

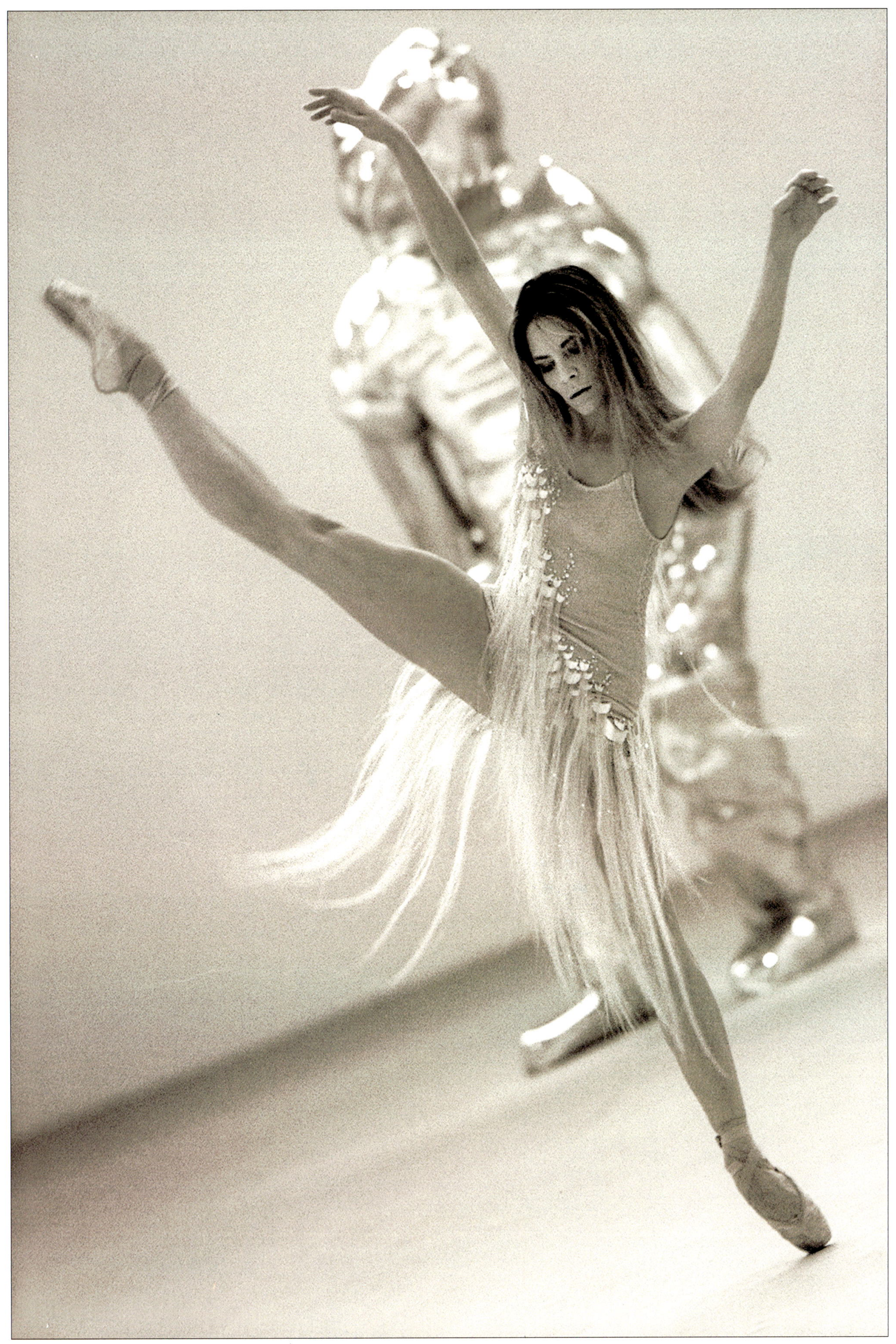

# R.D. LAING

Annie Brackx was the journalist conducting the interview for *City Limits* at his home in Primrose Hill. The psychiatrist was essential reading in the 1960s; we all had copies of *The Divided Self* and *The Politics of Experience*. I wished I had paid more attention to their conversation, but I do remember the cheery line ... 'Life is a sexually transmitted disease and the mortality rate is a hundred per cent.'

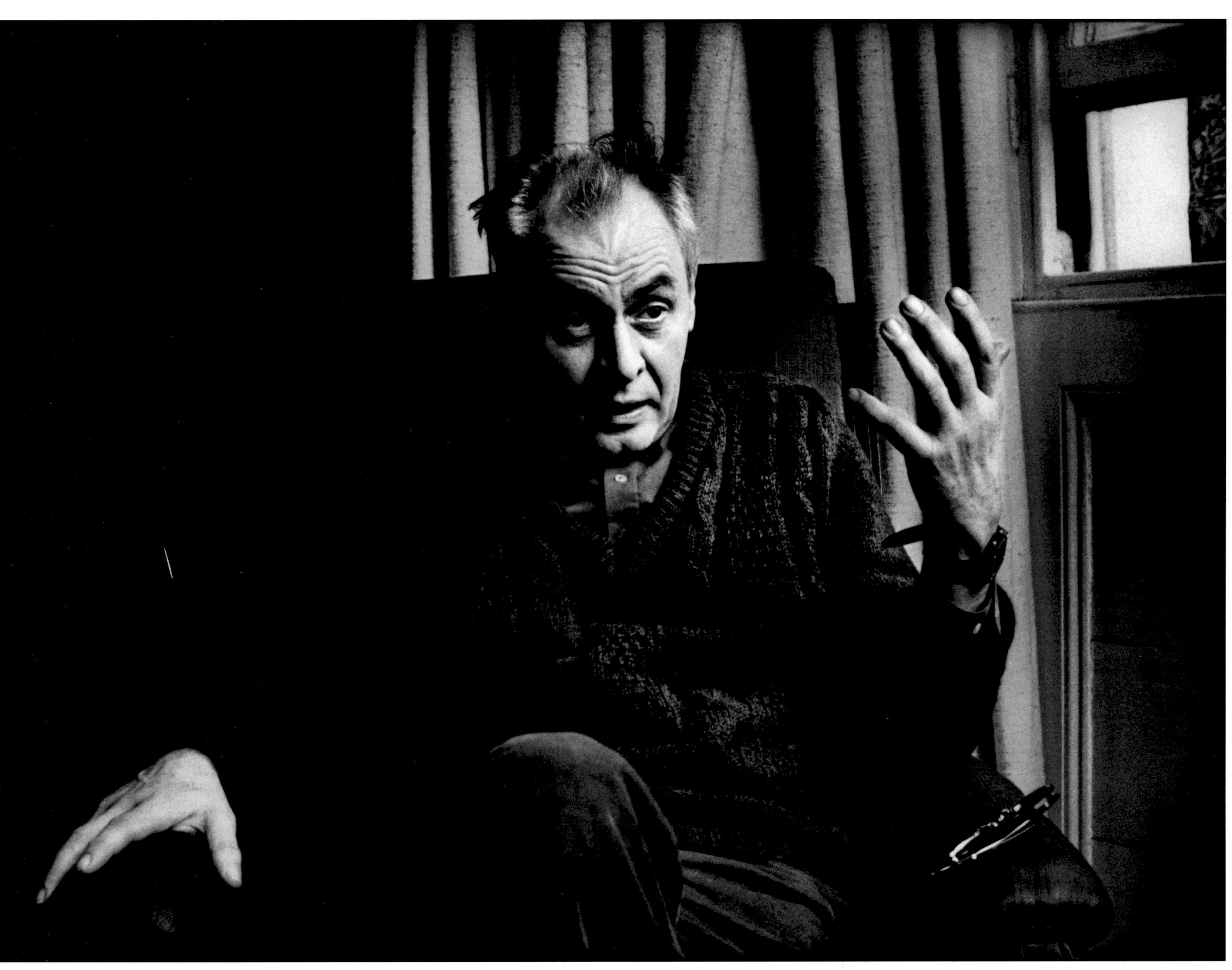

# CYNTHIA PAYNE

The door at Ambleside Avenue was opened by the Madame herself, a pert figure with a mischievous smile, waved us in. 'Would you like tea, dear?' It was a simple terraced house, not exactly a seraglio. The journalist, perhaps mischievously chosen, seemed genuinely shocked at the goings-on with vicars, barristers, ex-police officers and luncheon vouchers. For the picture I suggested changing into something against type. She reappeared in a demure white blouse and stood obligingly by the window.

About to leave, she asked, 'Going into town, dear?'

'Yes.' …

'Can I have a lift?' …

Chatting away, it happened we knew someone in common, which instantly made me family. She kept up a stream of outrageous stories, all the way to the Limelight Club at Cambridge Circus … 'Coming in, dear?' She was pals with Leigh Bowery and Boy George … more photographs.

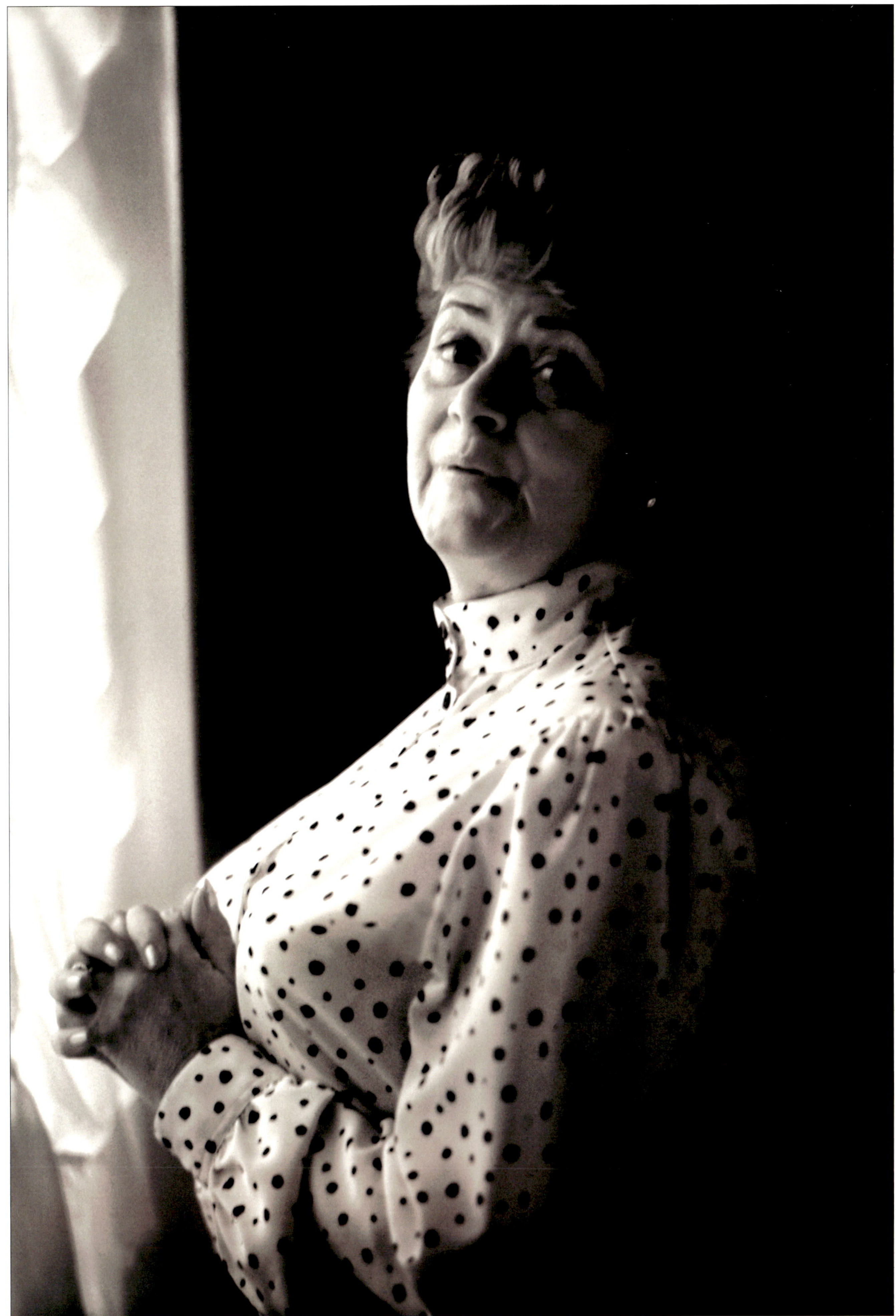

# SLAVA POLUNIN

In Russia, circus is most often performed in permanent purpose-built theatres. The proliferation of circus schools is another reflection of the long tradition there. The great clowns are national celebrities but little-known outside their own country. Slava Polunin is the exception, throughout the world the spectacular dénouement of *Snow Show* literally blows audiences out of the theatre. Pre-performance, the great mime artist gets into character, checks the make-up and waits for his cue.

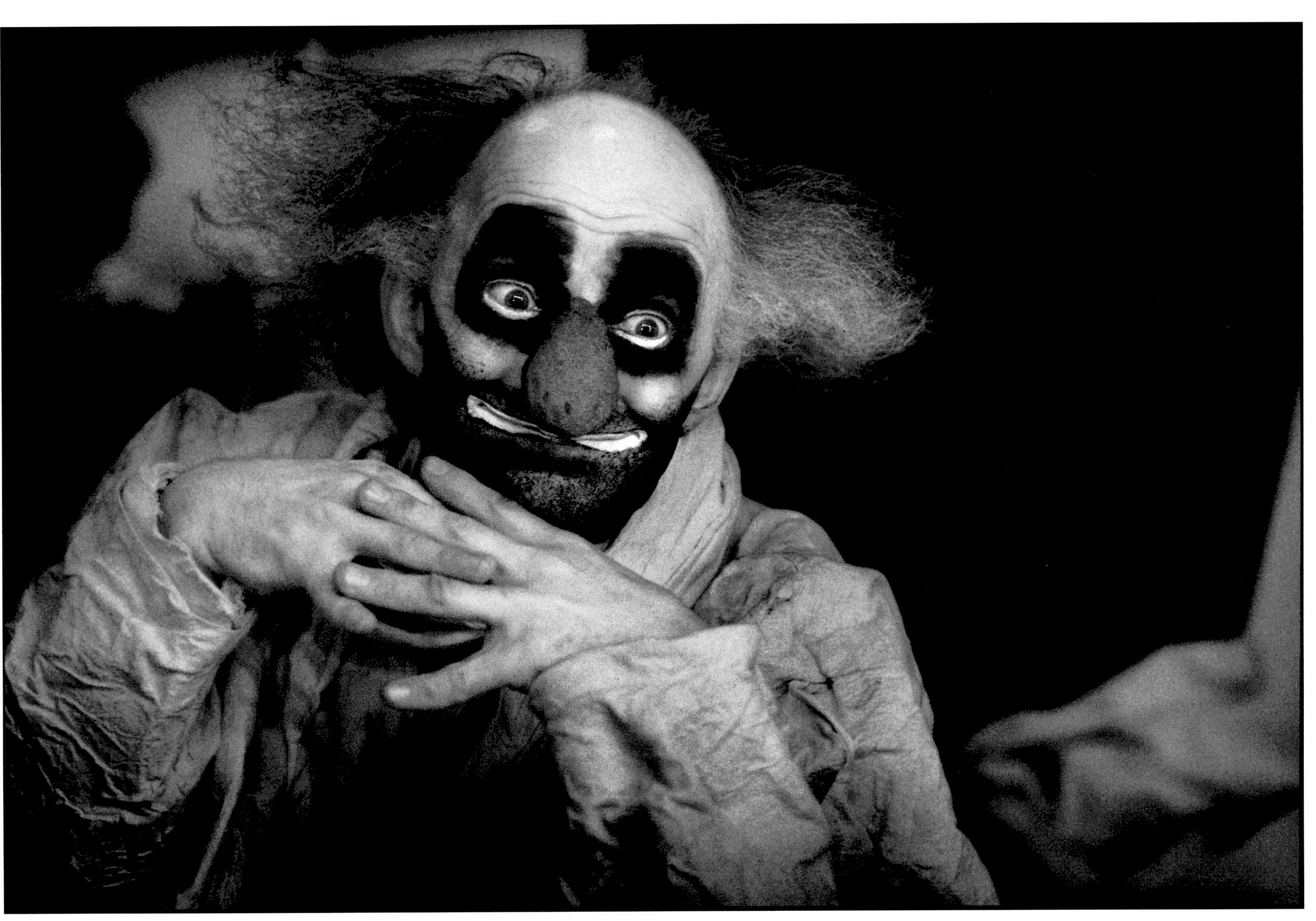

## KIM WILDE

A generation had slipped by since photographing her father, now here was his grown-up daughter in a daylight studio in Clerkenwell to promote a new record. Same name, same light and the music hadn't changed much either. She was more sophisticated than the songs she sang and the way she'd been promoted, so we decided to reflect that in the portrait.

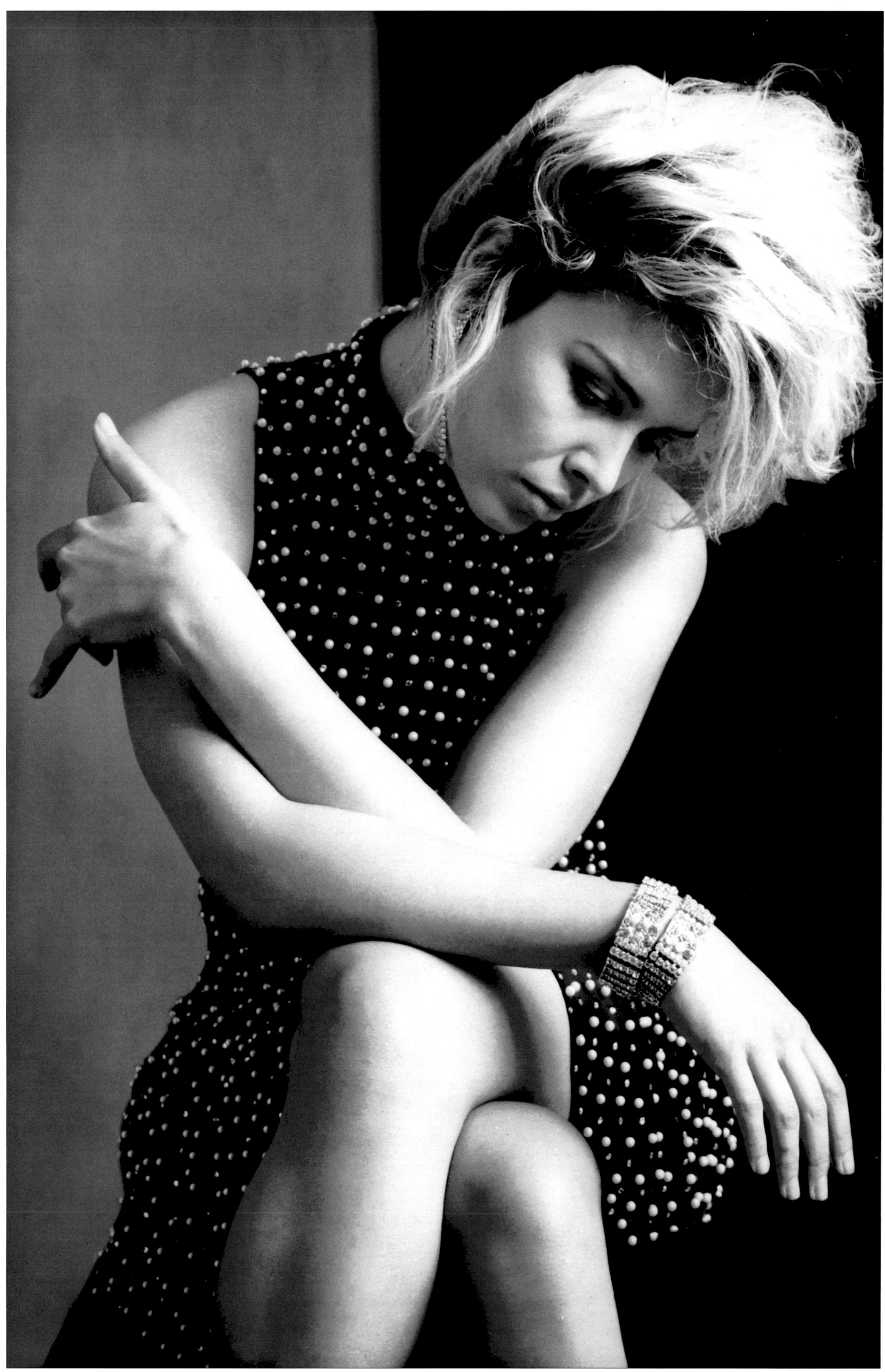

## DAVID & RICHARD ATTENBOROUGH

Given the choice of subject, Ivy Smith chose the Attenborough brothers for a commission from the National Portrait Gallery. The unveiling of the painting was a great opportunity to talk with the naturalist I'd been listening to since childhood. The 'Life of Birds' episode in New Zealand featured the kakapo, a large flightless parrot on the endangered list. The narrator faced the camera with the bird behind him, continuing ... 'the kakapo's only means of defence is to freeze, keeping absolutely still, till the predator moves on' ... the cameraman could be heard chuckling and the camera started to jiggle up and down as the bird unfroze and calmly walked out of shot. Unaware, Attenborough continued with an empty frame behind him as the rest of the crew fell about laughing. Full marks to the editor of the series for having the wit to leave it in.

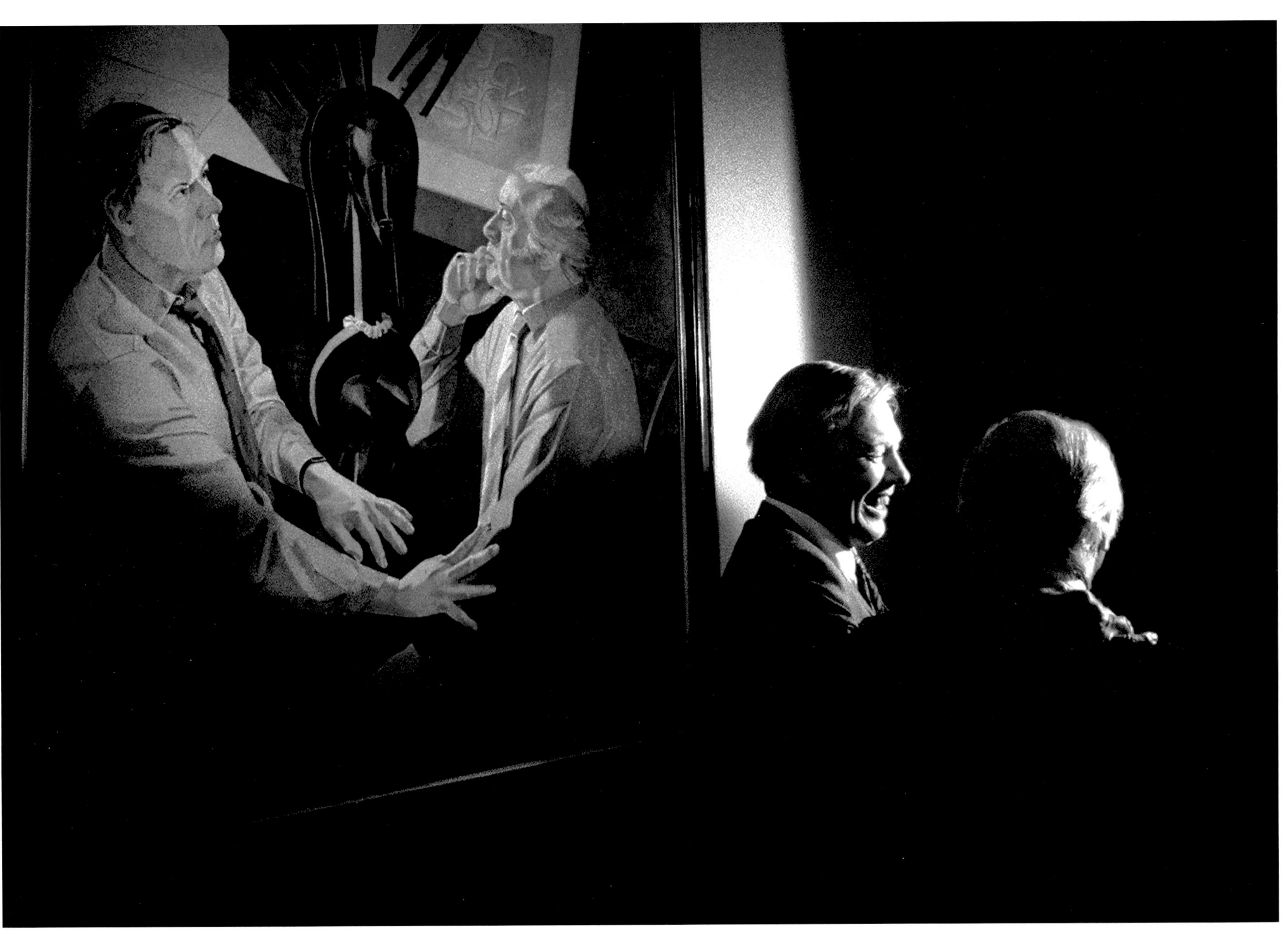

# GIANNI VERSACE

Maurice Béjart wrote a ballet for Sylvie Guillem based on the life of Elizabeth, the Empress of Russia, known as 'Sissi'. Versace was hired for the costumes and the premiere was to be at the Sadler's Wells Theatre. At the last moment a reluctant Sissi was persuaded by Tony Shepherd to accept at least one photographer, who arrived flustered and without any film. A quick call had my wife dragged out of her office and shanghaied into the rehearsal. Sissi danced the latter half in a simple slip as she descended into madness, whereas the opening had Versace and an army of dressers pinning and primping a champagne ballgown, transforming the prima ballerina into the Empress.

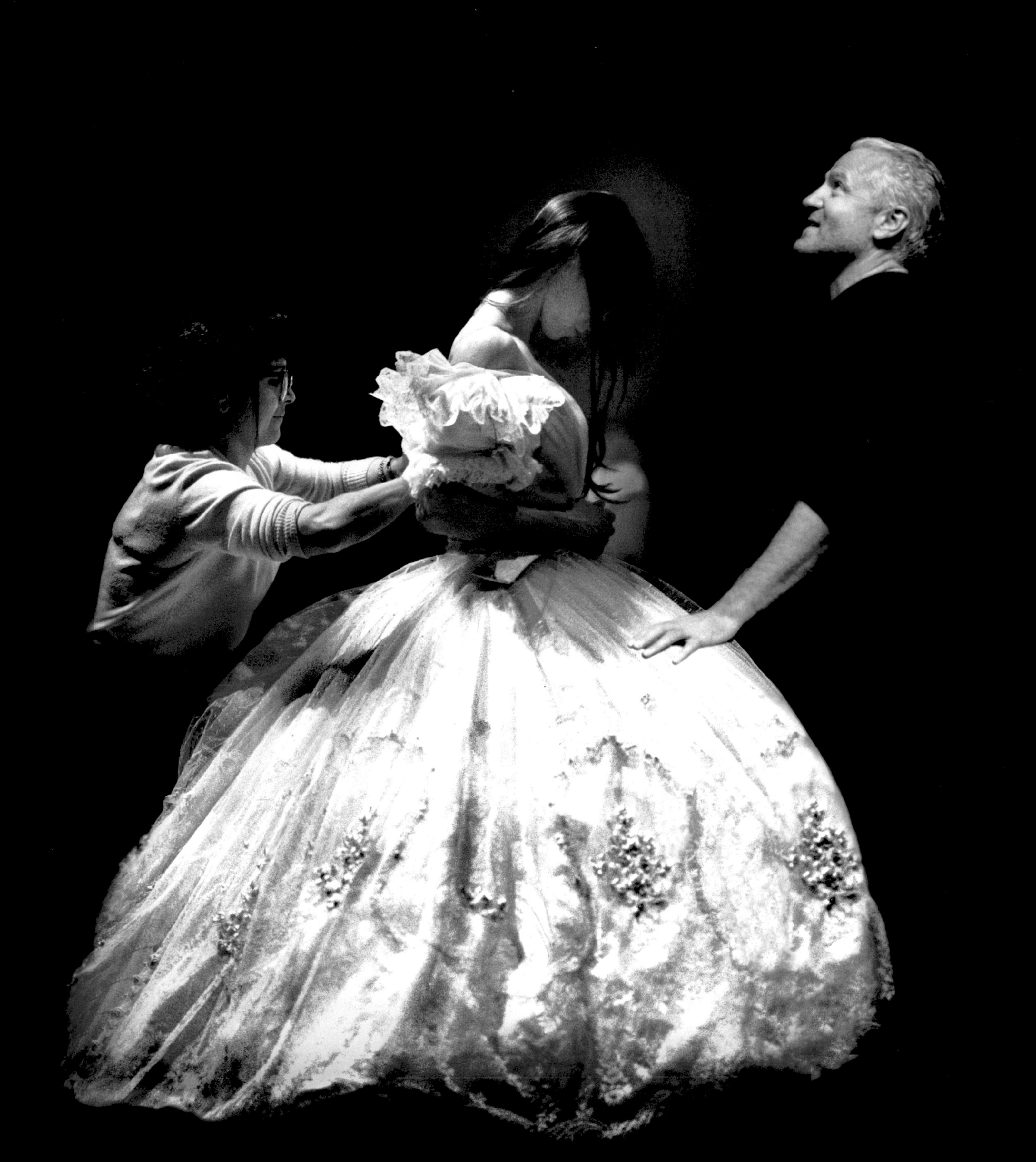

# MICHAEL FOOT

Since editing *The Evening Standard* at the youthful age of twenty-eight, it was his habit to read a paper on his way to work from Hampstead to Westminster. The Leader of the Opposition on the top deck of a number 24 bus ... what a gift. I, too, was on the way to work, for *The Independent*, so it was appropriate he was reading about Margaret Thatcher in that newspaper.

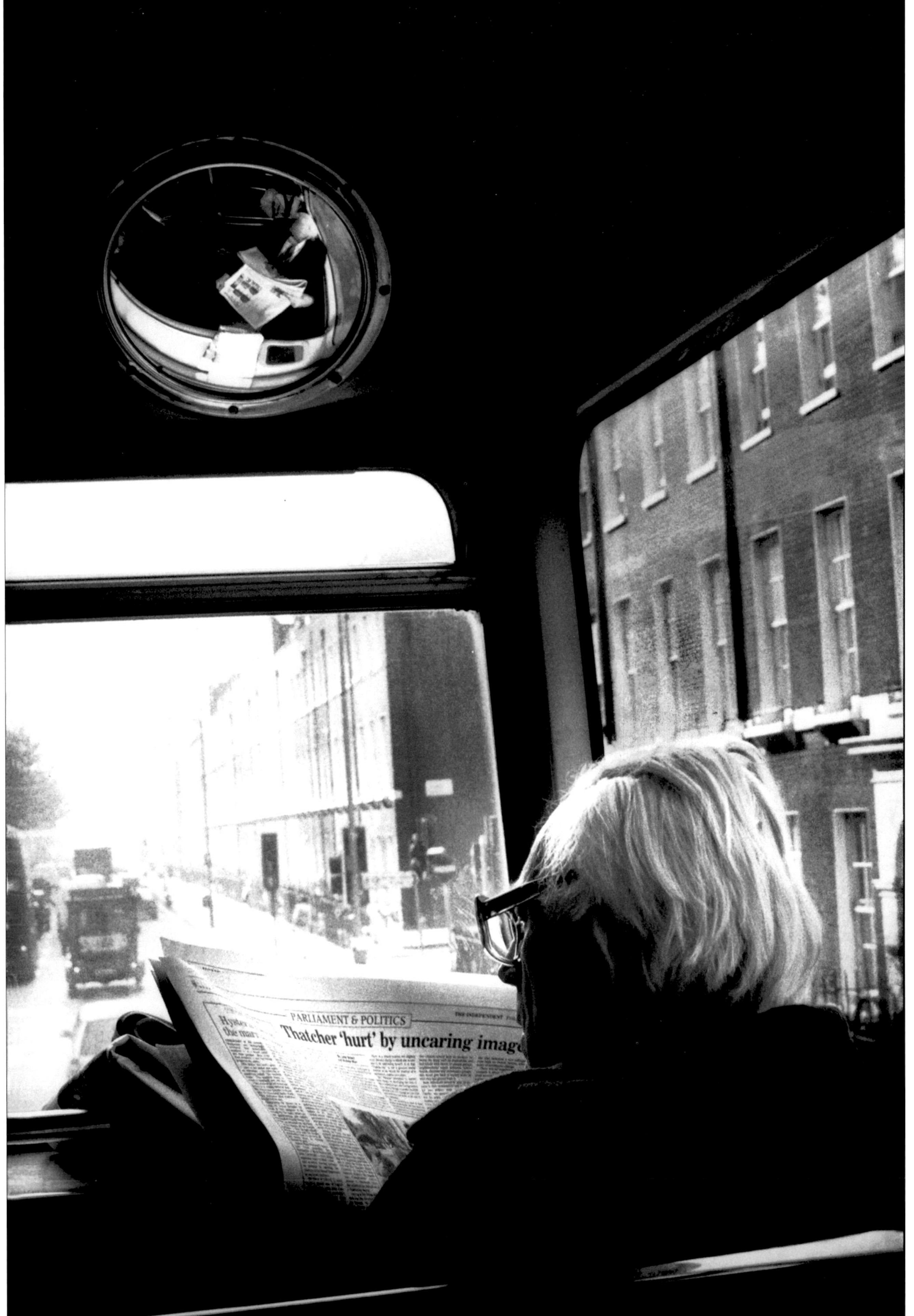
PARLIAMENT & POLITICS
Thatcher 'hurt' by uncaring

## JERRY LEE & LINDA GAIL LEWIS

When I saw him in the early 1960s the Killer was playing small clubs in the UK, like the Flamingo in Wardour Street, too jam-packed to dance, just a mass of bodies swaying as one, but you could see his hands flying over the keys and the sound came from the piano rather than an amplifier. A decade later, playing the first ever gig in a British sports stadium, he stomped, hollered and blew the crowd and the piano right out of the arena. Fresh as a daisy, he sat with his sister for the camera backstage, as if ready for a prayer meeting.

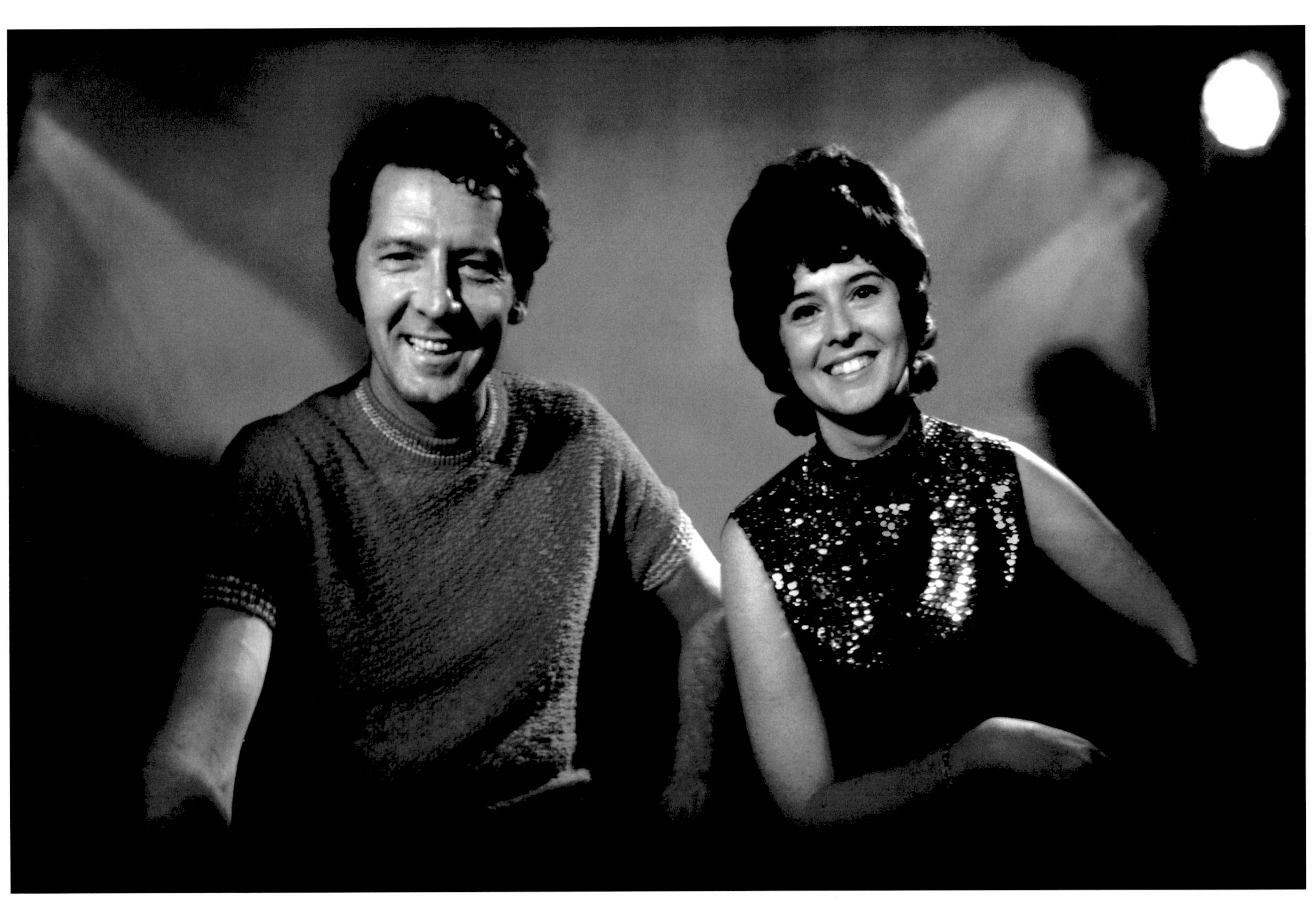

# LUCIANO PAVAROTTI

Earlier that morning, dressed in a peasant blouse and surrounded by village maidens, he was singing Nemorino in Donizetti's *L'Elisir d'Amore*, now struggling to leave the theatre he was dressed like Nanook of the North, surrounded by matrons seeking his autograph. One dared to ask for an encore of 'una furtive lagrima' but he demurred, apologising he must protect the voice and made his escape into the street theatre of the piazza.

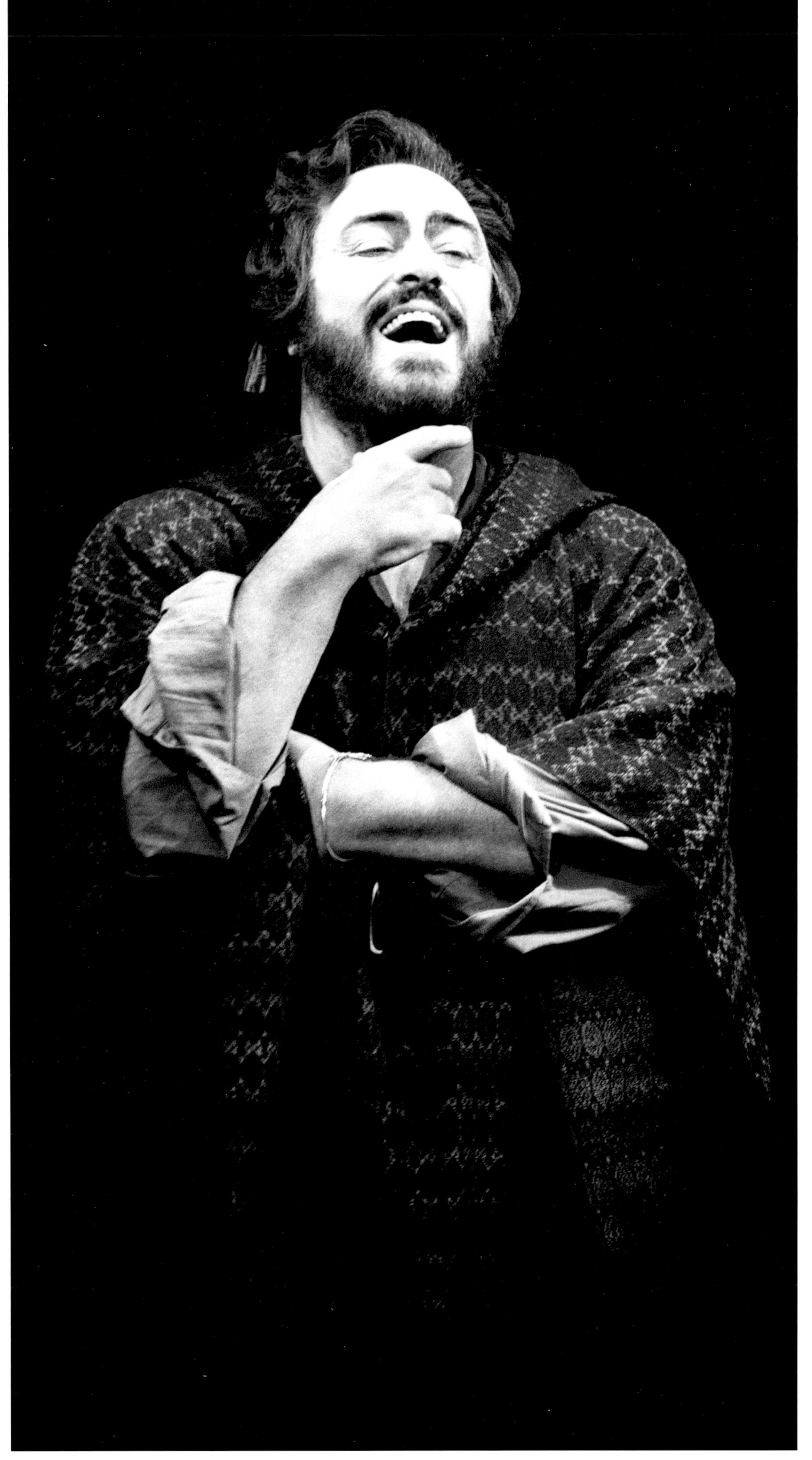

## JENNY SAVILLE

She was twenty-three years old when Charles Saatchi purchased her entire exhibition. Sitting in the gallery, dwarfed by her self-portraits she appeared self-contained and shyly confident. I liked her work, particularly the witty *Plan*, a nude figure whose contours were drawn like those on an Ordnance Survey map.

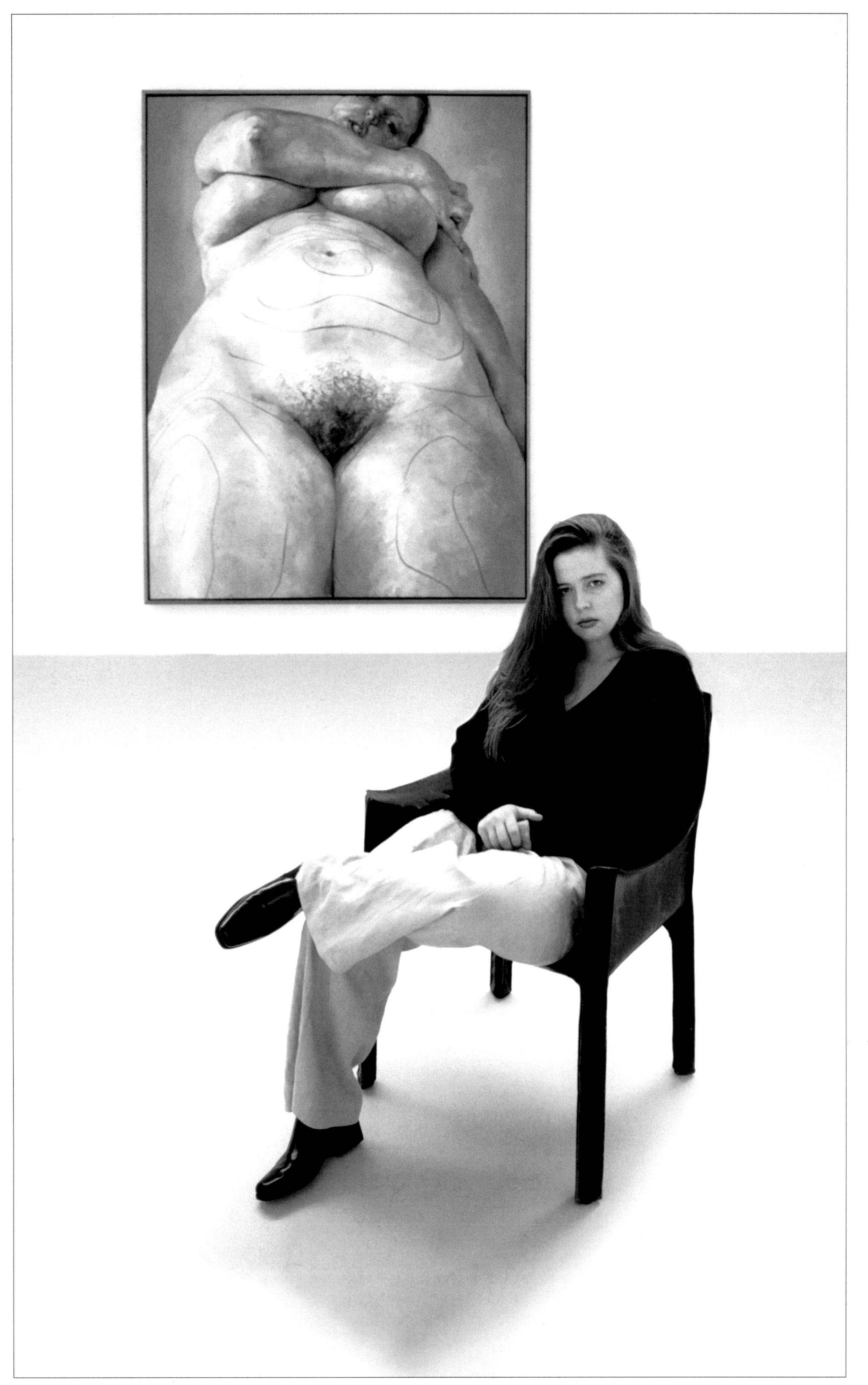

# FLOYD PATTERSON

He was the youngest-ever undisputed Heavyweight Champion of the World and the first to lose and regain the title, as Muhammed Ali did years later. Patterson was ringside at Madison Square Garden as guest fight commentator. I was in New York working on the 'Time-Life Great Cities' series when a man approached and said his photographer hadn't shown, would I fill in? The local film laboratory had a breakdown, many rolls were ruined ... this had never happened before or since, this one survived.

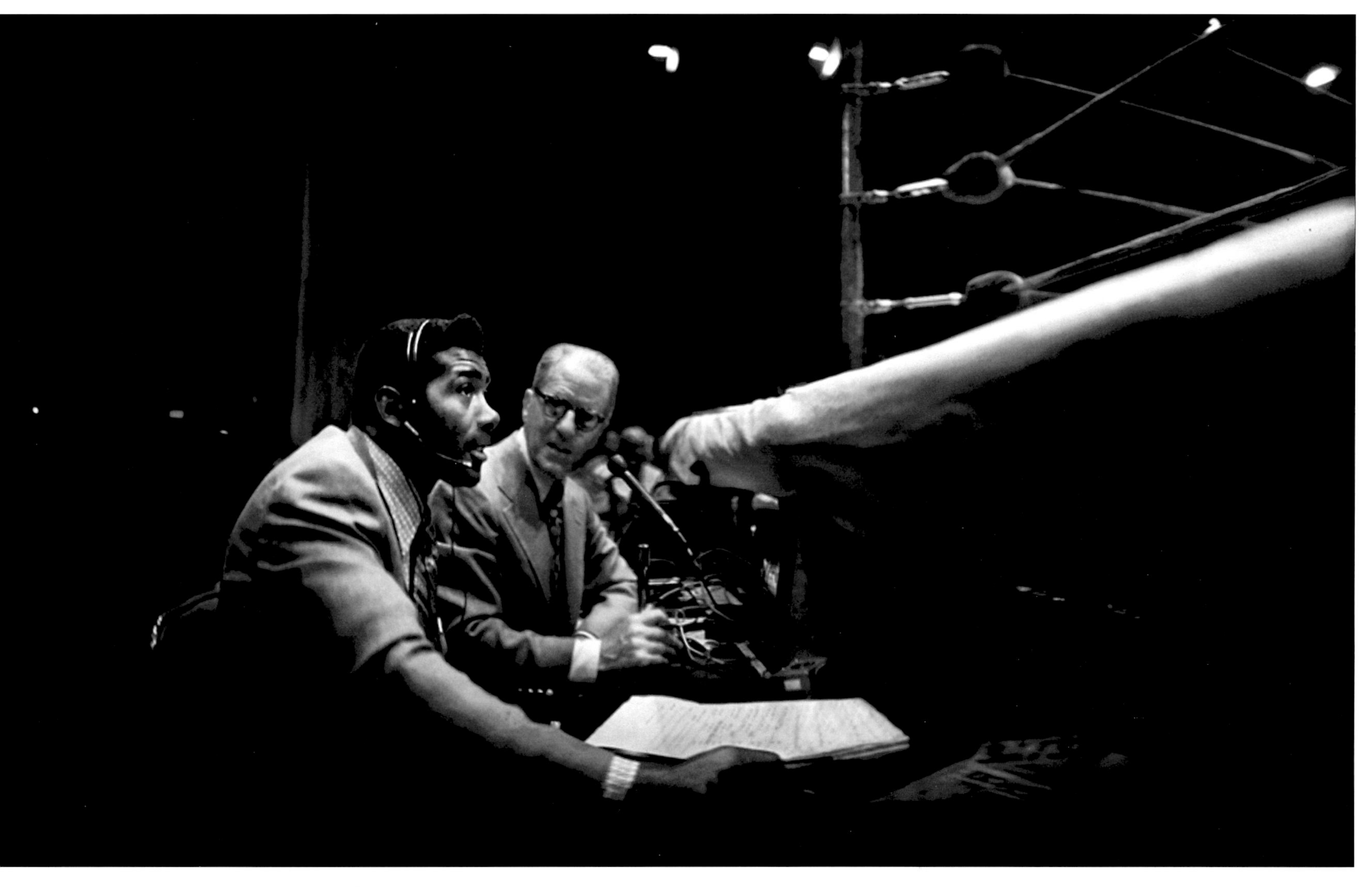

# JULIE WALTERS

'… It's no problem, love' …
I had asked her to sit in front of the dressing-table mirror and she burnt her bare shoulder on the hot lights. Anyone else would have kicked me out. A great start. Uncomplaining, she graciously moved to the safety of the window, an utterly charming and forgiving professional.

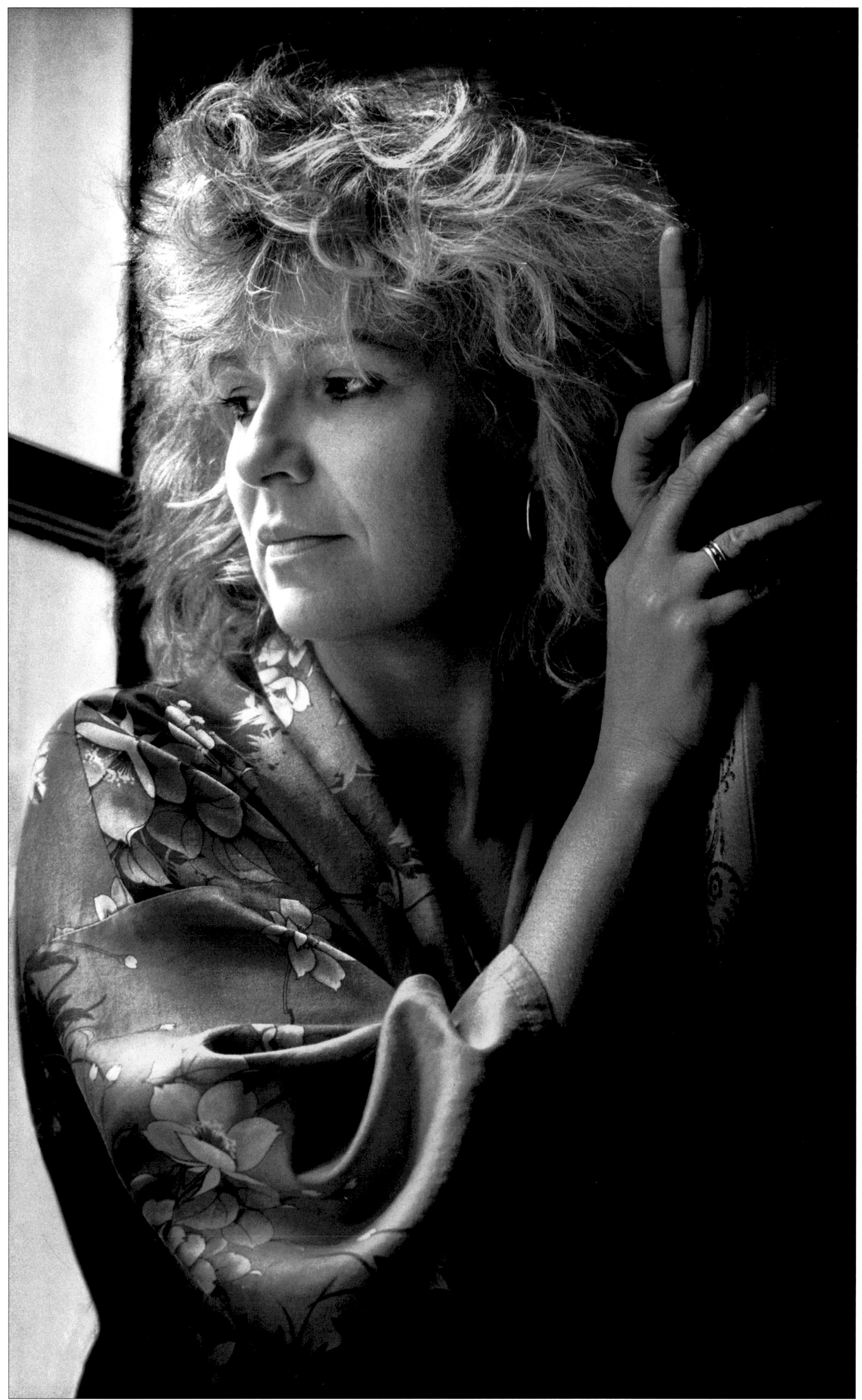

# ORNETTE COLEMAN

No surprise ... it was at art school I was hearing free jazz for the first time and his *Change of the Century* was the first important album. It's still fresh and slightly dangerous, even now. An enlightened soul at the Royal Festival Hall chose the musician and composer to curate the Meltdown Festival of Music on the Southbank. There were the usual obstacles for a picture ... not on stage, not backstage and this was just a rehearsal. There was a cast of managers, producers, technicians all saying 'impossible, no chance' ... during a lull, I asked him directly would he spare a few moments for a portrait in the foyer? He smiled and said, 'Why not?' ... natural light was more sympathetic than the follow spots, he leant on a banister, smiled once more, shook my hand, and was away.

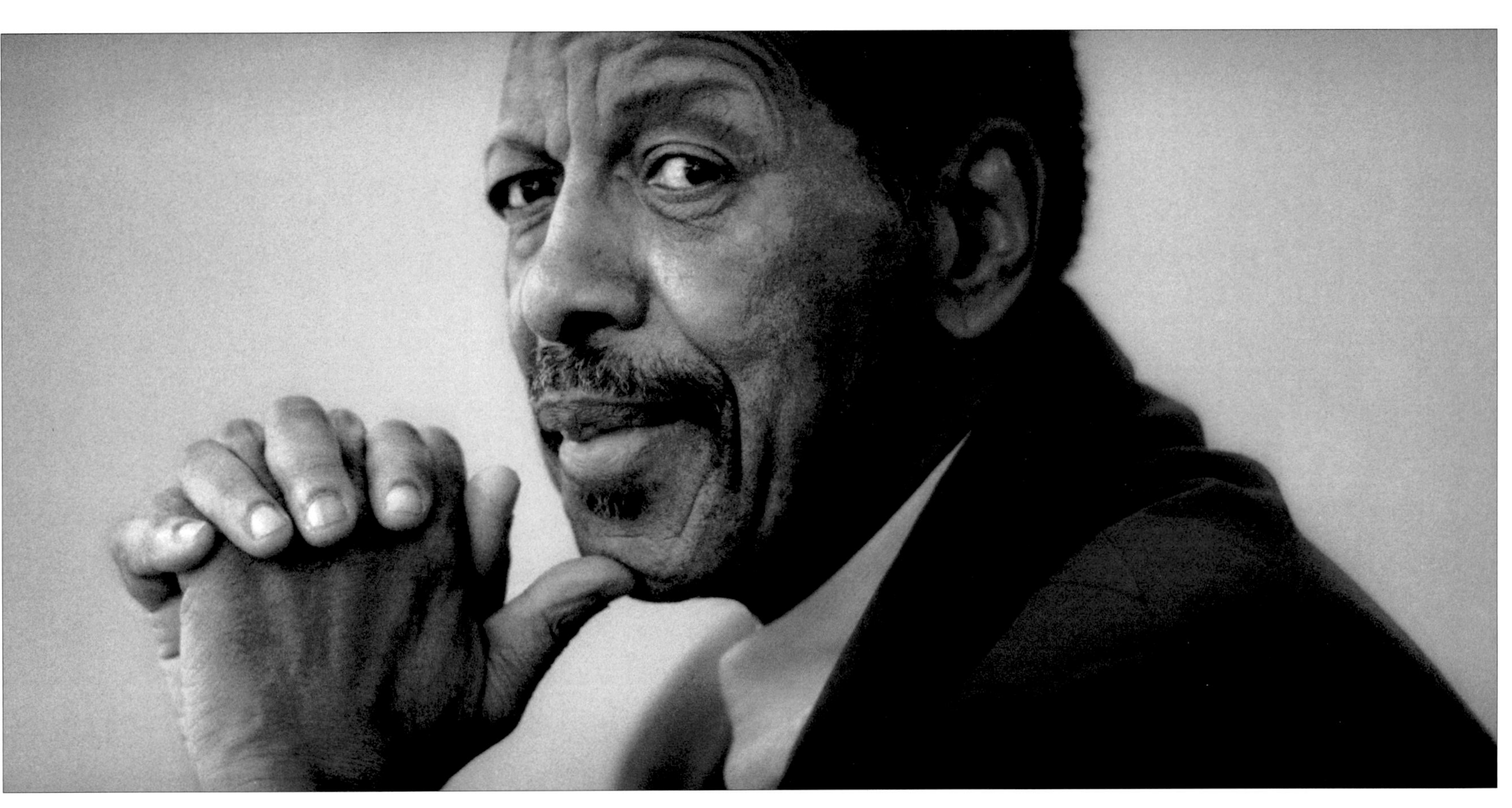

# THE BALLET BOYZ

I'd worked with Michael Nunn and William Trevitt a number of times at the Royal Ballet and later in their own company George Piper Dances, action pictures and portraits, so this was going to be a relaxed occasion. I'd planned some tight close-ups inside the studio and was about to wind it up when they both said, 'there's some great graffiti around the corner' ... Reluctantly agreed to take a look. They were right; it made a better shot in the evening summer light with the additional gift of Banksy's deep-sea diver between them.

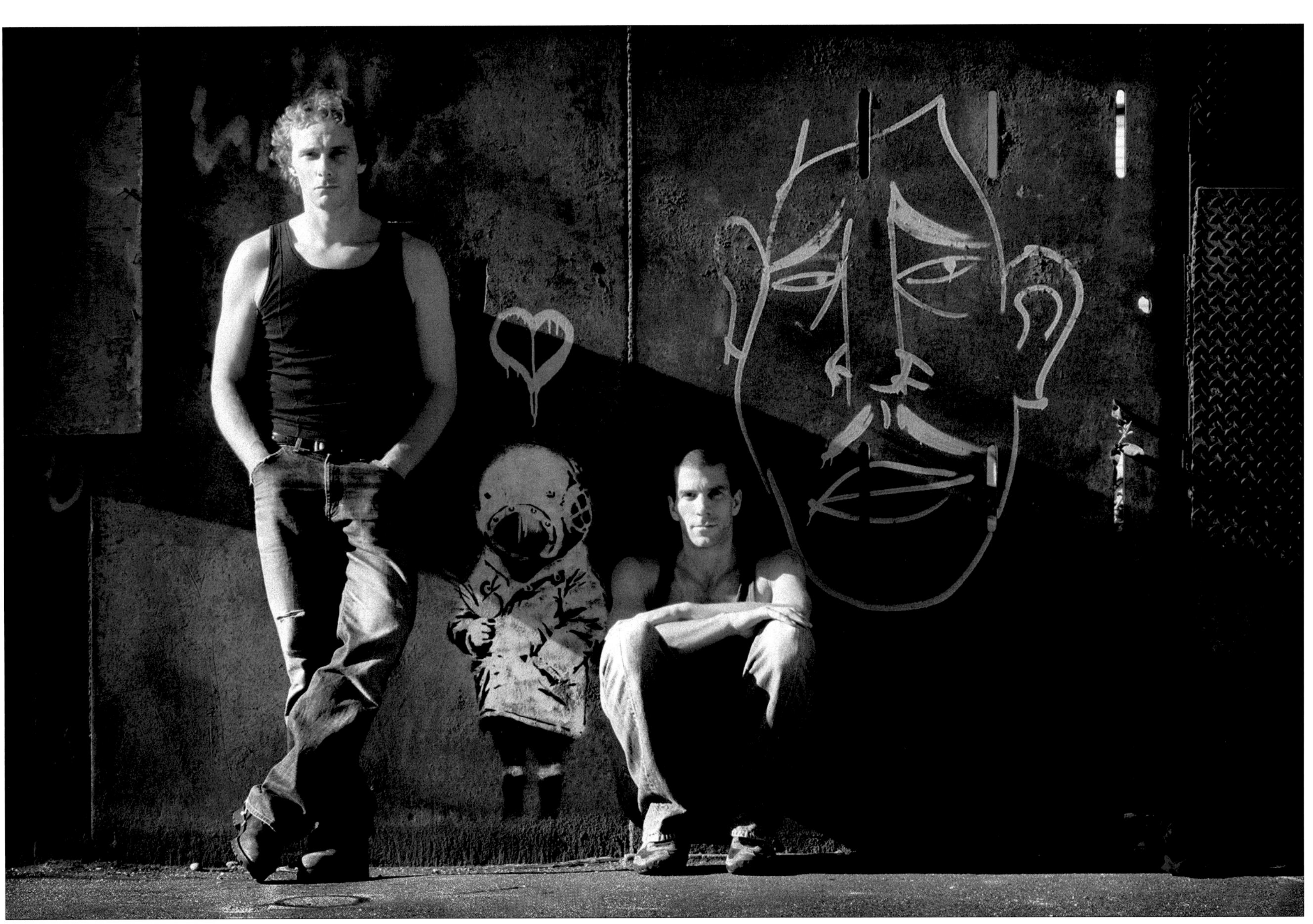

## MELISSA PHELPS

An unexpected burst of sunlight through the filigree shutters made the shot. The celebrated cellist was being made a Fellow of the Royal College of Music, and the session at Leighton House, Holland Park was to mark the occasion. Phelps works as a soloist, recitalist, chamber musician and teacher, having studied under Paul Tortelier and played with the late Jacqueline du Pré.

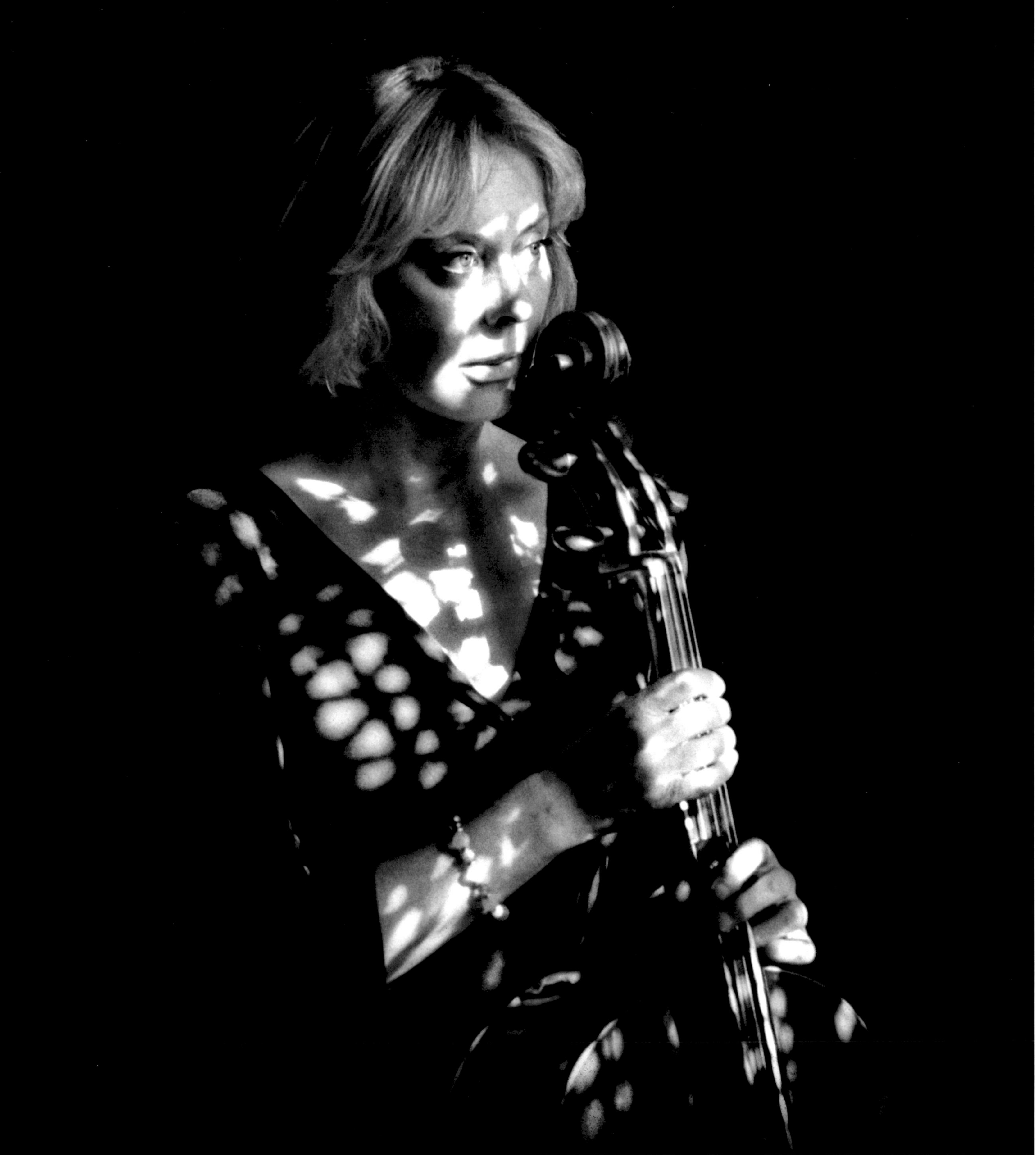

## RUDOLF NUREYEV

While the columnist interrogated his manager, I glanced up and saw him leaning out of a high window. We were lakeside in a converted convent at Lago del Orta, north of Milan. I took the hotel lift to the top floor and he stepped in. On the ground floor was a portrait of the Mother Superior, her hand with the dancer's own made a triangular shape which completed the composition. He went out of his way to be hospitable, escorting us in a motor-launch to a tiny island for a pasta lunch. The journalist really upset him with some intrusive questioning which ended any chance of seeing him dance in Gogol's *Overcoat* that evening. I made my apologies and left. Sadly, the portrait was the last one published of him looking well.

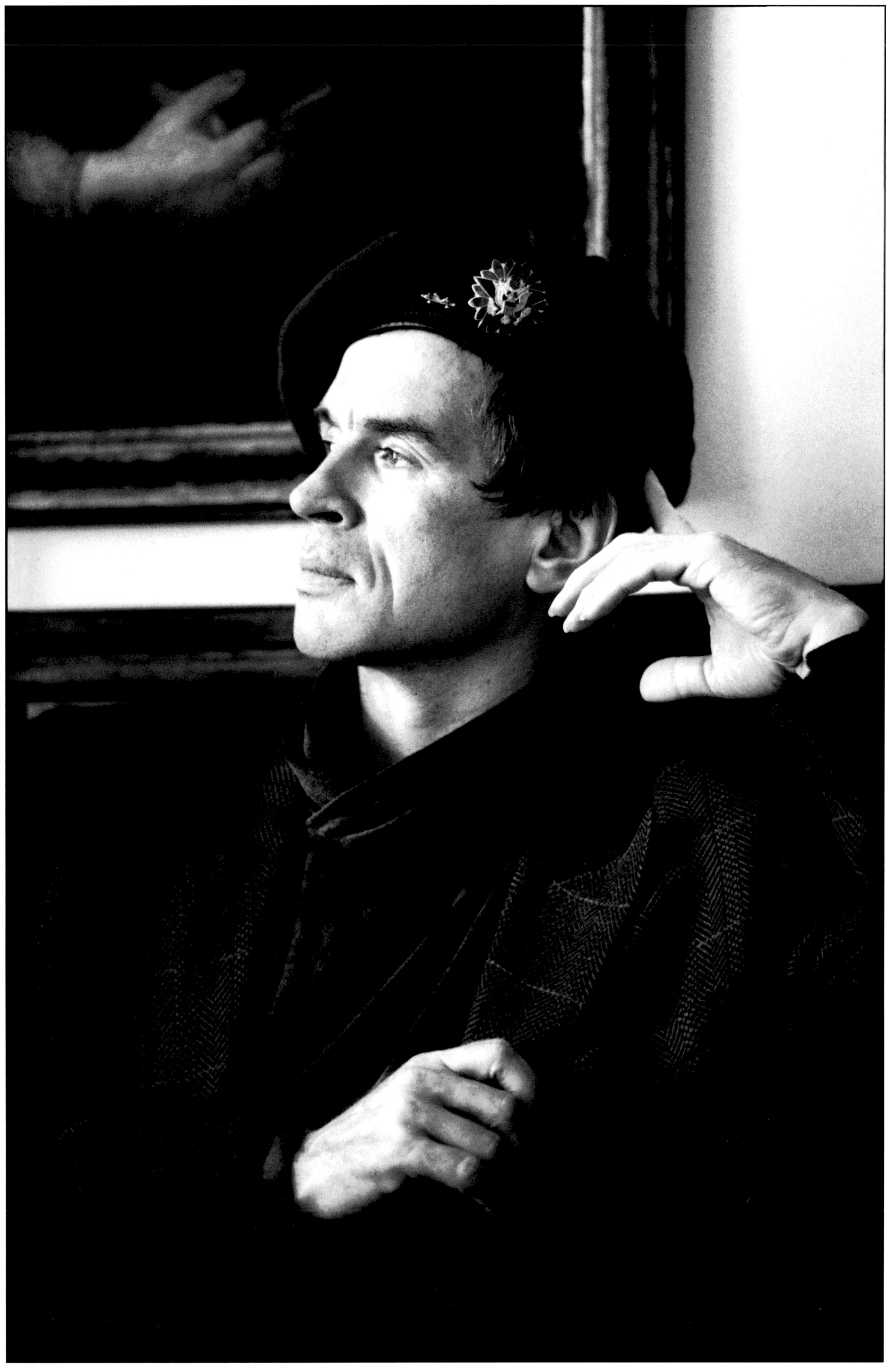

# NICOLA BENEDETTI

This was something of a contrast to seeing her with an excited audience and full orchestra at The Last Night of The Proms in the more formal atmosphere of the Royal Albert Hall. It was a blazing hot summer day and the Scottish virtuosi was to be found rehearsing in the relative cool of the Royal College of Music with just a conductor for company.

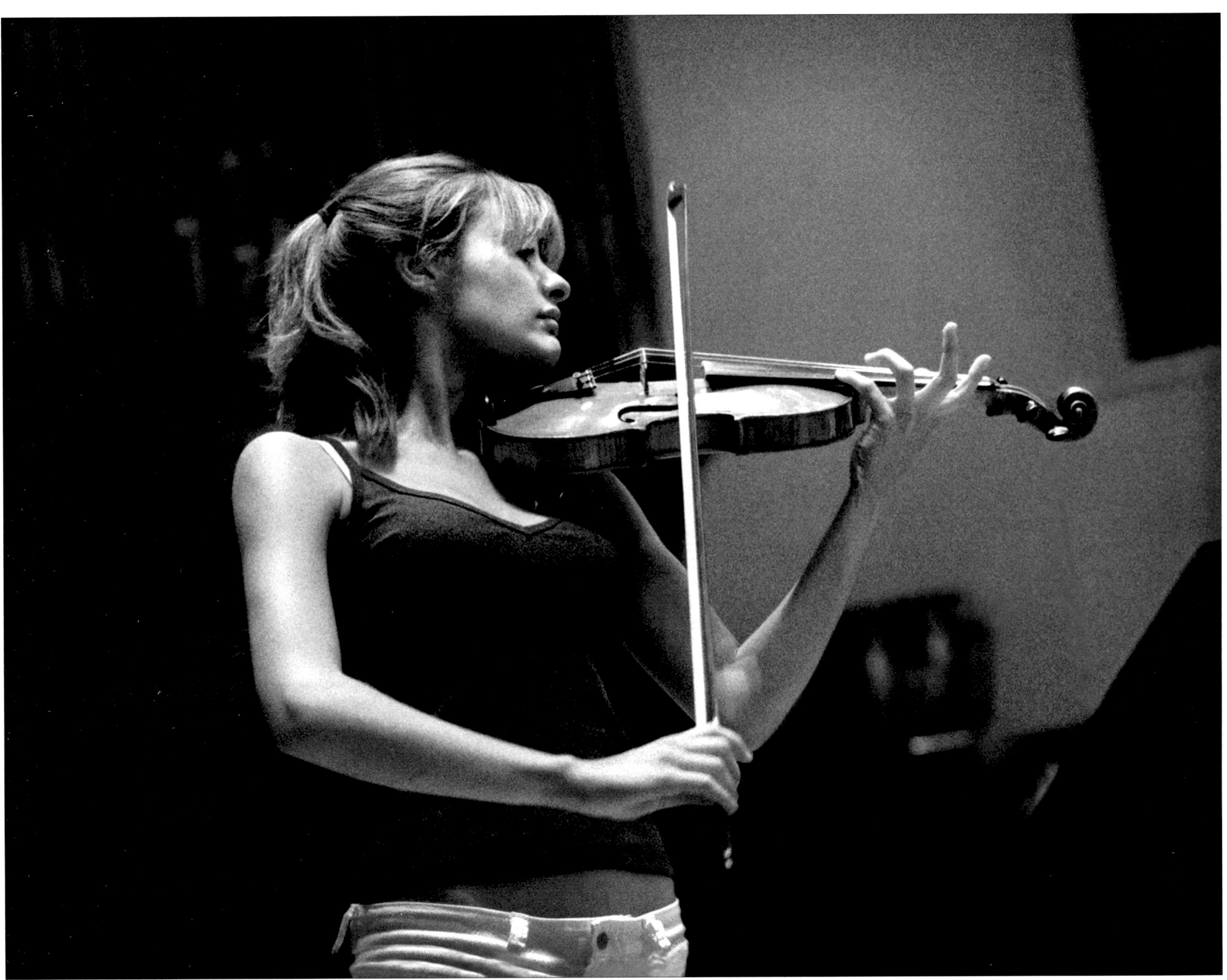

## STEPHEN SONDHEIM

News photographers regard pen-pushers as visual illiterates and journalists repay the compliment believing all snappers to be morons. Both views might be correct but some desk-bound editors do bear a slight grudge towards those out in the field ... 'He's camera shy, you won't get it' ... At the Phoenix before a performance of *Into The Woods*, the composer happened to be standing by the stage door, amiable and cooperative.

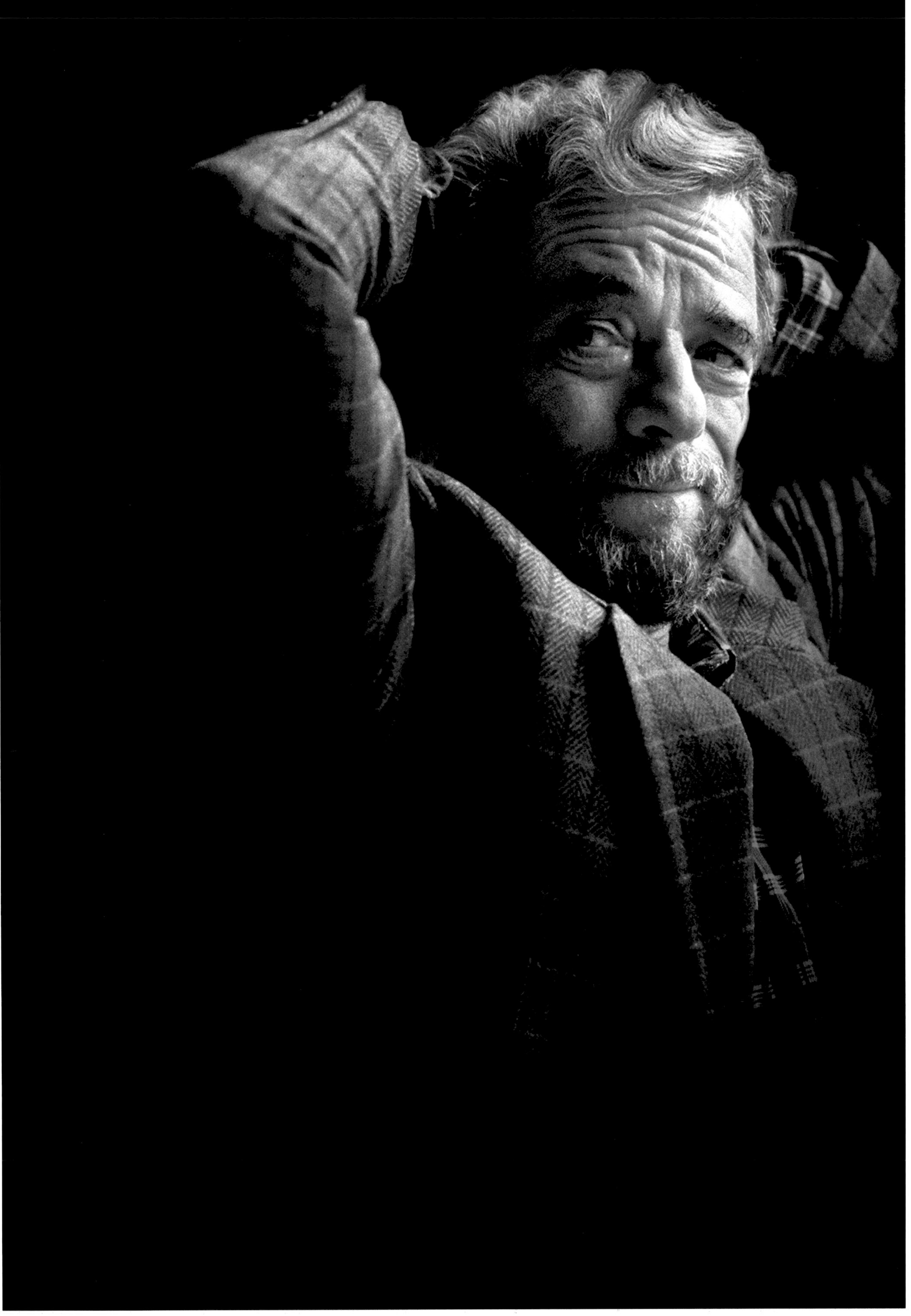

# BRIDGET RILEY

An intriguing quote by the artist ... 'Focusing isn't just an optical activity, it is also a mental one' ... yes, I would certainly agree with that. At the opening of her show at the Serpentine Gallery, I wanted to make the portrait in front of her well-known canvas *Cataract 2*.

'Ms Riley, would you please stand in front of this painting?'

'No.'

'Well, would you please stand in front of this poster of the painting?'

'No.'

'Ok ... let's do it right here, profile please' ... click.

Moments later, photographed the painting and superimposed it in the darkroom. She was right, the resulting image was much stronger than the first idea, the lines seemed to follow the contours of the face, like a bank note engraving.

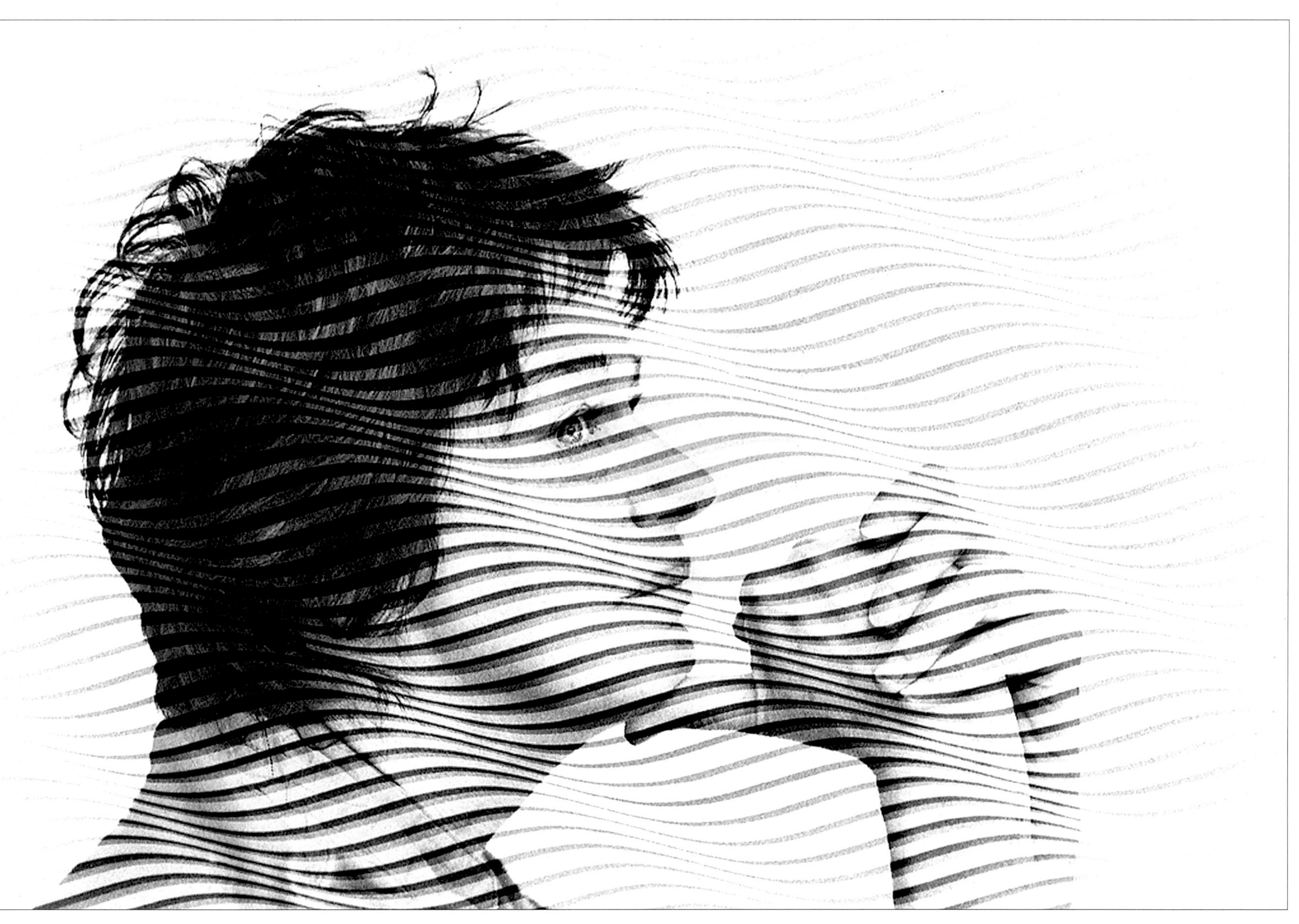

# CARLOS ACOSTA

It was a dream commission for the premiere of Acosta's *Tocororo* at Sadler's Wells ... fly to Havana, shoot the show at Gran Teatro, backstage rehearsals, portraits, morning class at the Ballet Nacional, on the beach with his family, break-dancing in the street, and ... a poster. The poster gave the most trouble, himself sitting on a 1950s chrome-covered American heap, with blue skies and palm trees. The onstage car was a green Chevrolet ... green?, it had to be red. Crossing town with producer Andy Wood, I spotted a huge red automobile chugging along, leapt out and slammed both hands on the bonnet, tucked a $50 note in the driver's shirt pocket and in atrocious Spanish, '*Por favor*, please be at the Hotel Nacional, Saturday'. The dancer had twenty minutes, where was the car? Chugalug over the hill came the shiny red 1952 Buick saloon. Barefoot, Carlos sitting on the car with and without his co-star Veronica Corveas, blue sky, palm trees blowing in a cool breeze, it was a wrap.

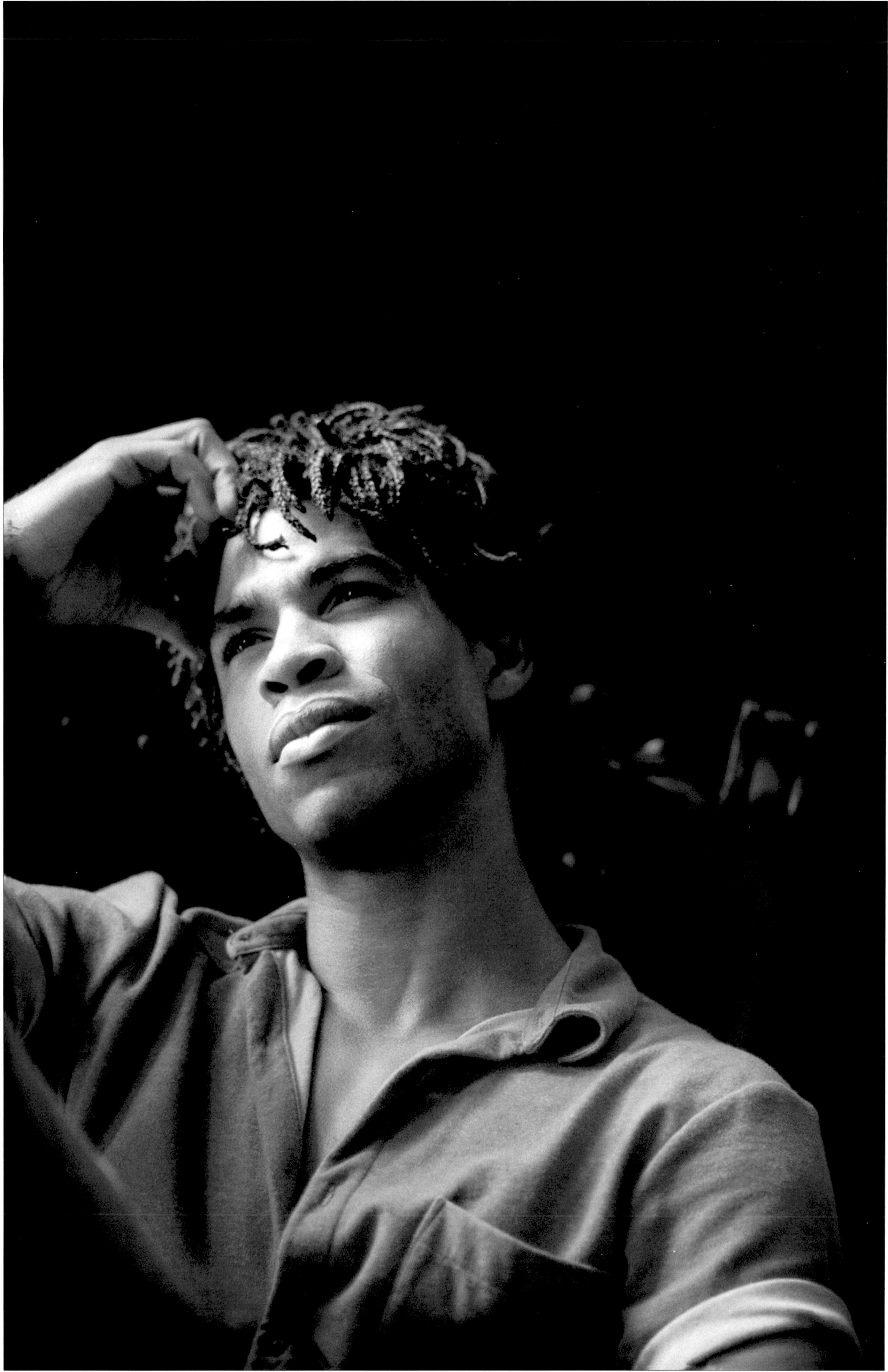

## MARTY WILDE, CLIFF RICHARD & DUFFY POWER

In the late 1950s Jack Good returned from America with the idea of a rock'n'roll show on British television, recruiting three cool cats, Marty Wilde 19 years old, Cliff Richard 18 and Duffy Power 17. Hanging around the 'Oh Boy!' stage door a fifteen-year old schoolboy watched The Drifters unload, picked up a guitar and Hey Presto was backstage with a Brownie 127 camera. The shooting script made the three soloists temporarily into a trio performing The Coasters' 'Three Cool Cats' written by Leiber & Stoller, themselves New York City teenagers.

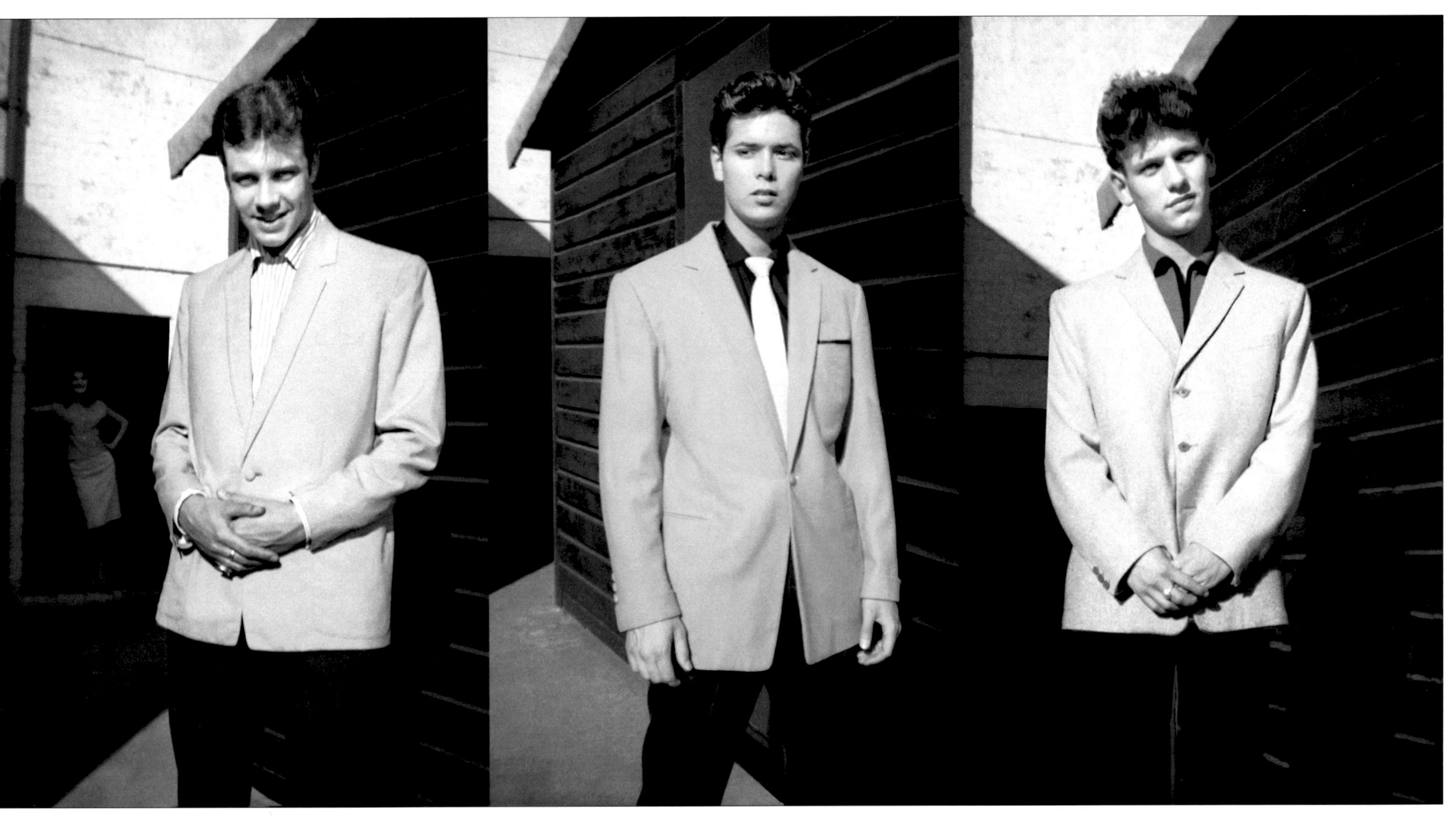

# DIZZY GILLESPIE

In the available dark at Ronnie Scott's Jazz Club, Dizzy held the floor. This was a commission for *Radio 3 Magazine*, the legend that played with Charlie Parker. I waited for the moment when he drew breath to avoid the puffed bullfrog cheeks, like waiting for an opera singer to close their mouth. He sang and played the piano but it had to be with his trademark bent horn. Despite the years in smoky clubs he lived to be ninety-three, an amazing man.

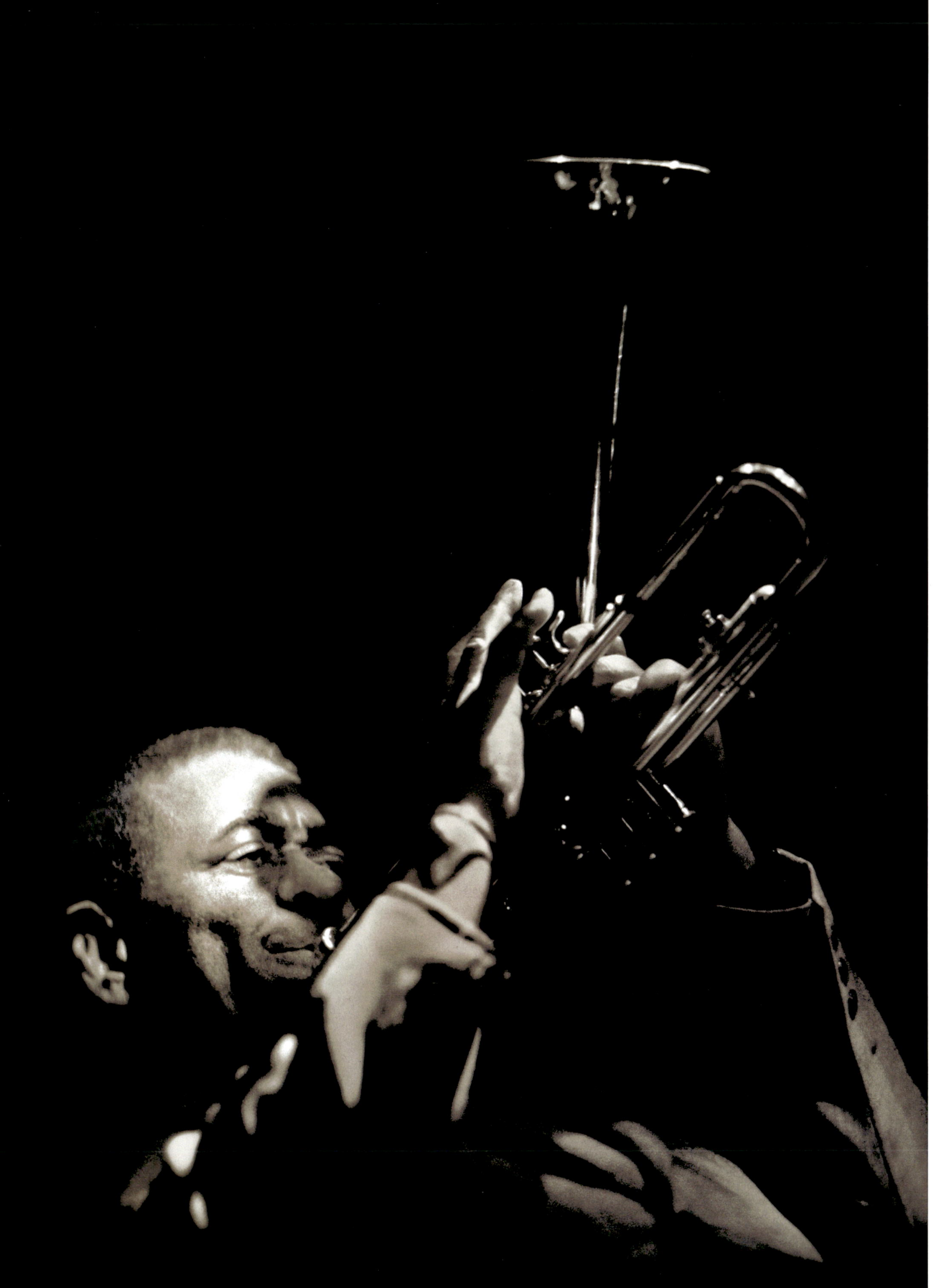

# JUDY TZUKE

For Ms Tzuke it was to be a long day in the studio. She arrived with hairdresser, make-up, wardrobe and accessories, very business-like with hair tightly pulled back into a snood, glamorous if a little severe. She made no fuss permitting the demolition of her coiffure, which dramatically softened the look, making her appear somewhat distant and vulnerable.

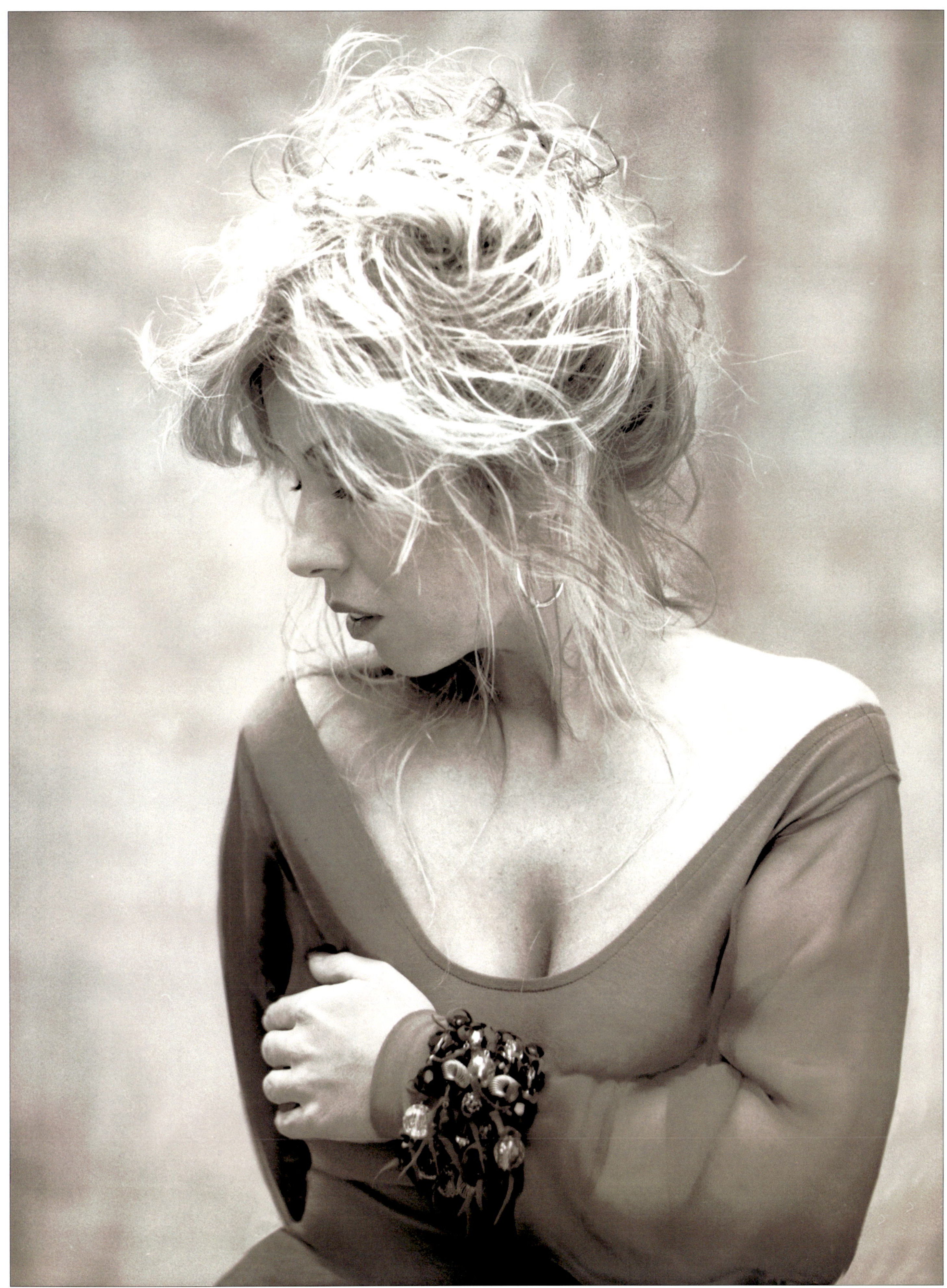

## IAN BOARD & DANIEL FARSON

Resembling a defrocked nun, the austere founder of the Colony Room Muriel Belcher persuaded the young Francis Bacon in the 1950s to recruit fellow refugees from early-closing pubs to the private intemperance club in Dean Street for relaxation in a malign atmosphere of fractious bickering and unrestricted drinking. Ian Board, the former barman, took over as ringmaster after she died and despite grumblings things carried on much as before. Daniel Farson, broadcaster and biographer, chronicled post-war bohemian Soho from its epicentre here at Muriel's. Perhaps the idea of a portrait prompted thoughts of mortality or vanity or both but climbing 'the filthy stairs' I was surprised at being honoured with an almost civilised reception.

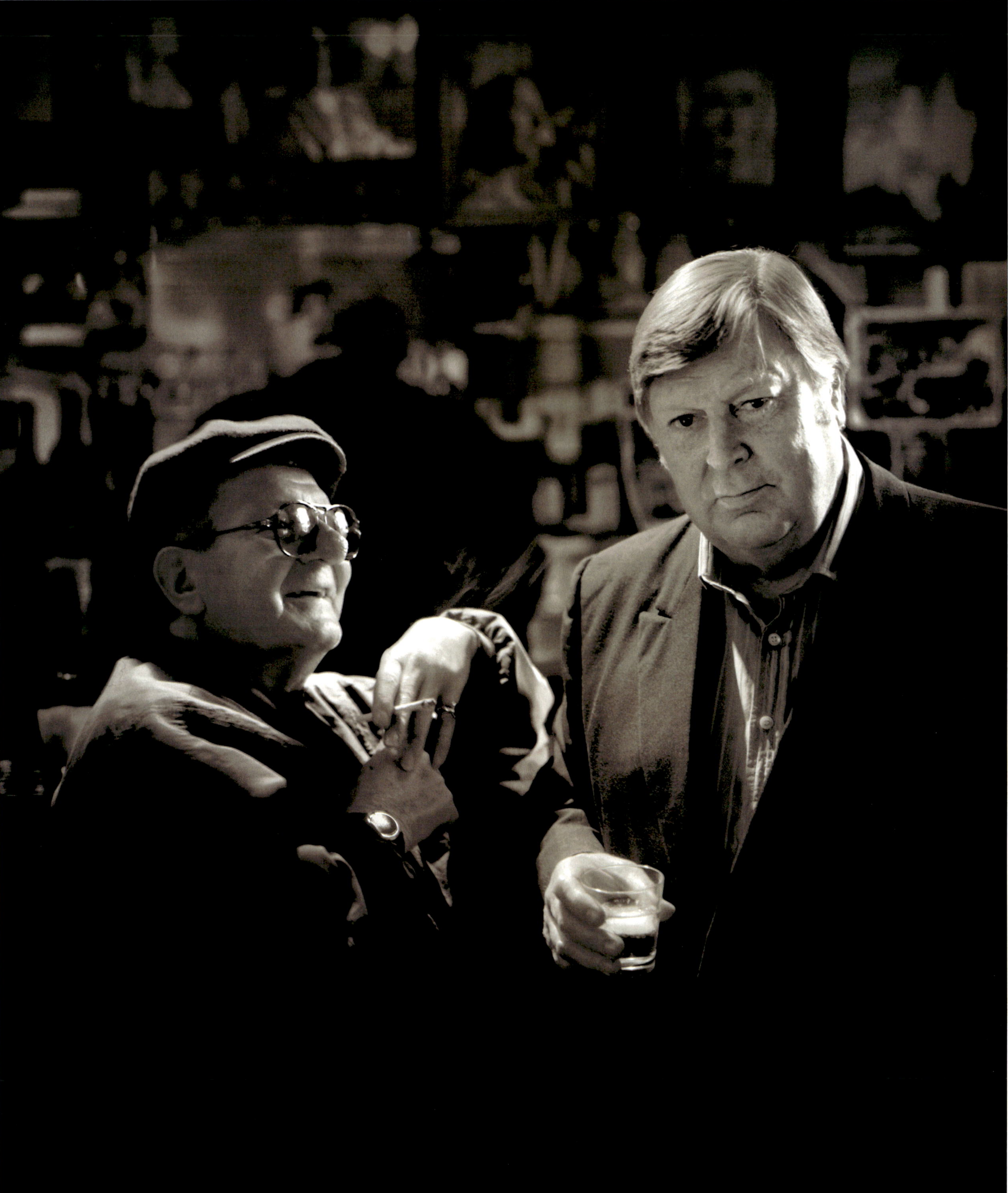

# RUBY WAX

I just listened ... for once I let the subject do the talking, she was like a shaken bottle of champagne, exploding over everything in the room, including Bette Davis who was hanging on the wall, a born comedienne. I hardly said a word, she fell naturally into position, next minute I was back out in the street. What a pro, her not me.

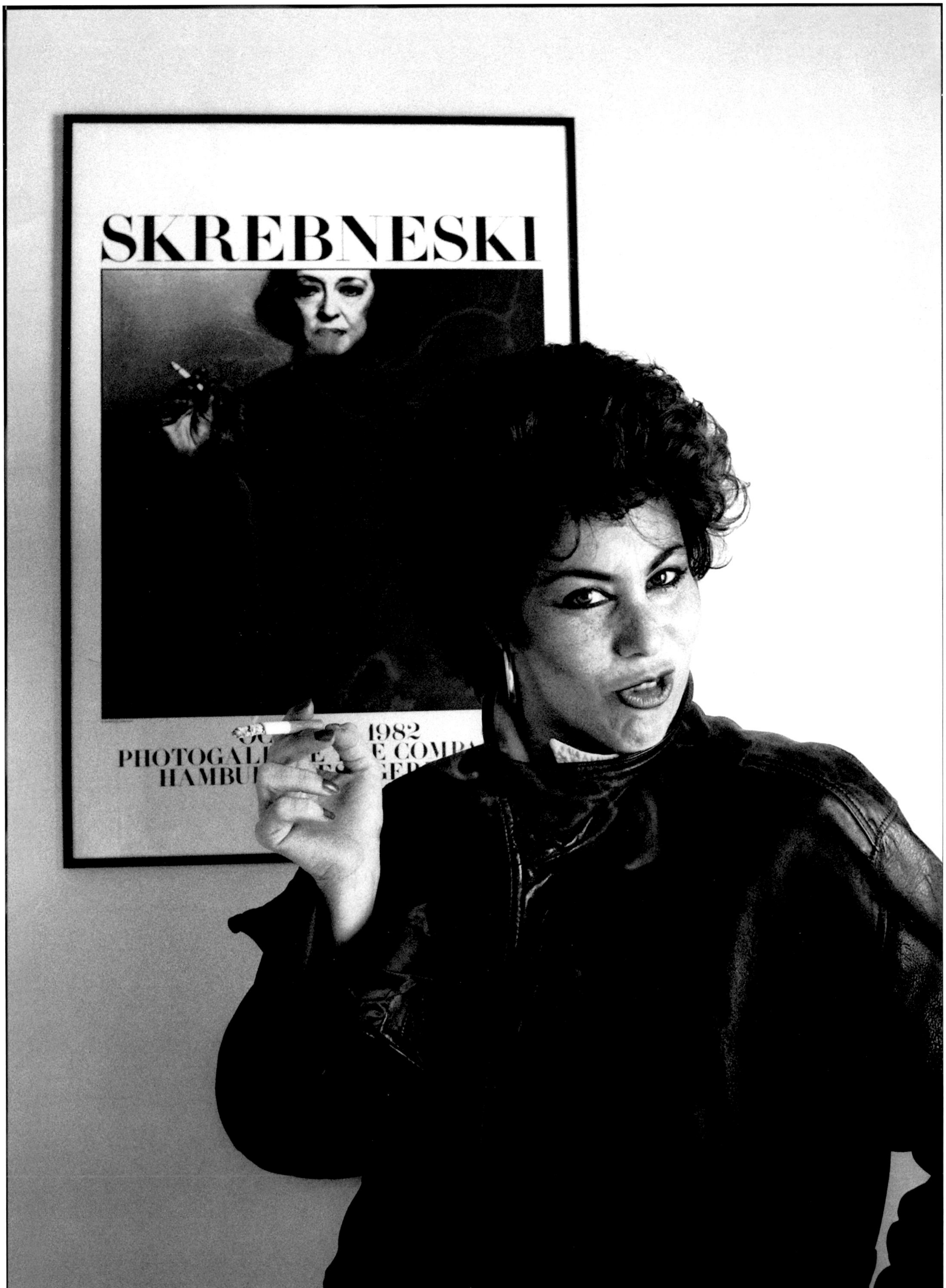

SKREBNESKI
1982

# HAROLD PINTER

The playwright was engrossed in the campaign against the war in Iraq, and not amenable to a portrait. Opening the front door he said ... 'Let's get it over with ... just here'. We were on the ground floor of his home in Notting Hill and the light was poor.

'May I look upstairs?' ...

'If you must.'

The light was right, he stood by the window prompting the memory of Vermeer's *Woman in Blue Reading a Letter*. Fortunately he was an admirer of the Dutch artist and as he picked up a letter, his mood changed and we chatted happily about his work and 17th-century painting.

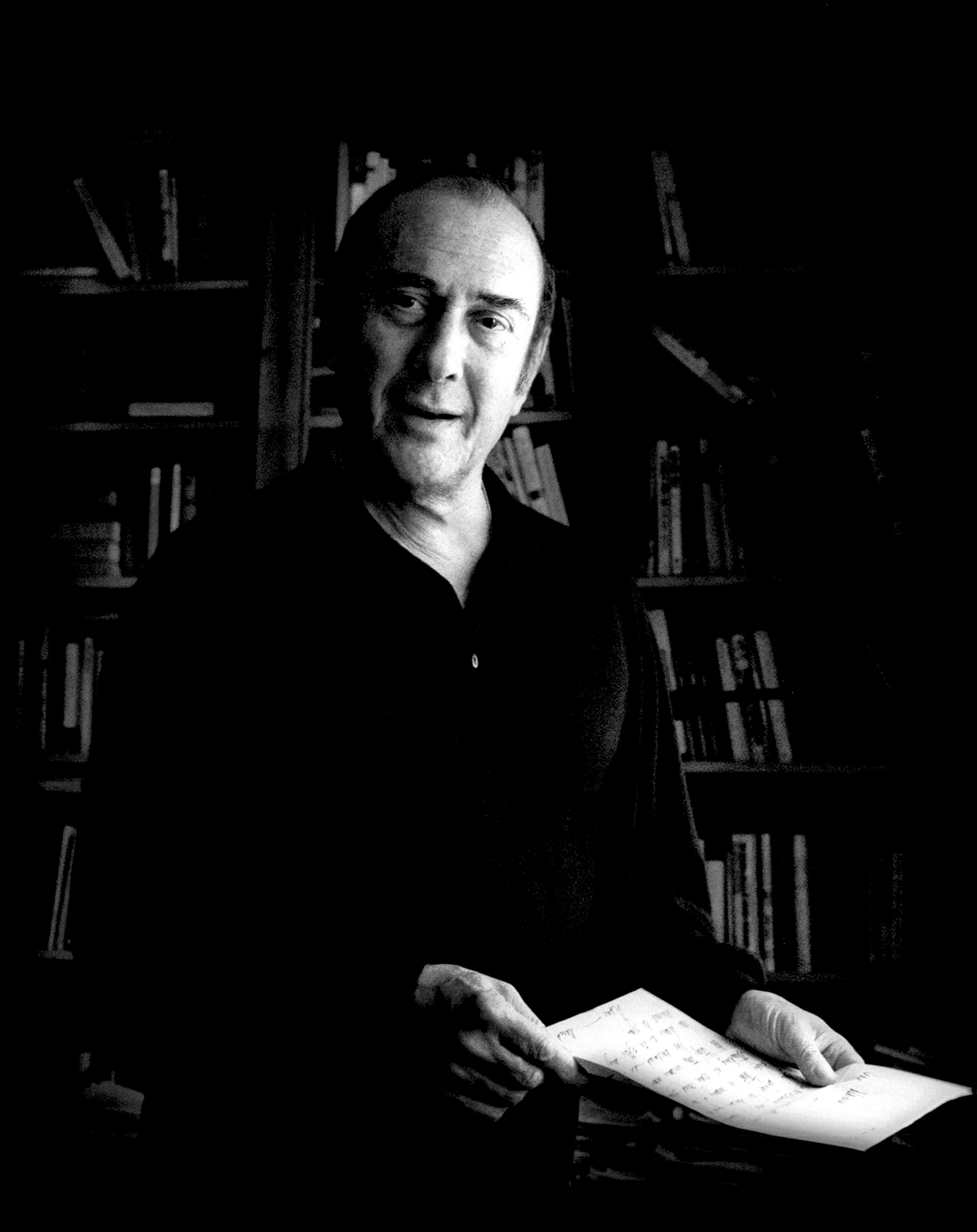

## VIVIENNE WESTWOOD & JOE CORRÉ

It was her idea to put Kirby grips in his hair to mimic her own. We were in the World's End shop on the King's Road, and Ms Westwood was teasing her son for being hours late. I liked the idea of reversing the man standing, woman sitting and so did she.

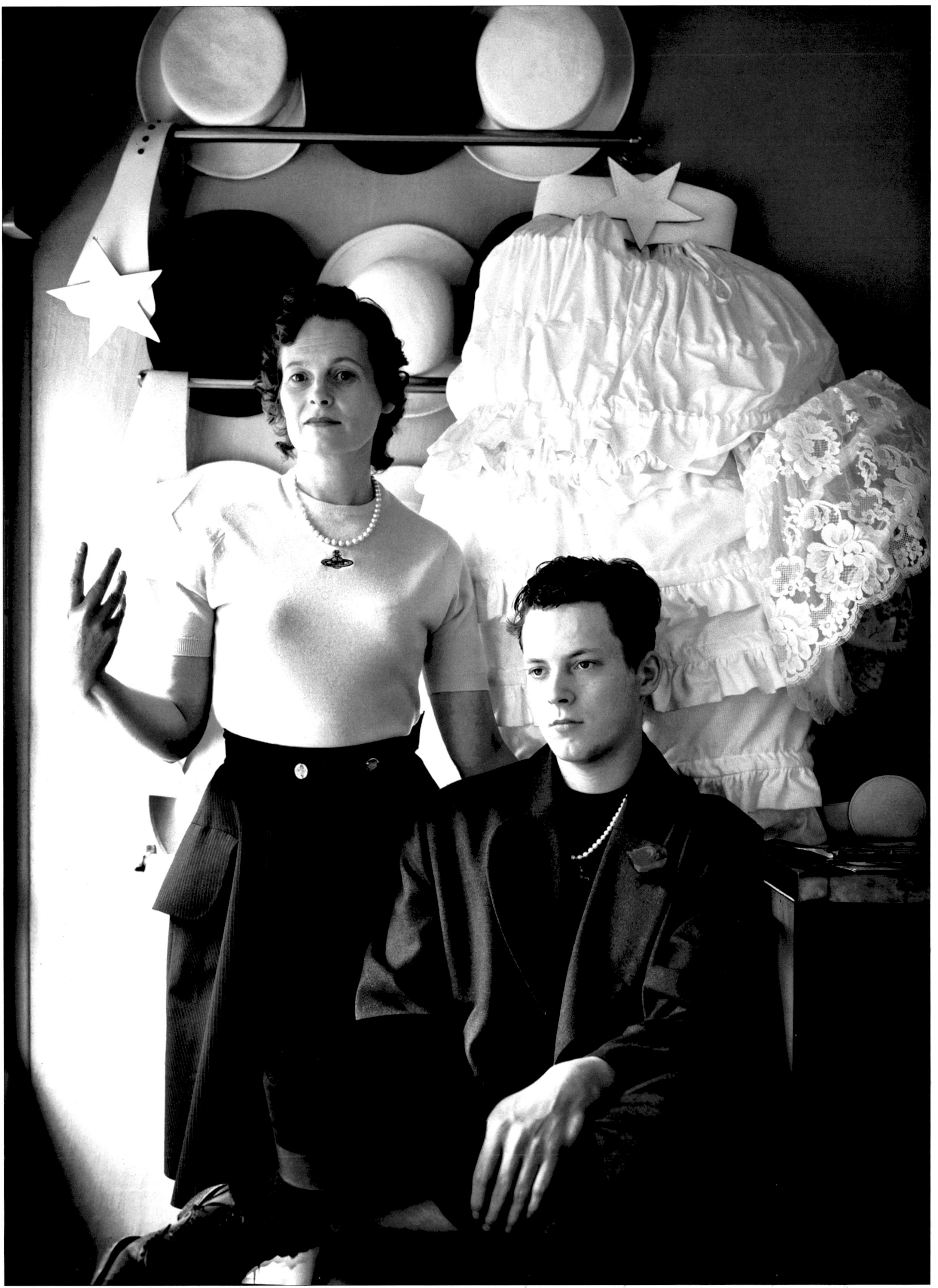

# BUZZ ALDRIN

When Edwin Eugene Aldrin Jnr was experiencing walking on the moon, I had to make do with watching him on television ... and it seemed unbelievable. Forty odd years later he was in town, to promote his book *Look to the Stars* in person, just standing there, near the River Thames and it still seemed unbelievable. *The Independent* newspaper leaned towards the eccentric detail to tell the wider story ... the close-up of his hands, with that ring, was spot on.

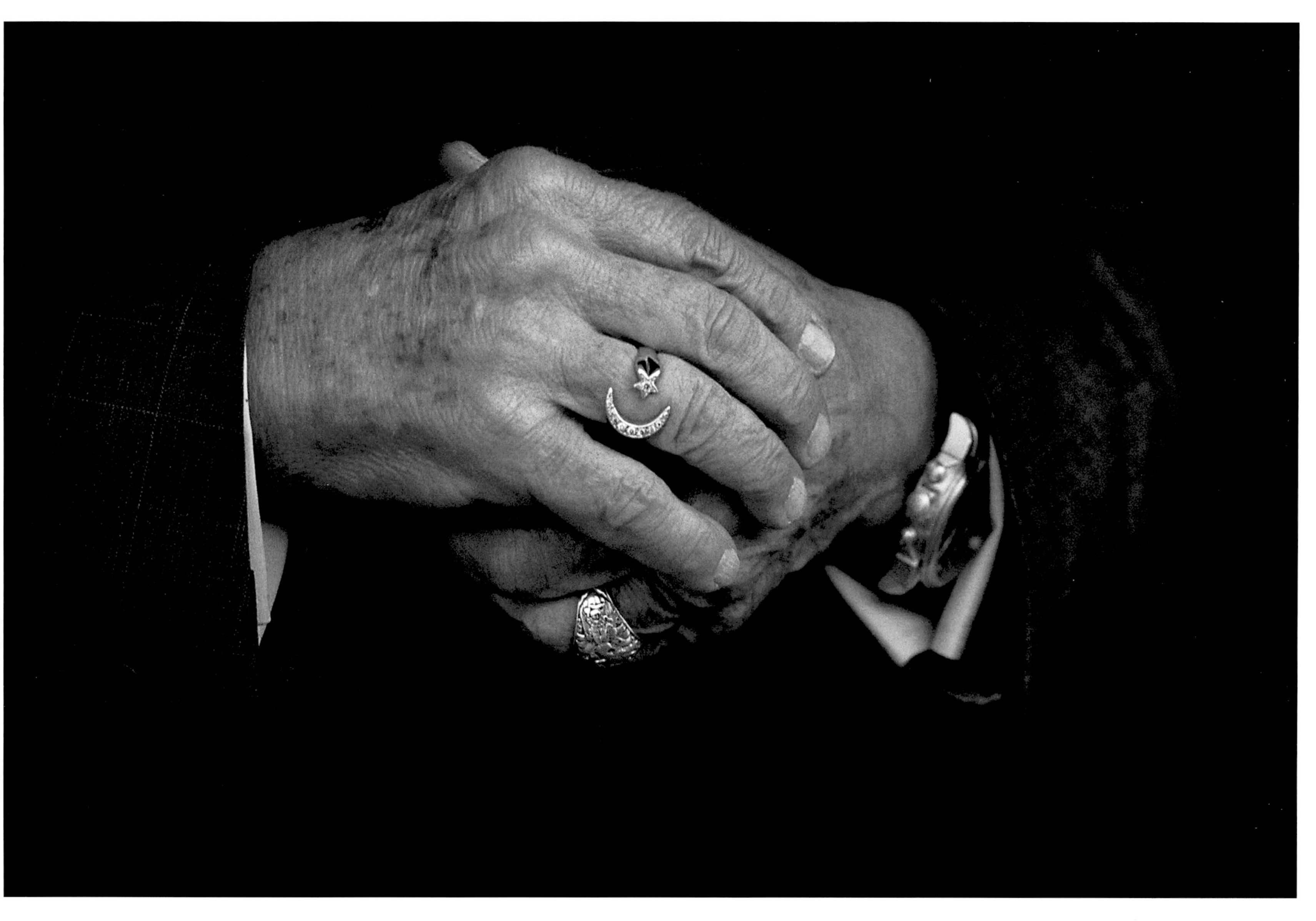

# NINETTE DE VALOIS & MARGOT FONTEYN

Margot Fonteyn and the Royal Ballet founder Ninette de Valois sat in the Royal Box in the company of Princesses Margaret and Diana for a performance of Macmillan's *Romeo & Juliet*. The evening was a Gala Benefit to honour the Prima Ballerina Assoluta, who had flown from Panama for the occasion. They watched Sylvie Guillem and Jonathan Cope dance the roles she and Rudolf Nureyev had premiered twenty-five years earlier. After meeting the press, Fonteyn returned to Panama, sadly dying the following year. I didn't see either of them dance but did photograph Madame waving her stick at dancers in rehearsal like a figure from a painting by Degas.

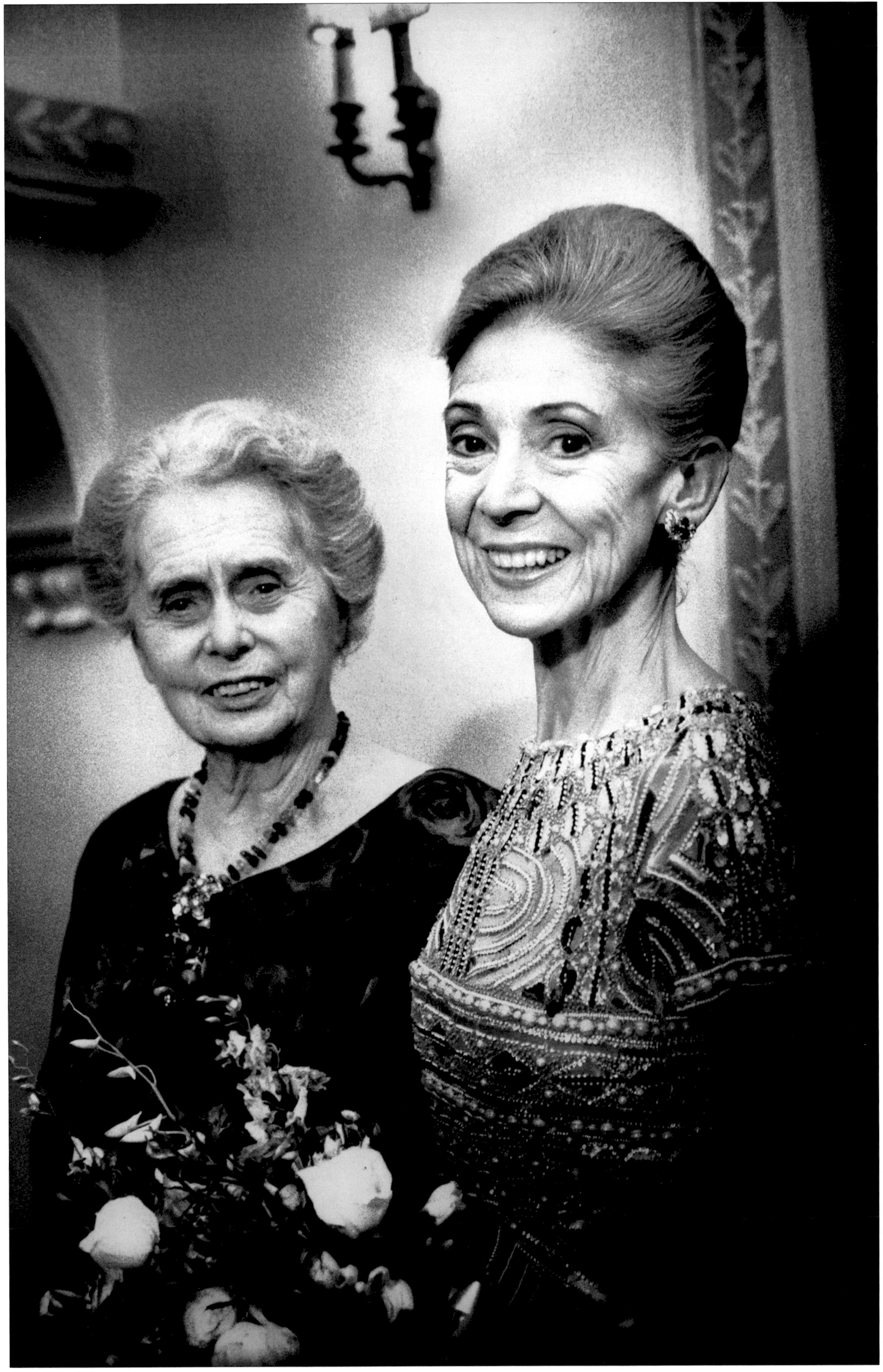

# CHUCK BERRY

Waking up in a room identical to the one a thousand miles away, and the one before that, same wallpaper, furniture, muzak, was debilitating to the soul of the most vital musicians, but that was how it was, not glamorous at all, just uniform and bland. No wonder some bands are provoked into bad behaviour. The booking agent had an obvious grudge with an itinerary that snaked across time zones with scant regard for our digestion or sleep patterns, making departure lounges seem like home. Bumping into Chuck Berry at Tampa Airport momentarily lifted the spirits. Listening to our crazy schedule he remarked, 'Been around huh?' Señor Berry cleverly turned his peripatetic life into rock'n'roll poetry.

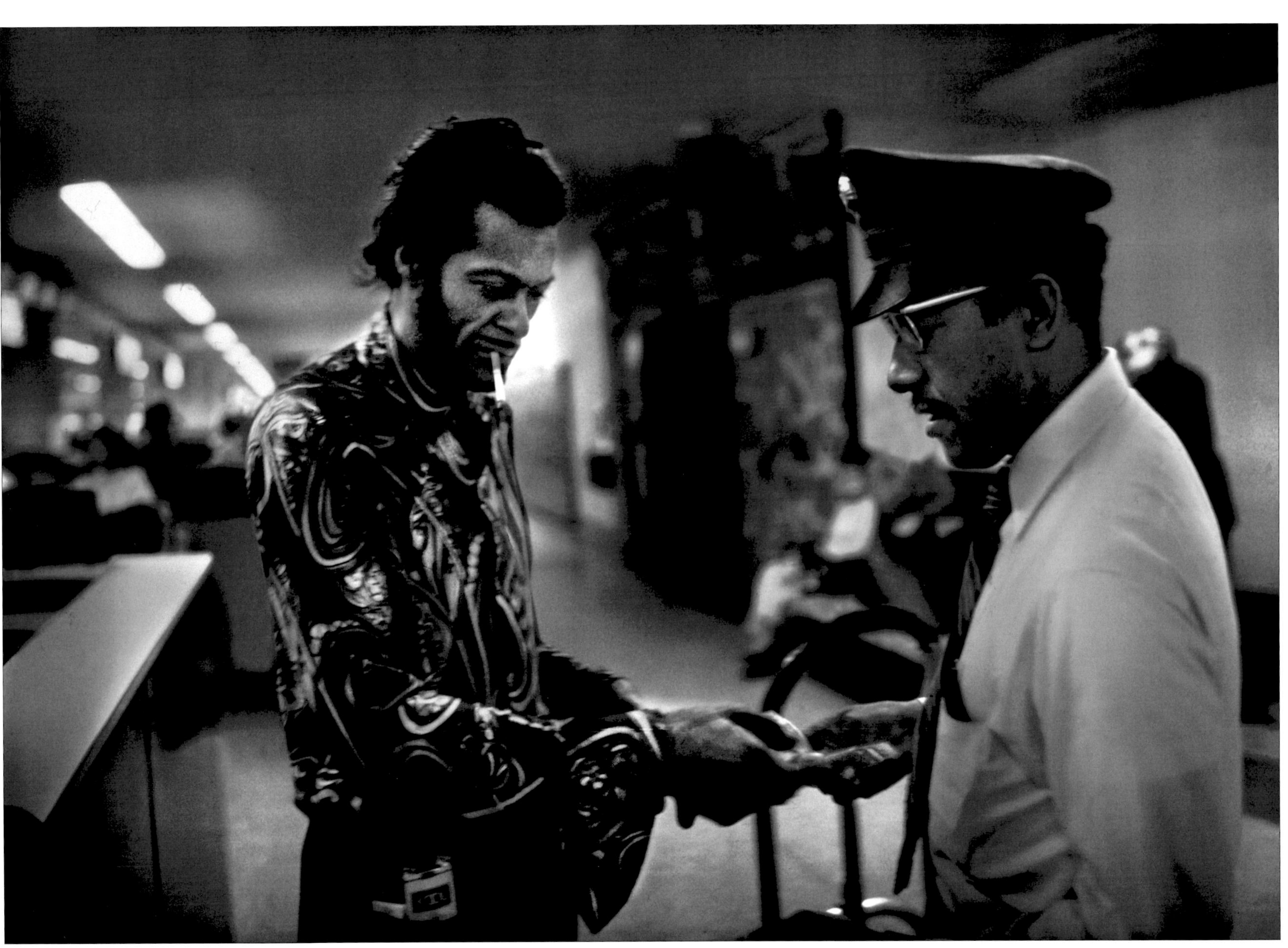

# TORVILL & DEAN

Johnny Weissmuller left the Olympic pool for Hollywood to become Tarzan; a few years later Olympic skating champion Sonja Henie followed him to star in *Thin Ice*. Jayne Torvill might have been inspired by the Norwegian but she didn't fly to California ... with Christopher Dean she soared even higher in their routine 'Flying Fish'. Dean remained ice bound while she drifted high over the audience, twisting, floating, pirouetting, while he steered her gently, seamlessly back to the ice, not so much aerial ballet but more like Esther Williams' underwater sequences from *Dangerous When Wet*.

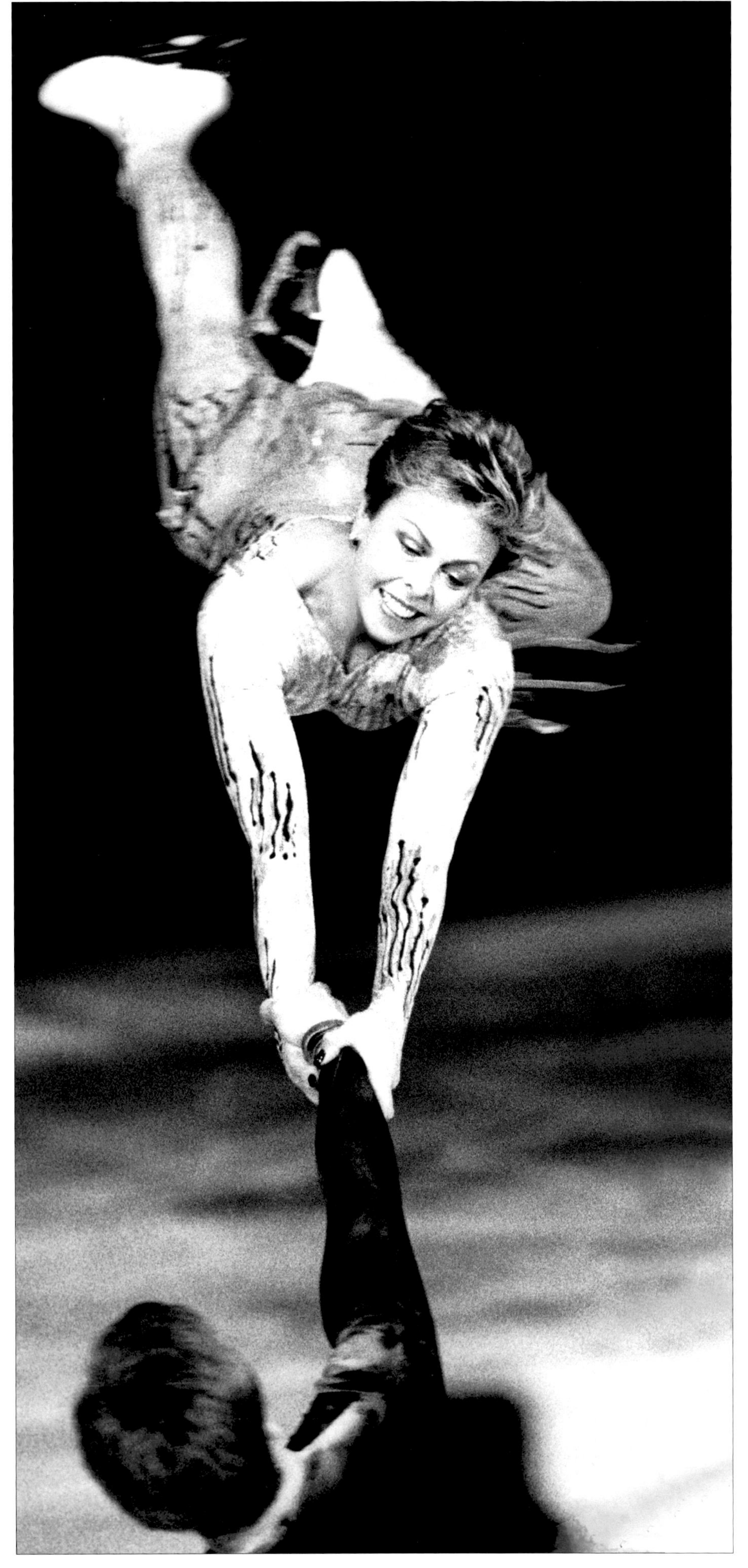

# JOHN PEEL

Peel kindly agreed to write an introduction to *The Concerts*, which involved a visit to his home in Suffolk. He looked at transparencies while I looked through his enormous record collection. During a musical drive back to London, he would glance at the weighty stopwatch on his wrist to time the lengths of tracks for the evening show ... 'There's not enough time in the day for timing and it's not something I care to delegate'. We went shopping, a great opportunity to follow him into record shops around Soho that I didn't know existed, buying twelve-inch reggae singles which naturally I bought too. Back at the BBC I was permitted to shoot preparations for the live broadcast.

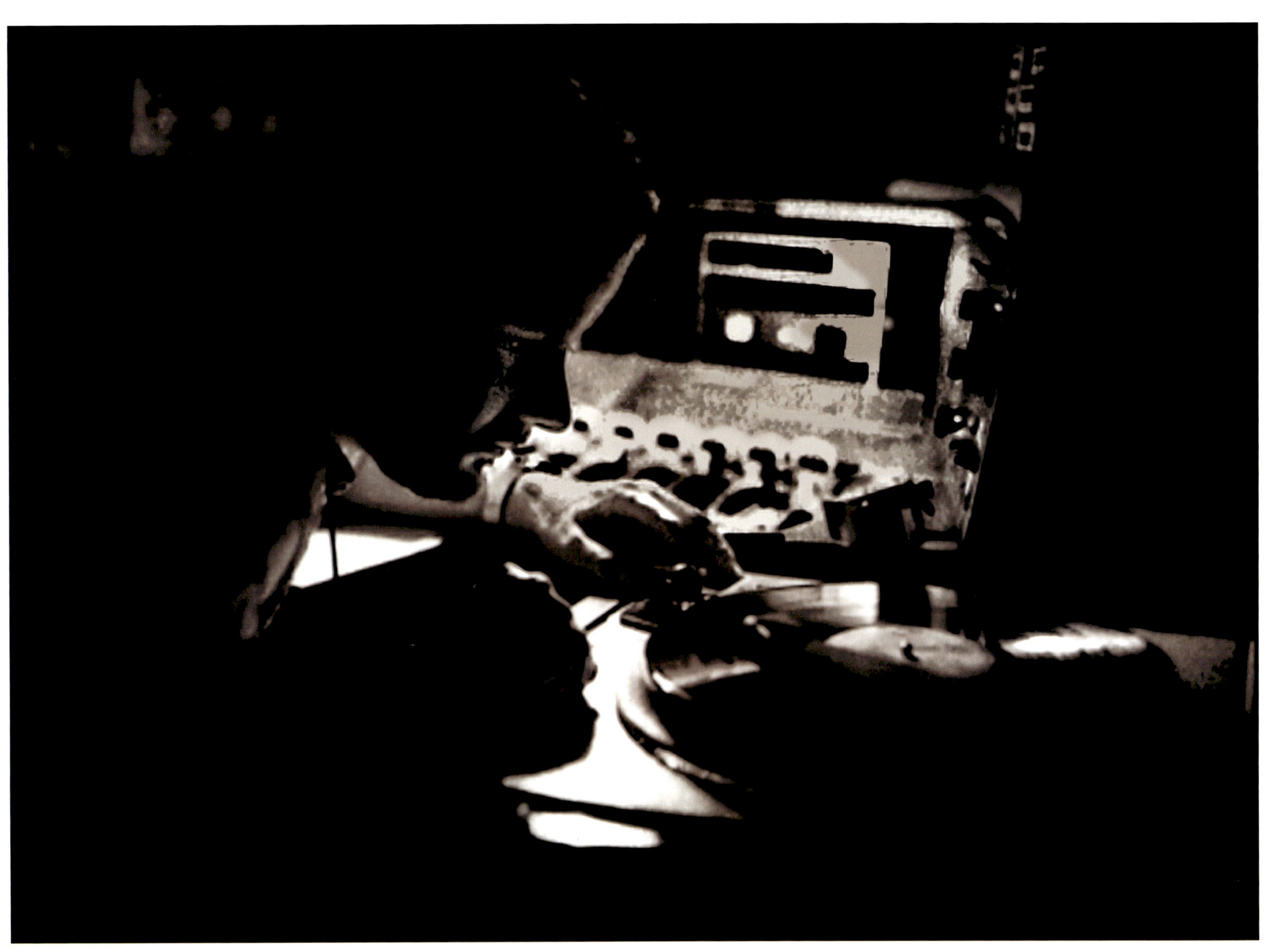

# CHARO ESPINA & PACO PEÑA

A cynic was heard to say 'When receipts were low at Sadler's Wells they'd put on a flamenco show'. The flamenco craze in Britain preceded *Strictly* by a decade or so, and still had thousands swishing fans and whirling in layered dresses. Leaving *The Independent*'s offices in City Road, bumped into picture editor Mike Spillard …

'Is that a front cover?' pointing to a box under my arm, …

'Yes' …

'Aah! but it must be black and white'.

Somewhat ironic considering all the paper's operatives had been bludgeoned with the edict … NO MORE BLACK & WHITE!, after the paper had gone 100% colour. He explained that *The Independent* had just won an award for 'The Best Use of B&W Photography in a British Newspaper'. It was the following day's front page.

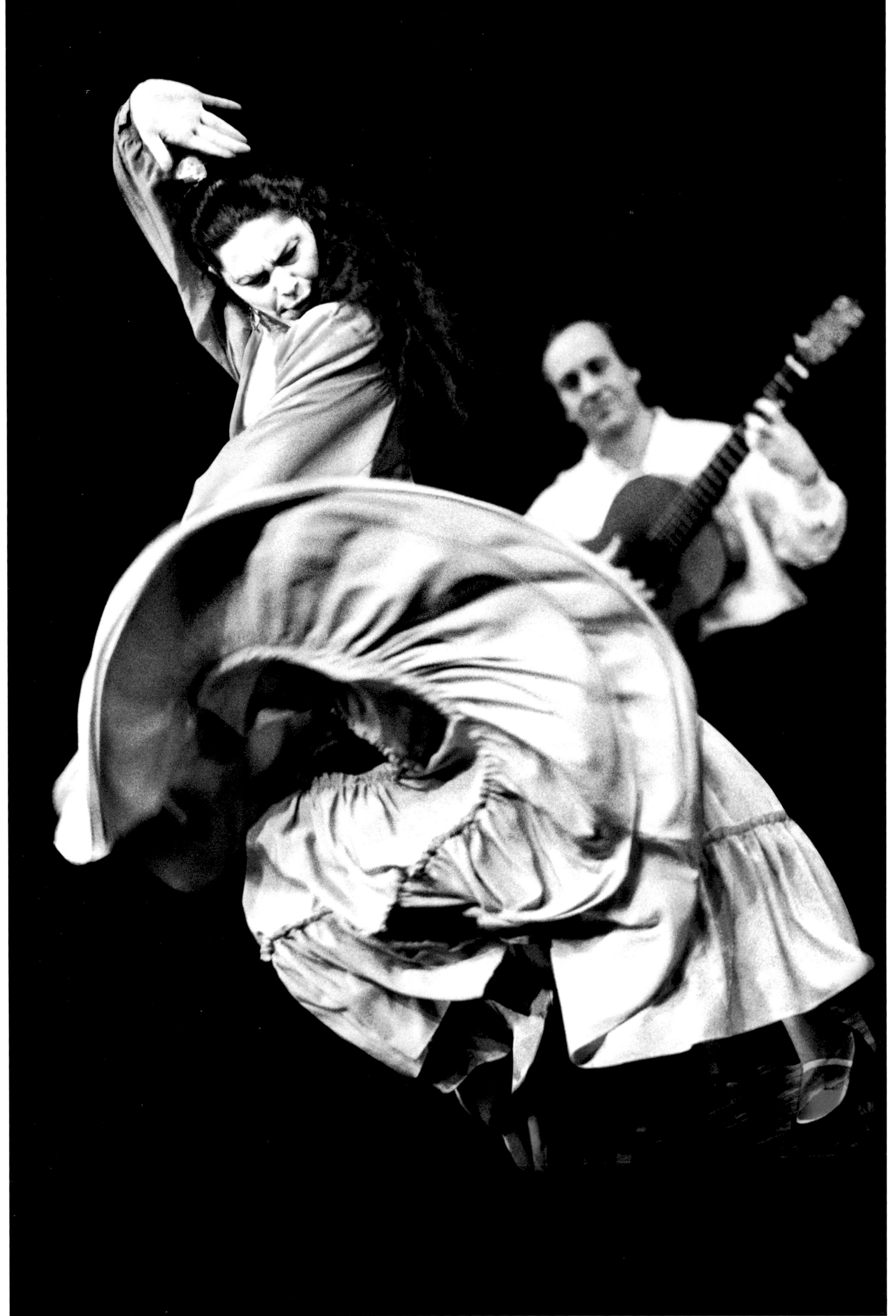

# SEGUN ADEWALE

Of the many picture editors I've worked with, the most memorable was Bruce Bernard, painter and photographer in his own right. Segun Adewale was one of his commissions for *The Sunday Times Magazine*. Adewale, born into a Nigerian Royal Family, moved to Lagos to practice as a musician and was in London to promote 'Yo Pop Music', part of the Afrobeat popular in the UK during the 1980s. The portrait was lit with a tungsten soft-box, shot on medium format in the upstairs foyer of the Hammersmith Odeon. He had a regal grace which appeared to reflect his background. Bernard remarked ... 'It's like a painting, a figure from a Delacroix.'

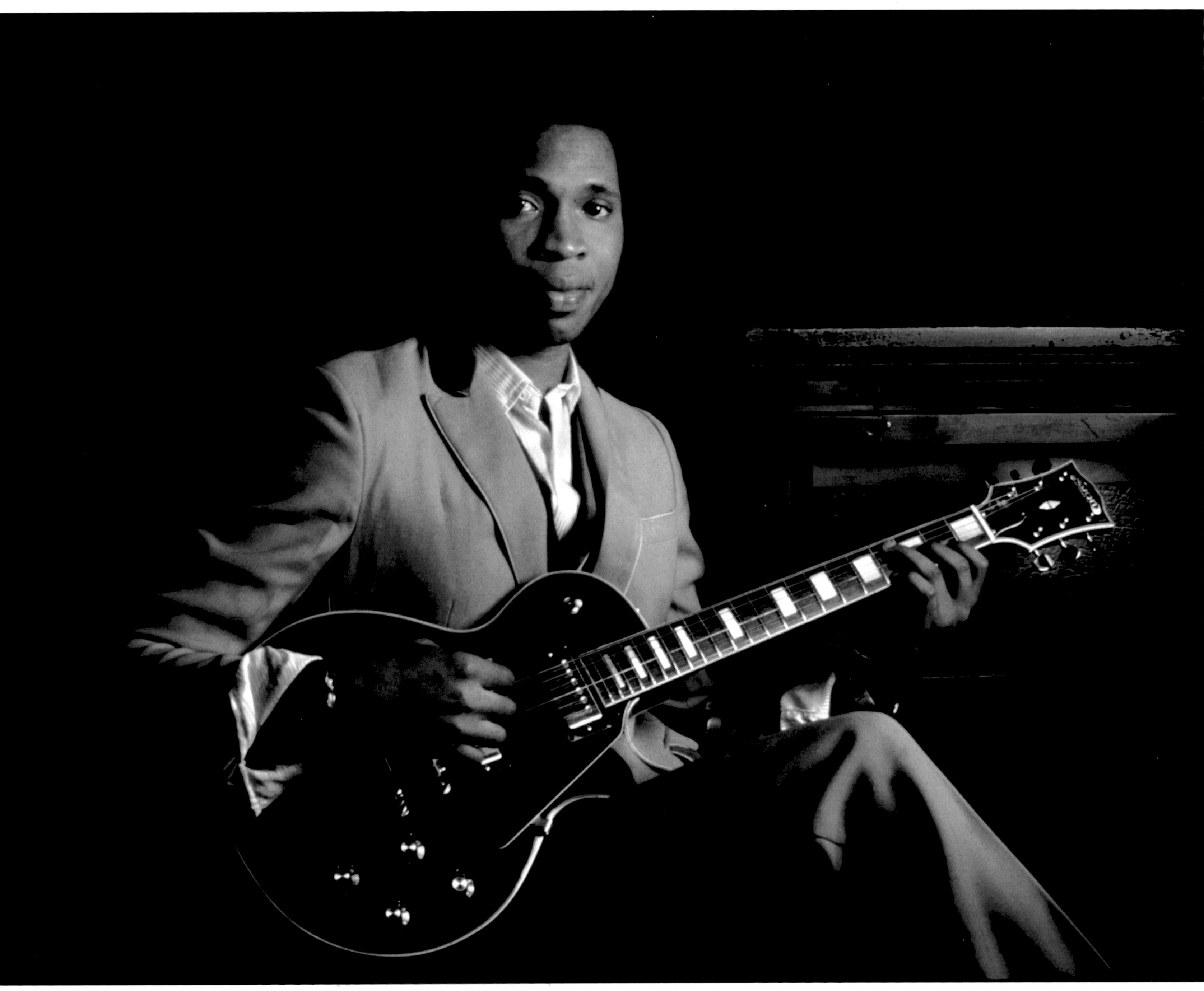

# MARINA ABRAMOVIĆ

Ten-foot high Polaroid self-portraits with Egyptian heads against a gold background are on loan from the Metropolitan Museum, New York, to the Tate Gallery. The Serbian performance artist liked the idea of blurring through the exhibit on a panoramic time-exposure, which we did but seen here in a conventional frame, without the movement. The following year Marina and her partner Ulay walked the Great Wall of China from opposite ends to meet in the middle and part forever ... meanwhile she accepted a lift back to her hotel in Russell Square, recounting tales of her exotic life.

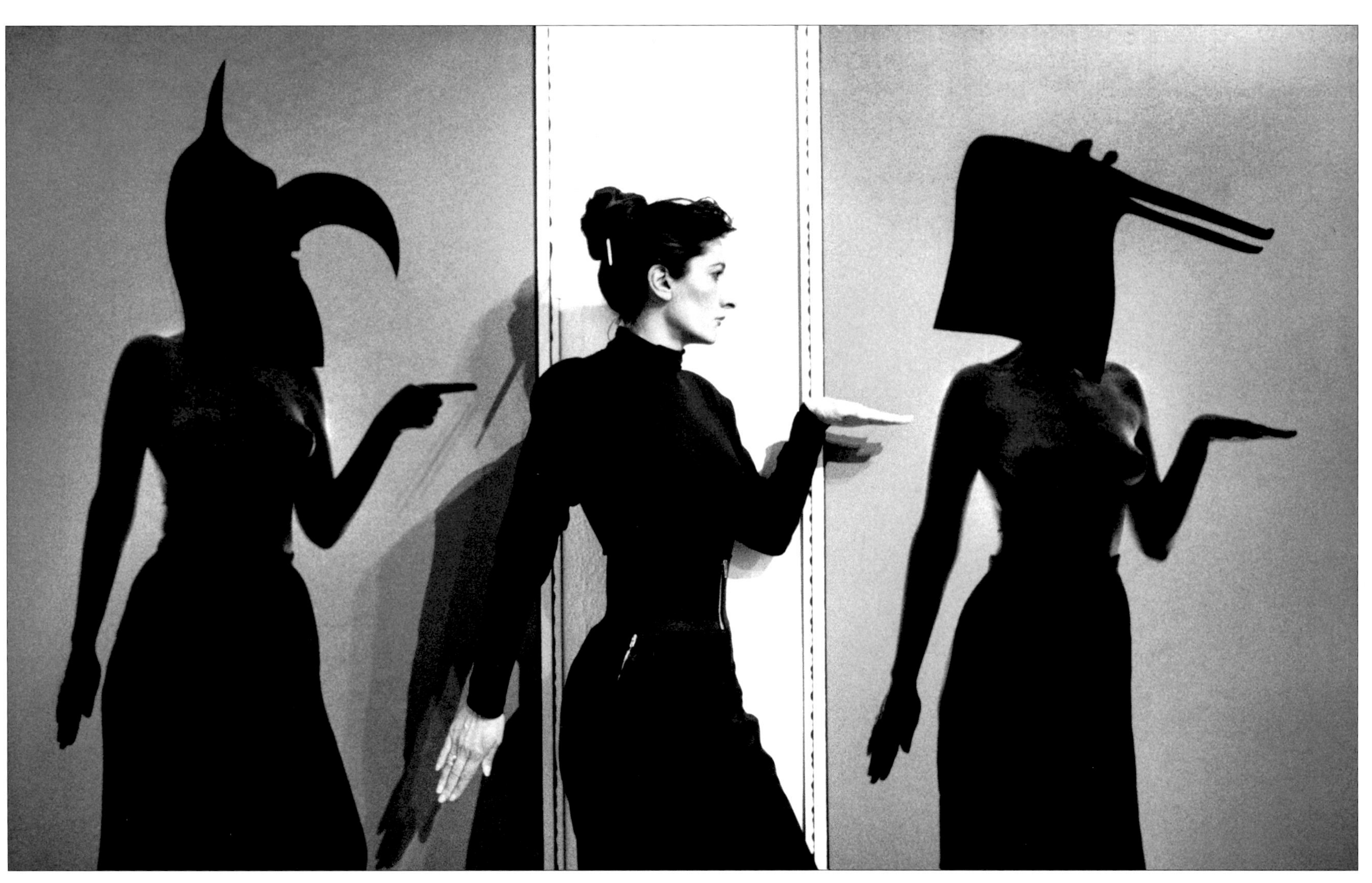

# JOHNNY CASH

The Man in Black walked on to the Albert Hall stage, took the microphone and in a rumbling bass-baritone said … 'Hello, I'm Johnny Cash'. He was one of the 'Million Dollar Quartet' at Sun Records with Carl Perkins, Jerry Lee Lewis and Elvis Presley where he began as a country singer. Now some forty years later he continued with 'Long Black Veil', a sorrowful country classic accompanied by his wife June and his son John Carter, the last concert he played in London.

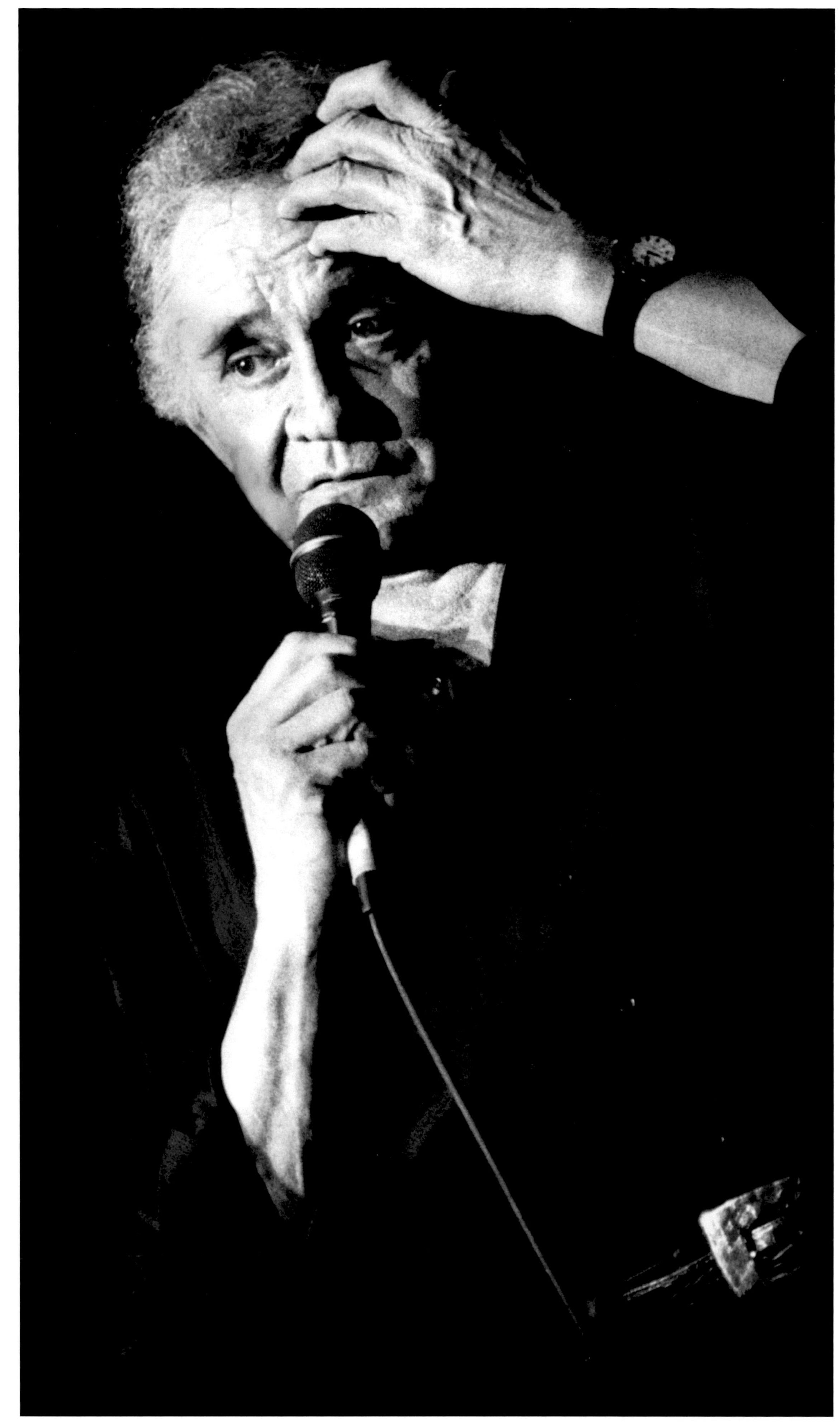

# MARIA BJÖRNSON

It was another of those 'you've got ten minutes occasions' and I'd bought a tungsten soft-box, mid-format and tripod, so needed some time to prepare. I had the car ...'If I run you to your next appointment, could I have another ten minutes?' She was the owner of a wonderful profile, shades of Edith Sitwell but was self-conscious and very grumpy. Ms Björnson was an extremely talented designer for opera, ballet and theatre, the magazine wanted to see her at work. The bust was sitting by the fireplace, with the drawing and the profile it made a triangular shape. Two weeks later ... 'I'm really sorry I was so horrible to you, may I have a print?'

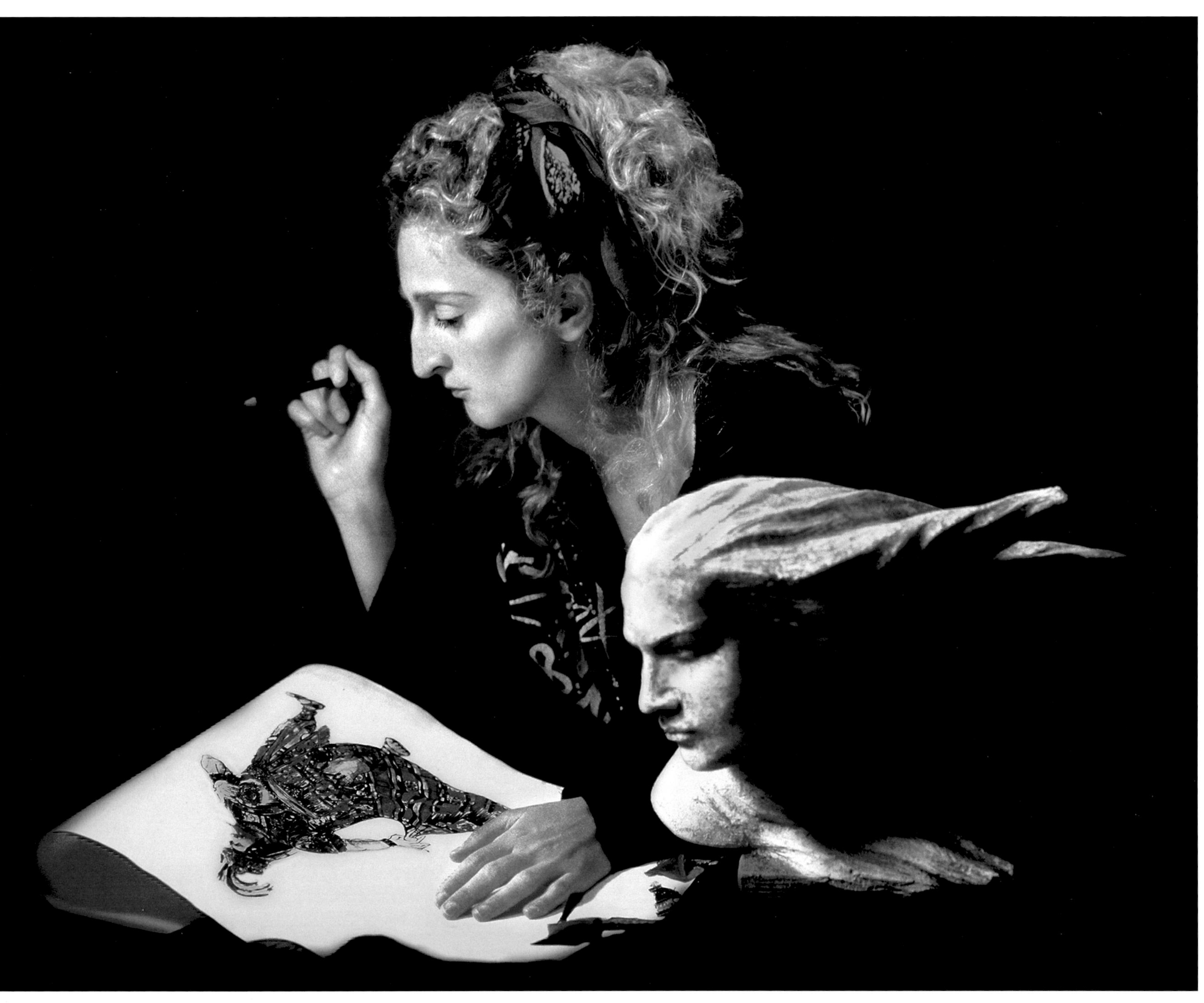

# MICK JAGGER

The view over London was dramatic, the one hundred thousand fans below like ants. Legs dangling over the roof of Wembley Stadium, I was waiting for a close-up on the video screens each side of the stage, to show the scale. A policeman was yelling to come back … 'Won't be a minute' … Evidently the owner had spotted the figure on the roof and ordered its removal. En-route the command had been garbled into … 'There's a terrorist on the roof'. Manhandled and frogmarched away, we descended the stairs and bumped into The Leader of the Opposition, Neil Kinnock … 'What seems to be the trouble, officer ?' … arms freed, showed the Access All Areas pass, everyone relaxed and I was backstage in time to catch Mick Jagger.

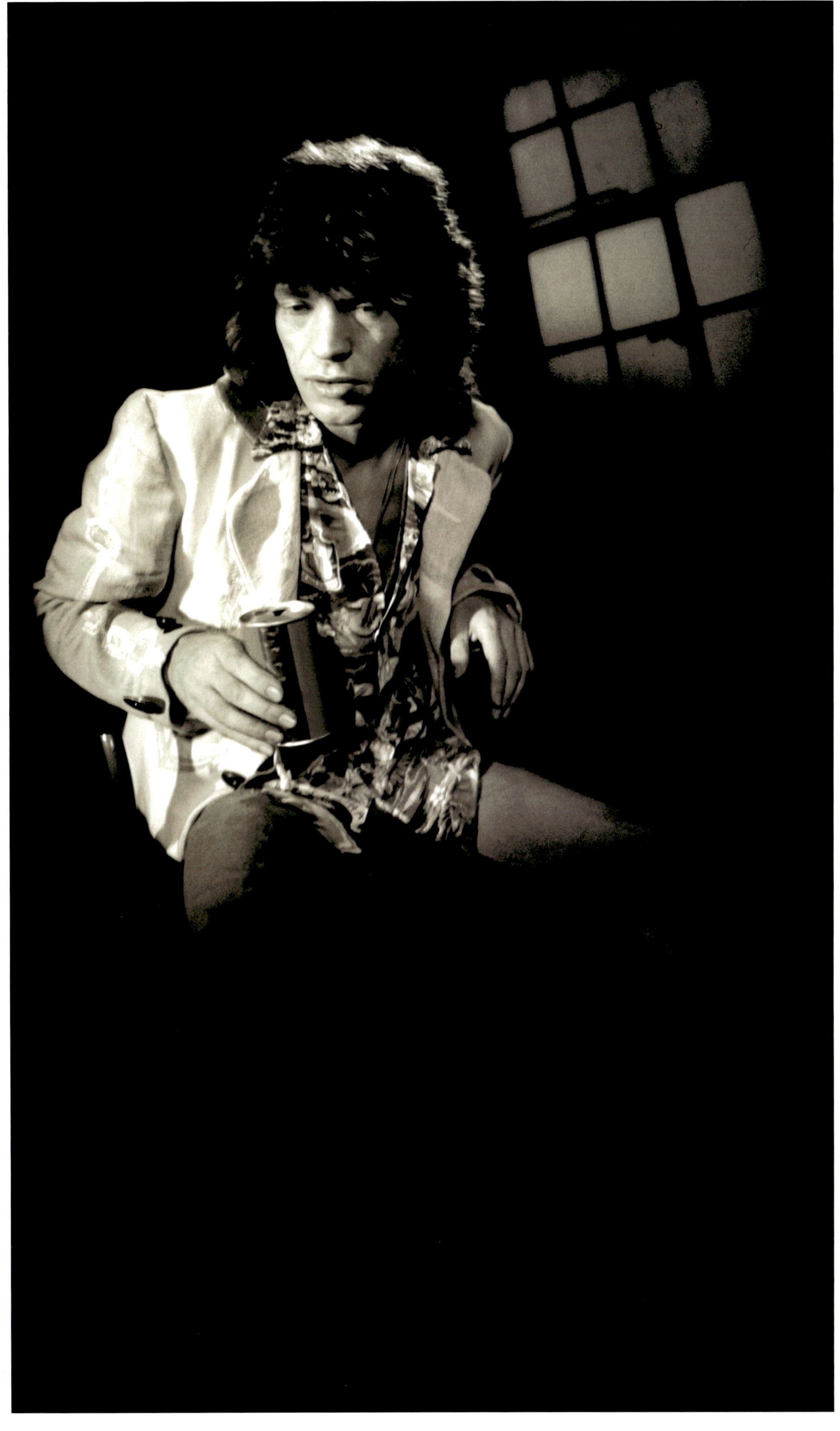

# DELPHINE SEYRIG

When I learned that Mme Seyrig would only be photographed during an interview and the assigned journalist would not work with a photographer, my heart sank. The simple solution was to accompany a writer from another magazine. The actress was in London to promote Chantal Ackerman's film *Golden 80s*, the interview to be held at Brown's Hotel, Mayfair. Twenty-five years after seeing her in *Last Year at Marienbad* she was still beautiful, though it was her smoky contralto that you remembered ... 'Did you know the first telephone in the UK was installed here, at Brown's by Alexander Graham Bell ... and that Oscar Wilde, Bram Stoker, J.M. Barrie, Arthur Conan Doyle and Robert Louis Stevenson came here to use it?' she informed us, with that voice.

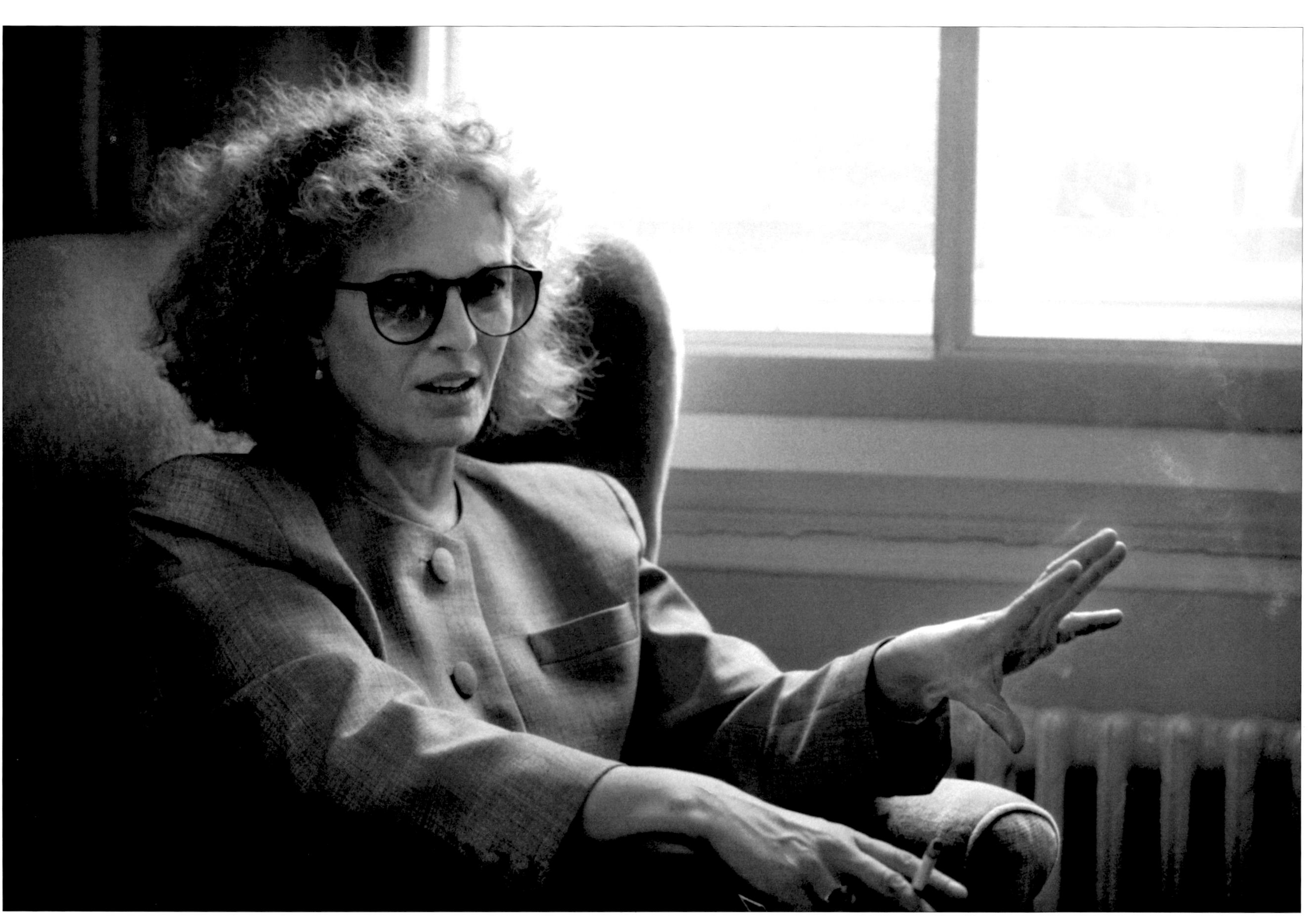

# PILGRIM

Despite the temperature being -20°C, there was no snow just white powdered dust. Pilgrims had descended the mountains to Kumbum for the First Mid-Moon Festival, the devout circumambulating the lamasery three times, prostrating themselves after each step which left them looking like spectres. It seemed an impertinence to interrupt their devotions, so this gentleman remains anonymous.

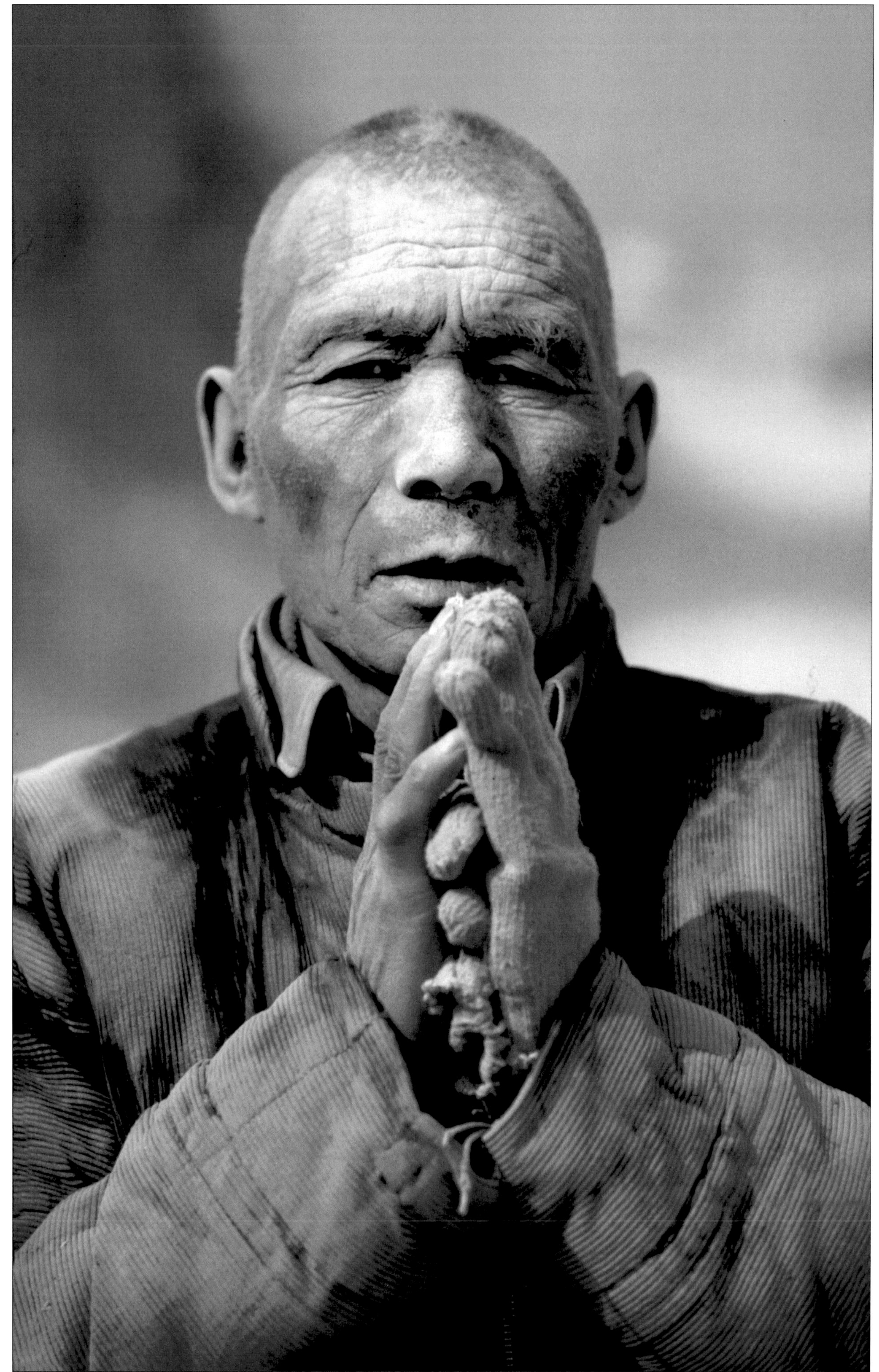

## SYLVIE GUILLEM

Mlle Guillem would insist on getting her own way, which most often she did, earning the sobriquet 'Madame Non'. Rudolf Nureyev promoted her at the Paris Opera Ballet to *Etoile* ahead of her seniors, and soon after she defied her mentor and left for Britain. *Marguerite & Armand* had been premiered by Nureyev and Fonteyn with the Royal Ballet, which was then considered off-limits for anyone else until Guillem, partnered with Nicholas Le Riche, dared to dance the revival. There were mutterings from the ballet establishment, forgetting that as understudies Lynn Seymour and Christopher Gable had also danced the roles.

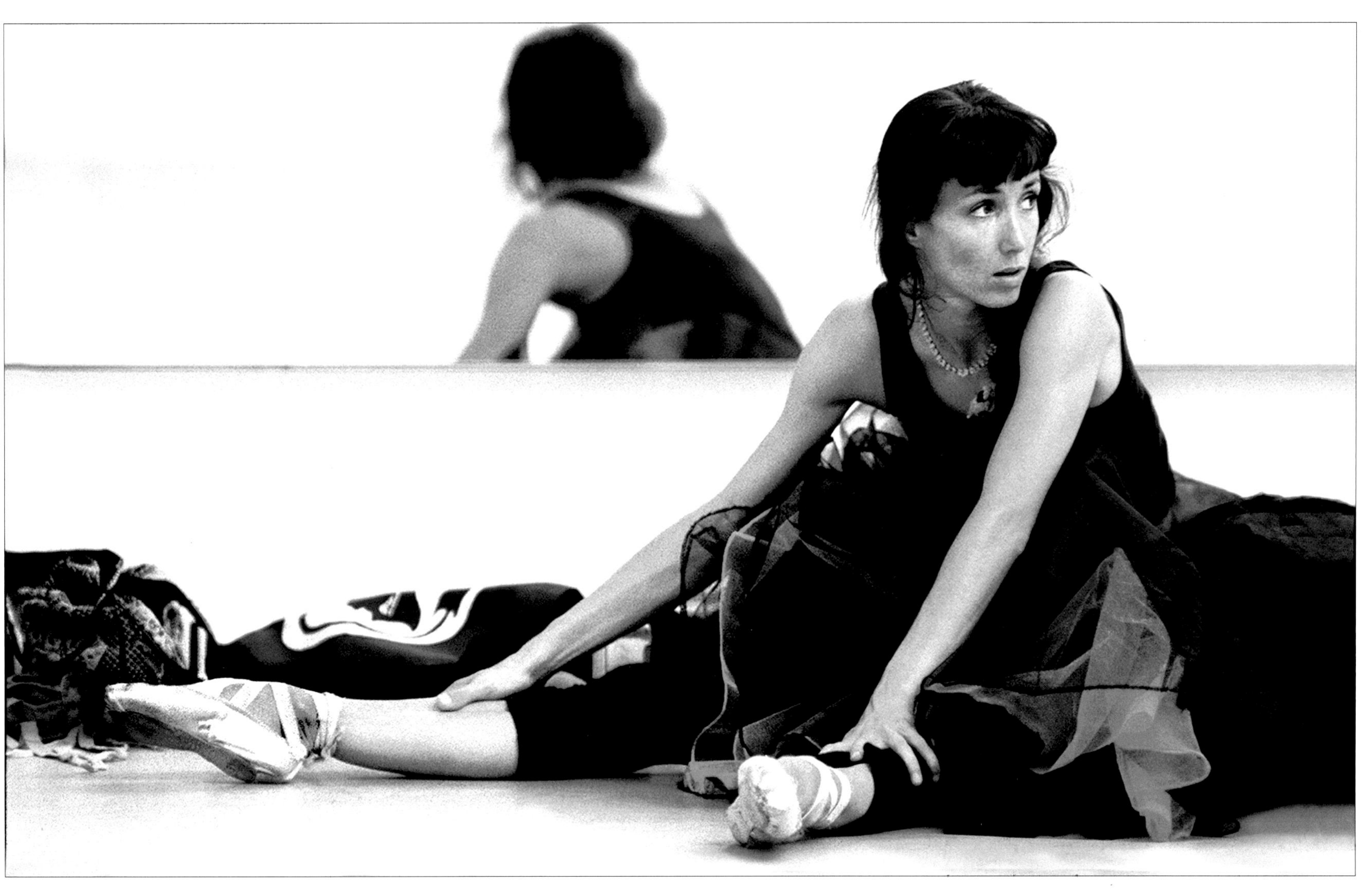

## BOBBY McFERRIN

With both parents as singers, he was off to a flying start. Bobby McFerrin was one of Ornette Coleman's inspired choices for the Meltdown Festival on London's South Bank, and if you were obliged to categorise him, jazz vocalist would be close. However, his *a capella* polyphonic gymnastics with beat-box style percussion using his mouth and body, places him in his own unique category. The composer Carl Stalling needed the entire LA Philharmonic for the *Bugs Bunny* soundtracks as well as an array of sound effects ... Mr McFerrin performs solo.

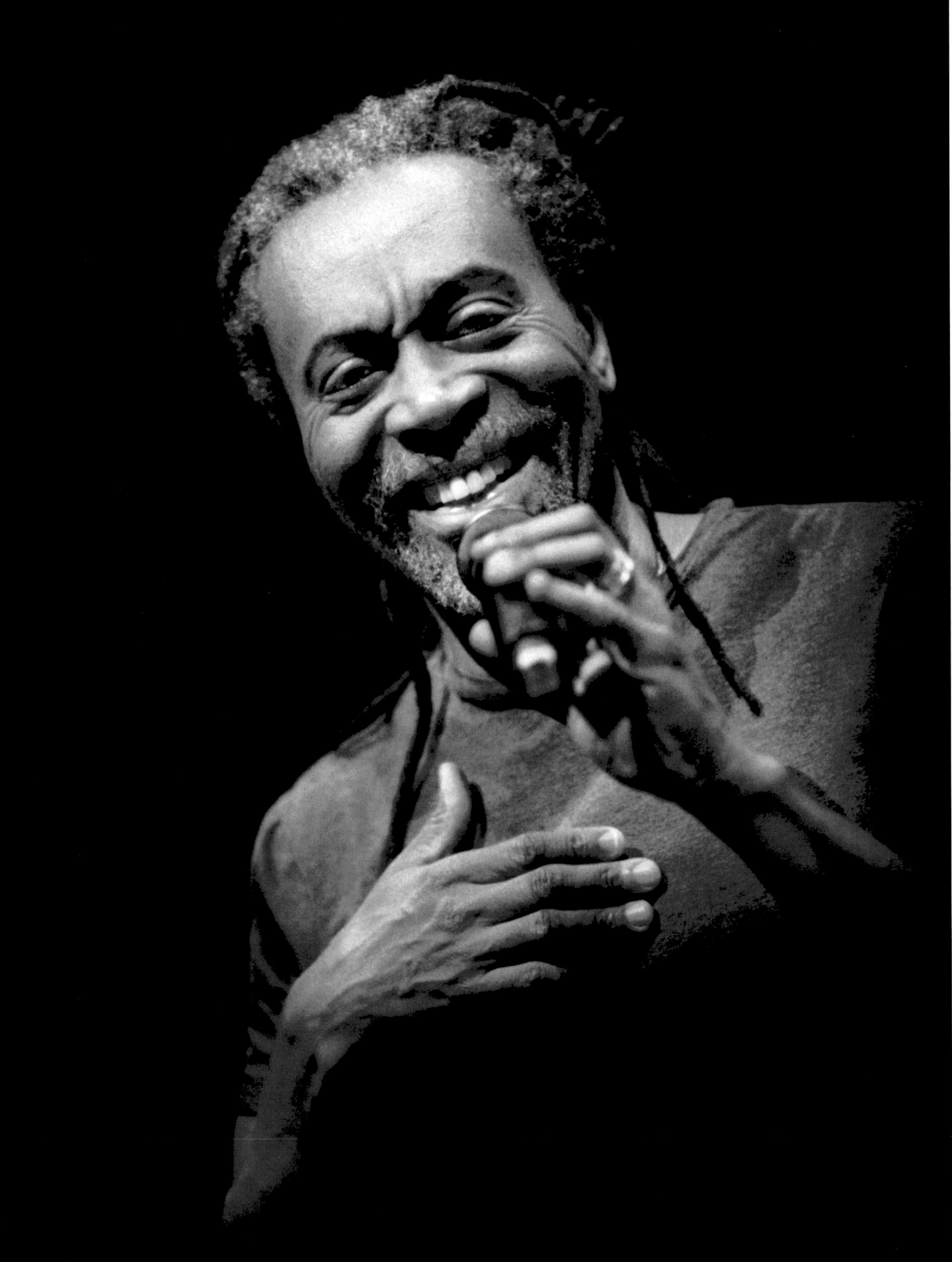

# DIANA ROSS

There must have been twenty-five people in the hotel suite ...
I dared to ask 'Could we go into a quieter room?' ...
'You want me in my bedroom?' she growled.
... A dull grey filtered through the curtains, not unlike a soft studio light, perfect. Her make-up was also perfect but I took a pad and powdered her face. She grasped my hand, examined the pad and said, 'Oh ...you've got my colour'. A lucky break, it was the only one I had ... 'Well, I suppose you want this' cupping her breasts and hoisting them up ...
'No, not really, in fact would you mind putting your coat back on?' ...
'You want me in my coat!?' ...
It was a beautifully tailored item. The agreement was that she had full approval. Two prints were made, sent to the Park Lane Hotel. She approved them both ... phew.

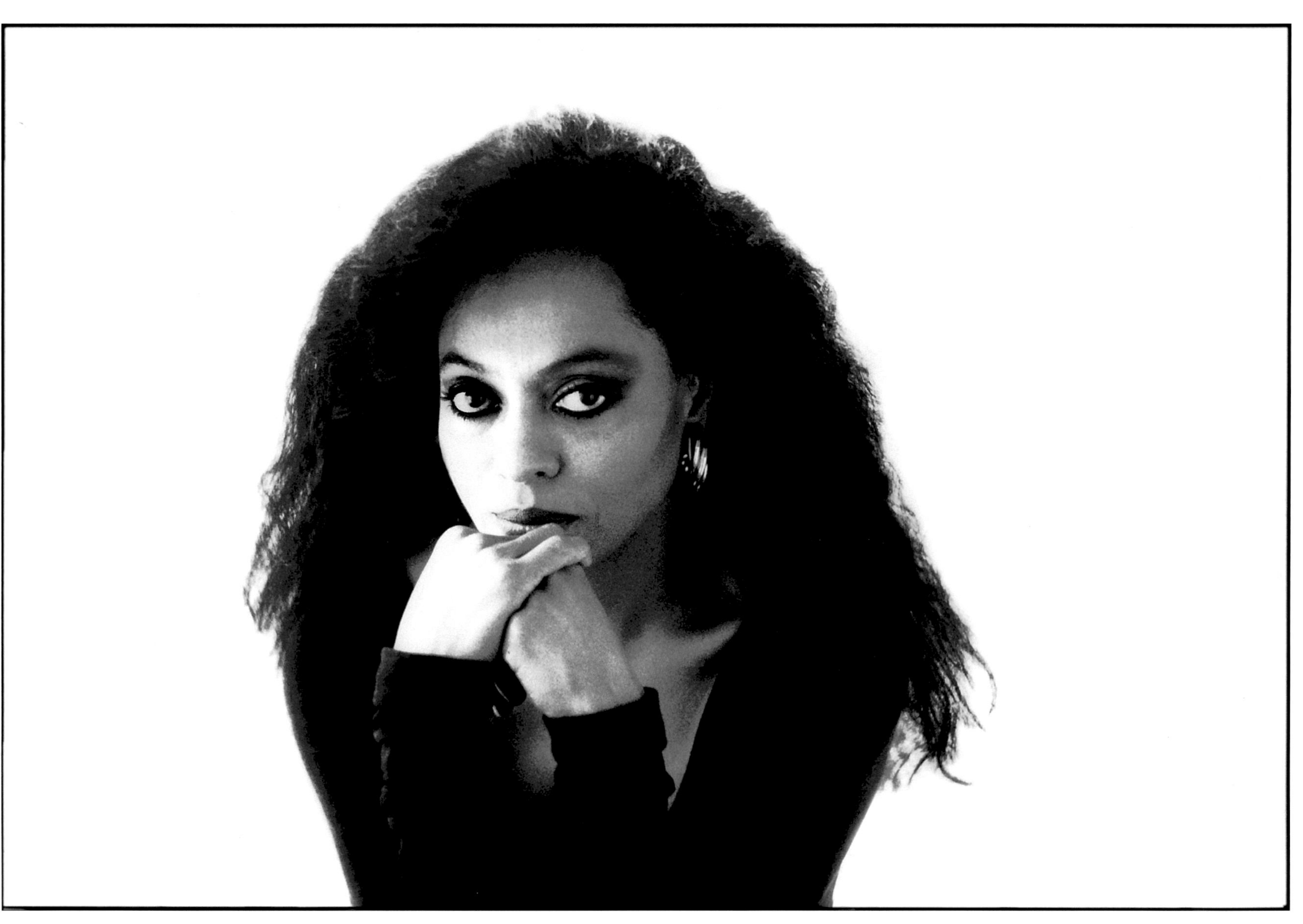

# ISAIAH BERLIN

Nobody mentioned it was a re-shoot, the world's greatest living philosopher had rejected the work of the previous photographer. They said he would be difficult, I'd have little time and the piece was to celebrate his eightieth birthday. He opened the door himself and stated … 'I won't stand and I won't smile and I want to be here with my books', indicating a dimly lit library.

'Well Sir, if you prefer to sit, that's fine, and if you don't want to smile that's also fine … but we won't be working by the books because the light is better here' … taking the Picasso off the wall and setting the tripod. Using a mid-format camera the session was over within minutes. Somehow, we became involved in a discussion about Alexander the Great, how close his troops had come to the Hindu Kush, the current inhabitants with green eyes and blonde hair … after some time he said …

'We're getting on very well aren't we?'

'Yes.'

'Now why do you think that is?'

'Well you do resemble my Uncle, so I feel I know you.'

'Your Uncle?! … What does he do?'

We discussed my Uncle and Alexander until it was time to leave. I'd been there for five hours. A month later his secretary rang and asked if they could use the picture for a book cover.

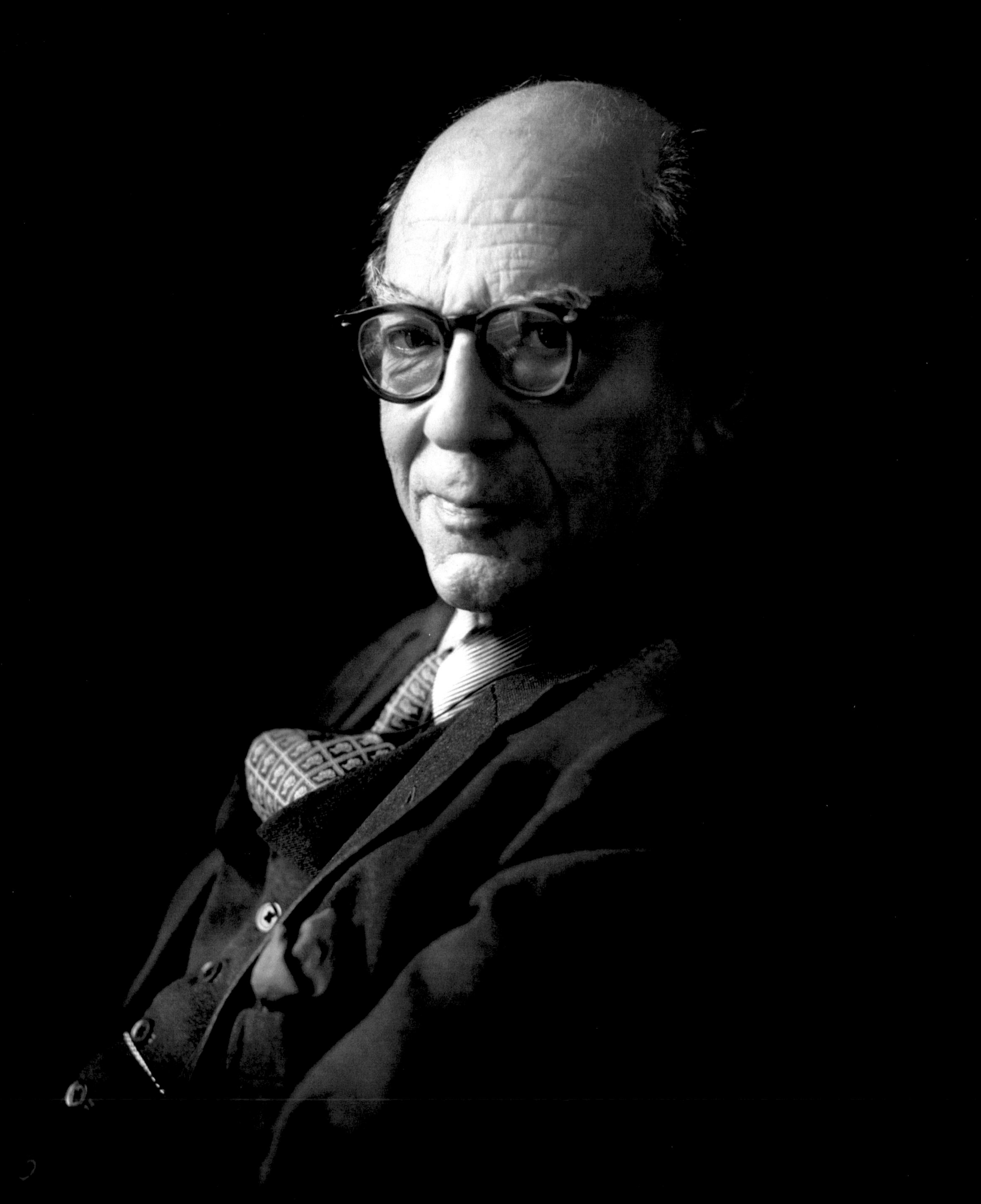

# LEA ANDERSON

The light level was so low she appeared like a transparent vapour trail in the subdued gloom. The picture editor had asked for a picture showing movement. A static object next to a moving one might strengthen the illusion, so two images were merged, a portrait and the other of her dancing. With the all female Cholmondeleys and the all male Featherstonehaughs she consistently choreographed the most witty and original modern dance in the UK.

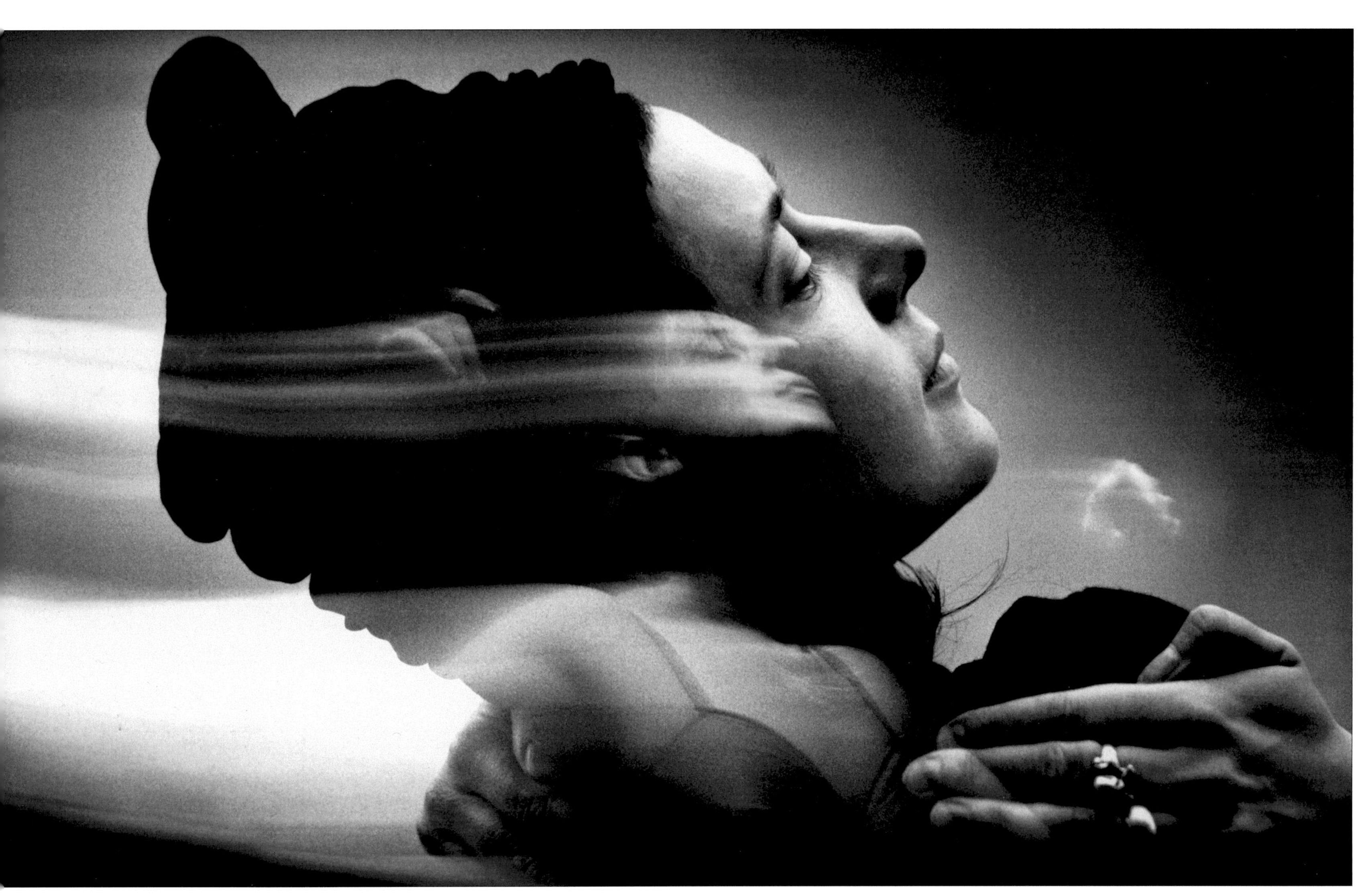

## TOM COURTENAY

The character he played in *Billy Liar* was so full of vitality it came as a surprise to find him sitting quietly in a dressing room reading a newspaper. Along with *Tracy's Tiger*, *Harvey*, *The Secret Life of Walter Mitty* and *Whose Afraid of Virginia Woolf?*, the film helped me with a college thesis titled 'Imaginary Friends'. For a thespian his demeanour didn't strike me as typical, he was courteous, almost shy. He was waiting to be called for make-up, portraying a Russian soldier but ... that's the point, he's an actor, metamorphosing into any person he's required to be. More recently saw him in *45 Years* with Charlotte Rampling, a beautifully understated film, a long way from *Billy Liar* but equally well observed and sympathetically played.

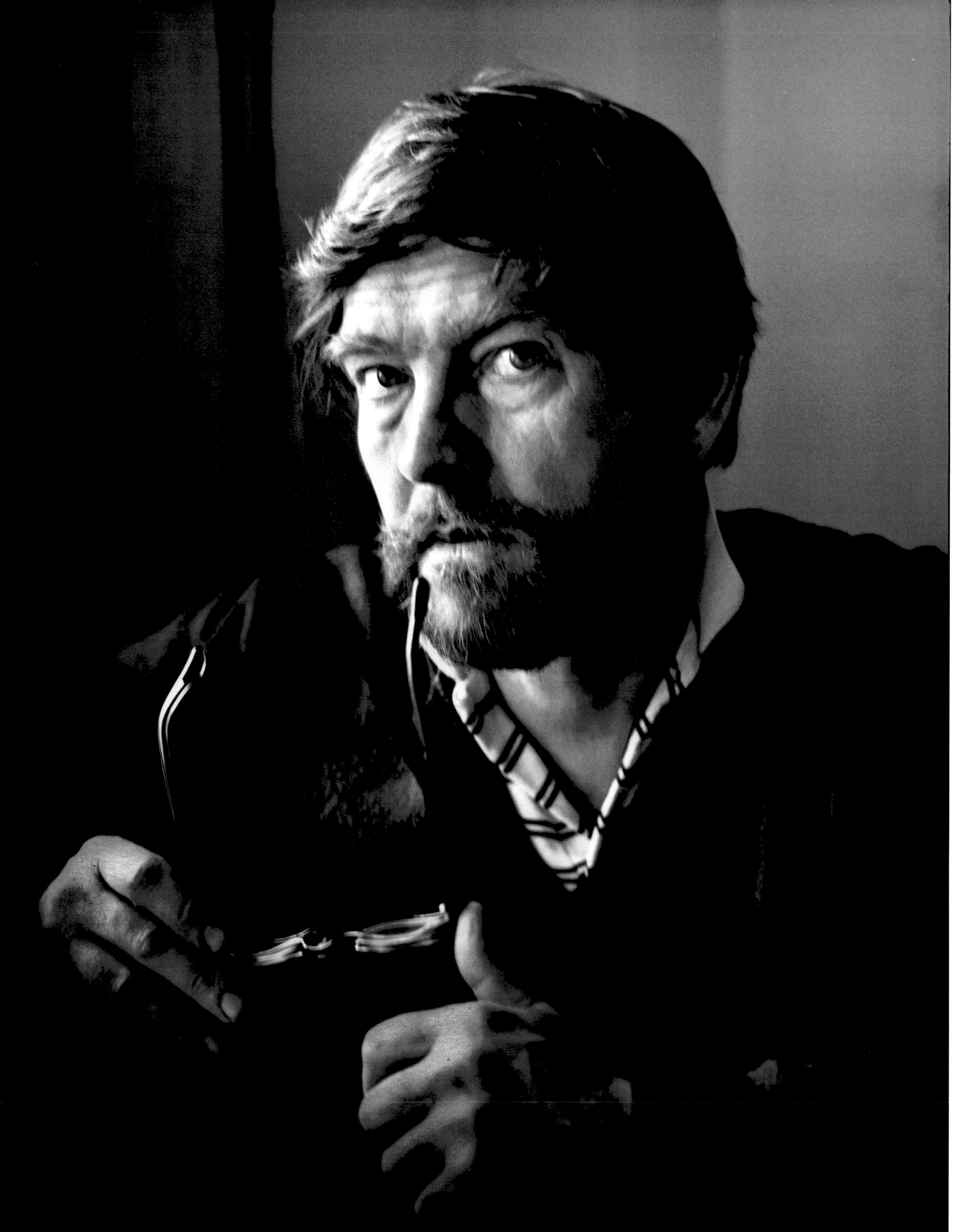

# LINDSAY KEMP

The image is from Kemp's satire on Hollywood *The Parades Gone By.* There is an interesting chronological line from the white-faced clowns of Commedia dell'arte to Harpo Marx, Charlie Chaplin, Stan Laurel, Buster Keaton, Jacques Tati, Jean-Louis Barrault, Marcel Marceau, Pierre Étaix, Lindsay Kemp and later Slava Polunin. Kemp has been described as a dancer, tragedian, comedian, thespian, choreographer, vaudevillian and actor-manager but I would say simply … a great mime artist.

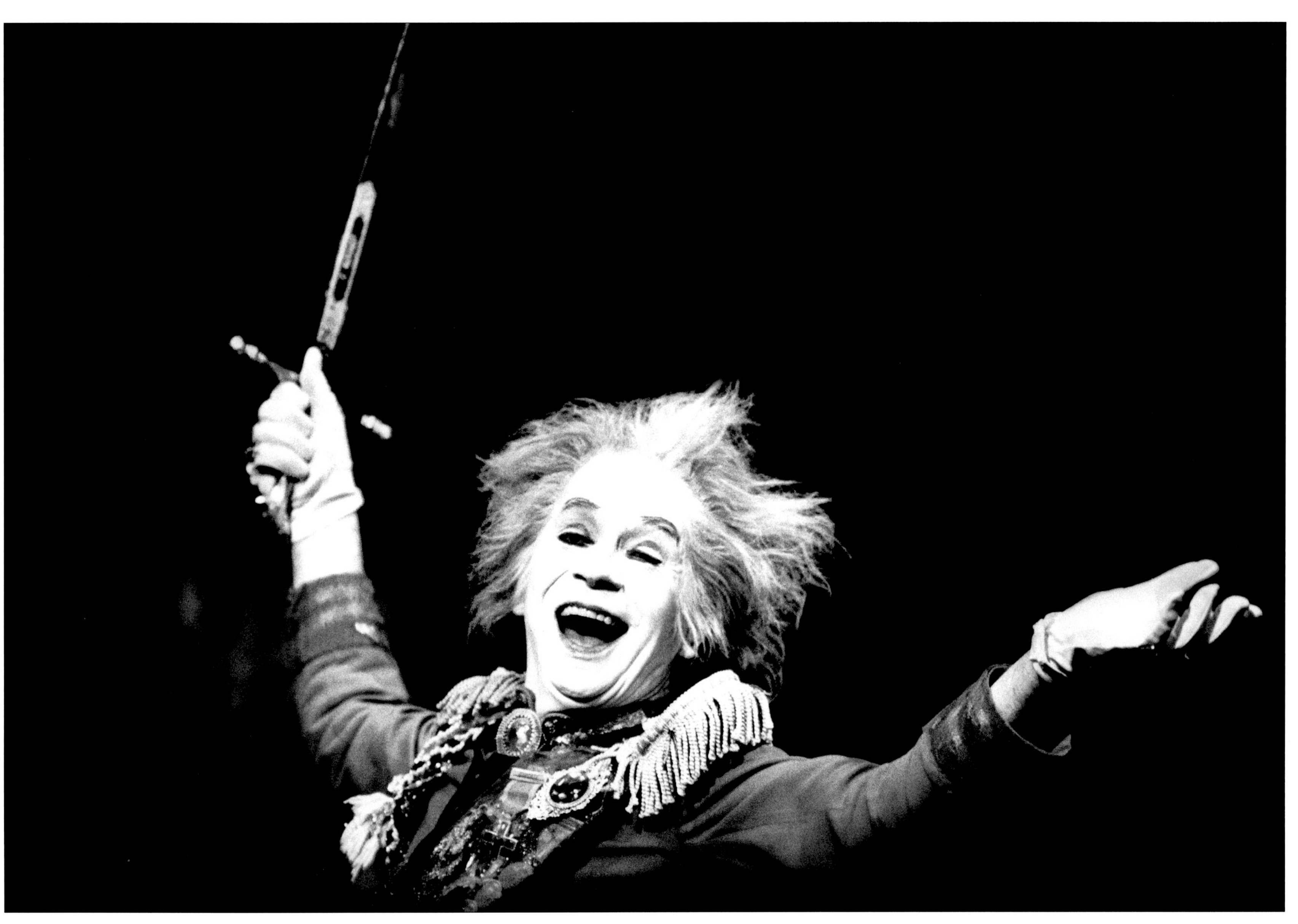

## DEF LEPPARD

On the last day of 1984, Rick Allen, the band's drummer, crashed his Corvette and lost his left arm. This was to be the first shoot since the accident and the record company warned it might be tricky. The session was over two days at the Windmill Studios in Dublin, the second an exterior along a railway track. Joe Elliott asked what I had in mind ... 'Well, let's shoot so we hide it, show it, and then down the middle and you choose what works.' Everyone relaxed and we worked through the night, using a bank of tungsten lights, much like a film set. We hired a talented local hairdresser, and Mark Clinton who managed the Irish band In Tua Nua, both helped keep the mood light. The pictures were used for the album *Hysteria* and the single 'Animal'.

Def Leppard, *Top, left to right:* Rick Savage, Phil Collen
*Bottom, left to right:* Rick Allen, Joe Elliott, Steve Clark

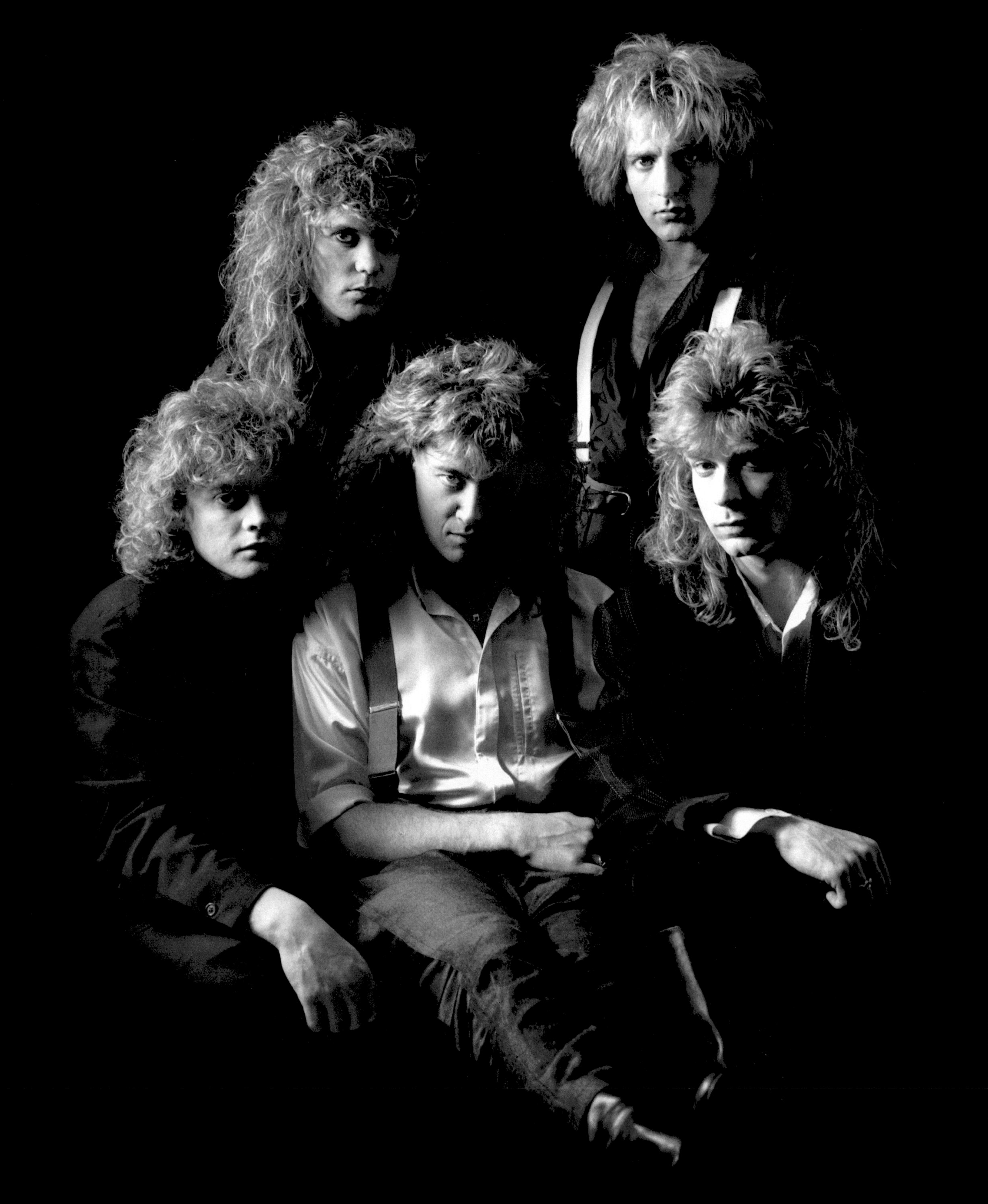

## PETER BLAKE & GERALD SCARFE

'The Big Draw' is an inspired UK wide project encouraging everyone to draw. The artists Blake and Scarfe had agreed to promote the event at the Victoria and Albert Museum for the newspapers. There were two set-ups, the first was drawing on glass in the sculpture hall. I'd seen a Picasso documentary where the problem of seeing the artist's face and the drawing together was solved by shooting through the glass. The V&A cleaning staff had been twitching in the background while the artists worked and were uncommonly swift in removing the drawings from the screens we'd borrowed. The following day, anarchy and mayhem as the same staff was traumatised by hundreds of youngsters running riot on hallowed ground, mothers changing nappies, tots daubing and splattering on giant rolls of paper rolled out across the galleries. The sculpture is by Canova.

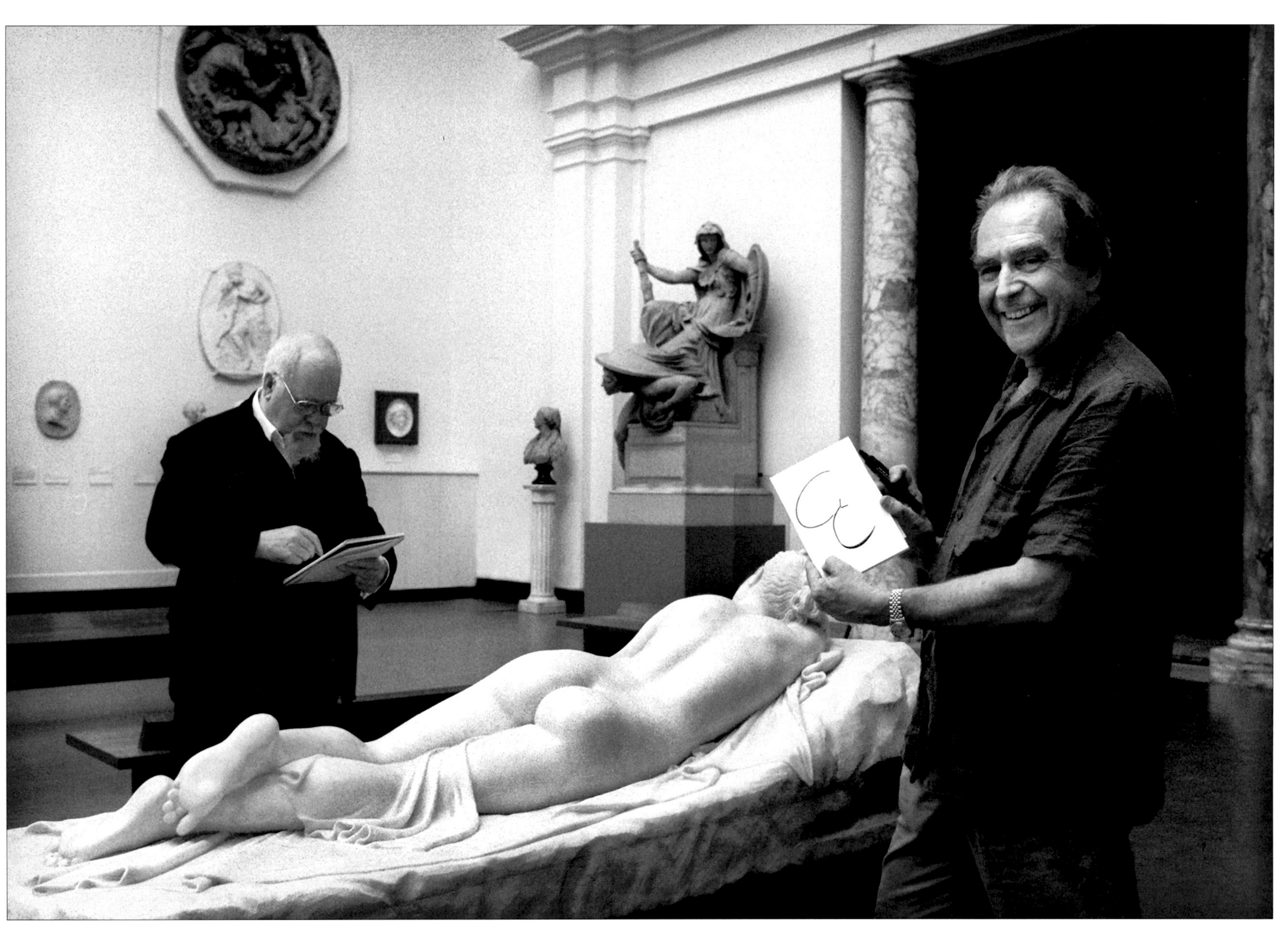

# GEORGE WEIDENFELD

The address was Flat 23b on the Chelsea Embankment near the Physic Garden, Carlos the butler opened the door saying ... 'He won't be long'... I'd been advised I would have ten minutes. Carlos led me through a series of rooms, containing some paintings that I recognised ... originals, and on through more rooms till it dawned on me he lived in the entire block. We found a suitable patch of light and the butler stood in for the subject, composed, focused, ready ...

'Where is he ?'

'He's arriving promptly, in the helicopter' ...

He marched in and barked 'Ten minutes!' ...

After a few moments polite conversation, he said 'I did say ten minutes.'

'Is it true you smoke a cigar?'

'Yes.'

'Would you mind lighting one?' ...

He did so, relaxing in the process.

Click, click, click, 'Thank you Sir', packing up ready to leave.

'Is that it?'

'You did say ten minutes.'

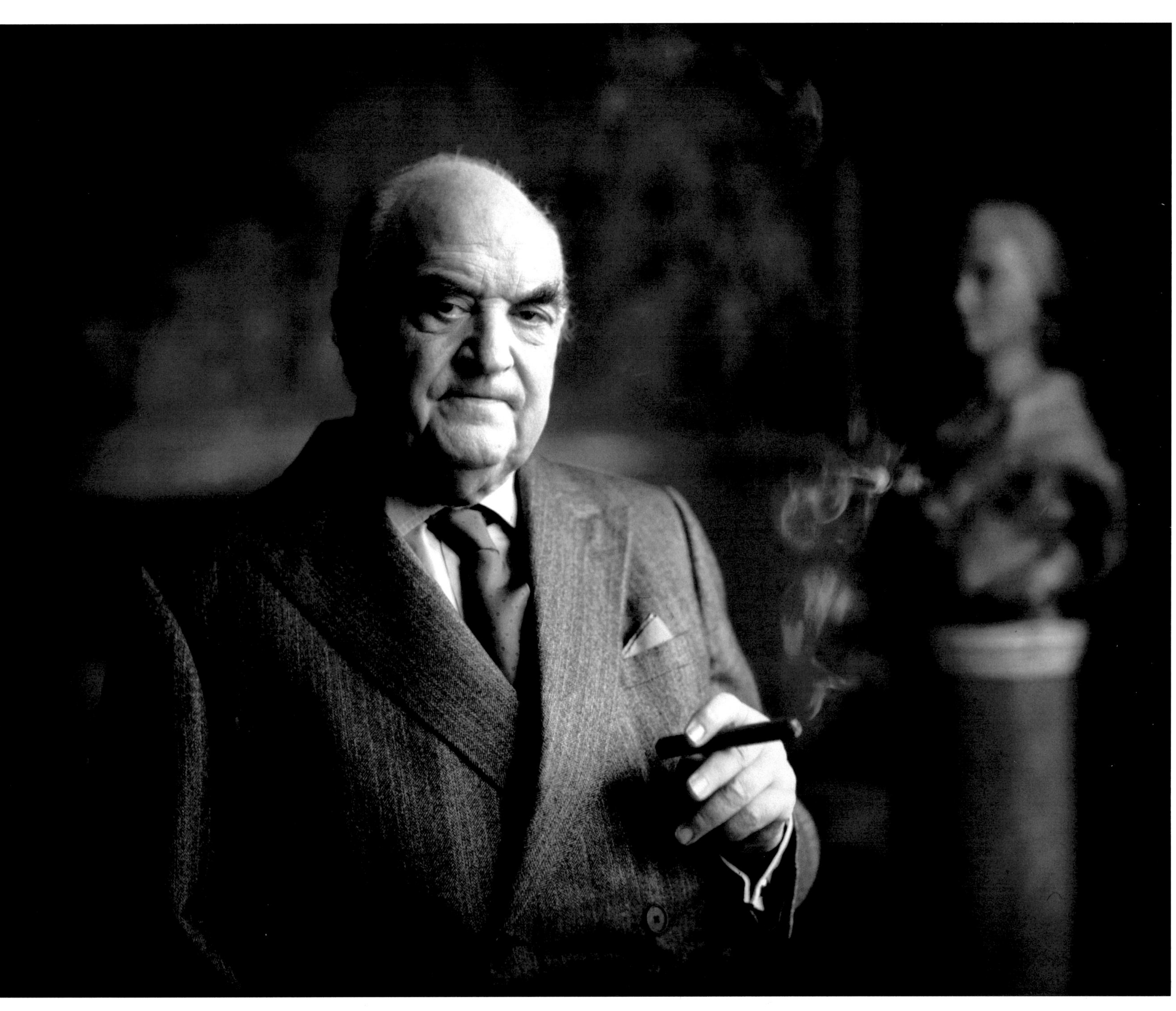

# IMELDA MAY

Baby Violet watches her mother get ready for the London Jazz Festival. Imelda May is changing more than her image; she still wears the kiss curl but tonight it will be soulful blues and torch songs. A few years later she'll change again; the look will be different and the music too.

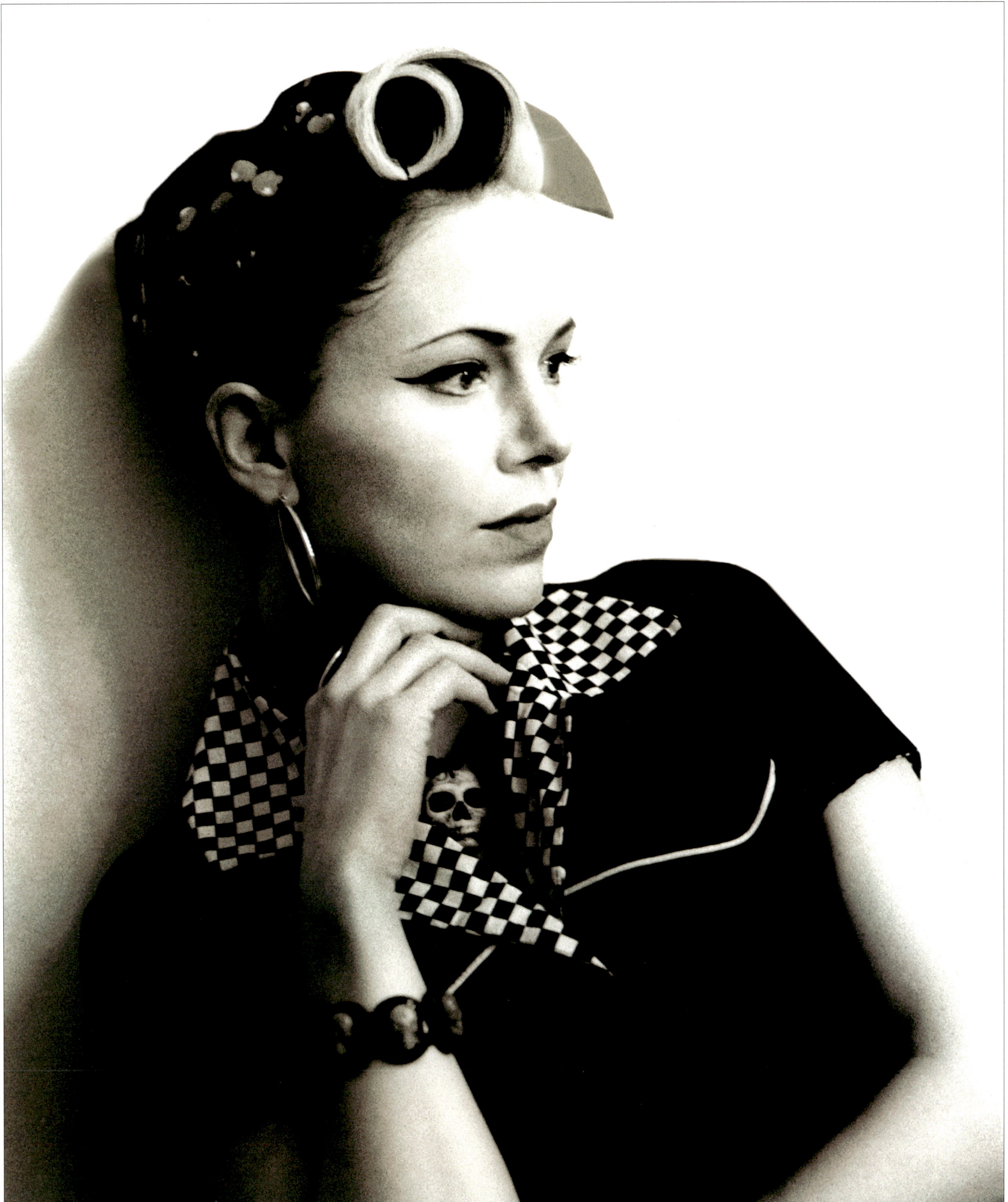

## KEN RUSSELL

The William Morris Gallery recently celebrated Walthamstow Art School 1955–66 with an exhibition. We had both attended as art students a decade apart. Ken went on to work for the illustrious *Picture Post* as a photographer before finding his *métier* in the cinema. The sombre rooms at Simpsons had us both improvising in a corridor bedecked with odiferous dragon lilies … 'dracunculus vulgaris', intoned the covert botanist …

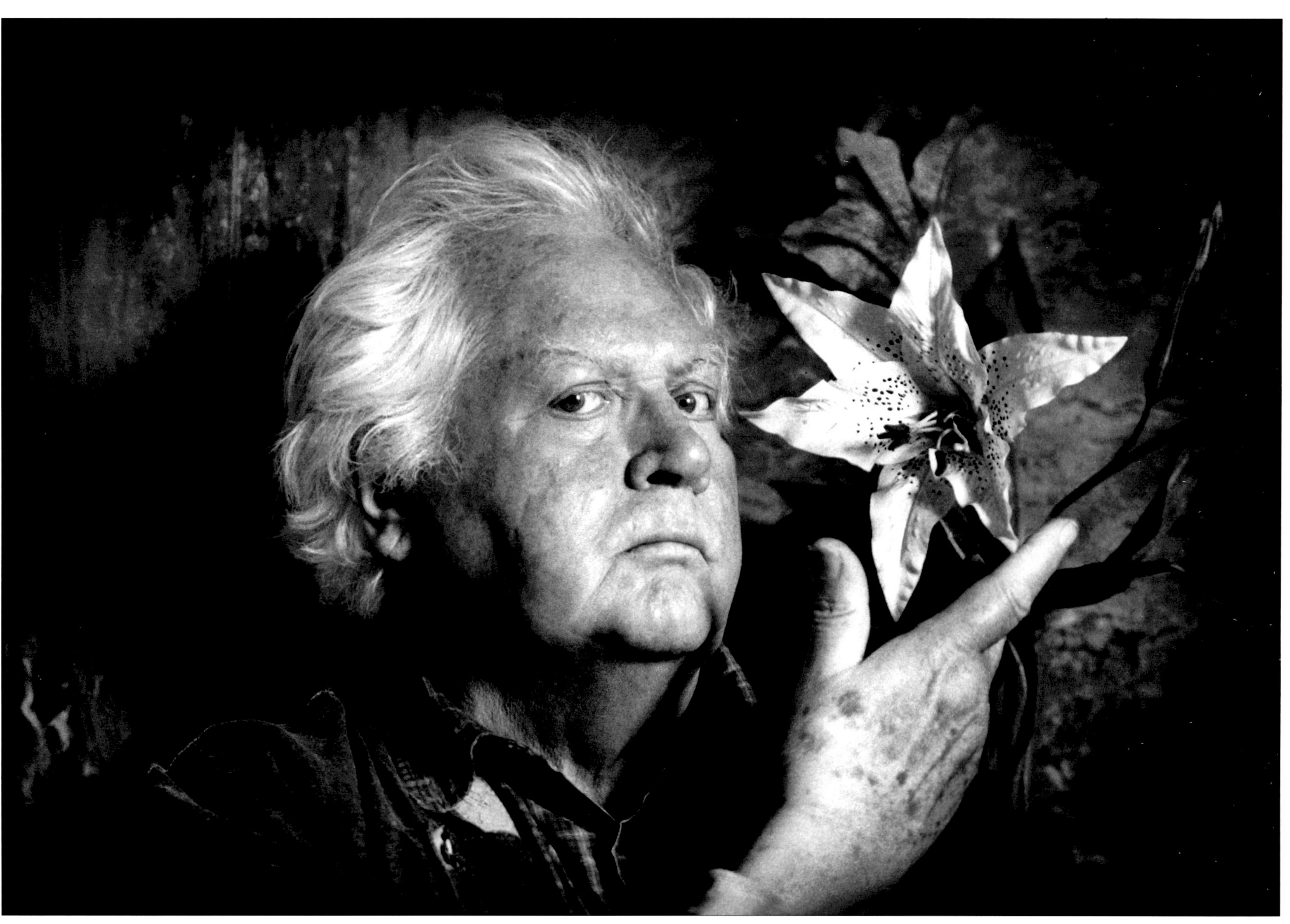

## ZAHA HADID

My daughter Sarah insisted on showing me Zaha's work at the Design Museum. I hadn't previously been interested in architectural drawing but this was something else, they were stunning. I went to her lecture at the Queen Elizabeth Hall, and later to the opening of her exhibition by the Serpentine in Hyde Park. She was gracious, pausing in front of *New York, Manhattan* for the camera.

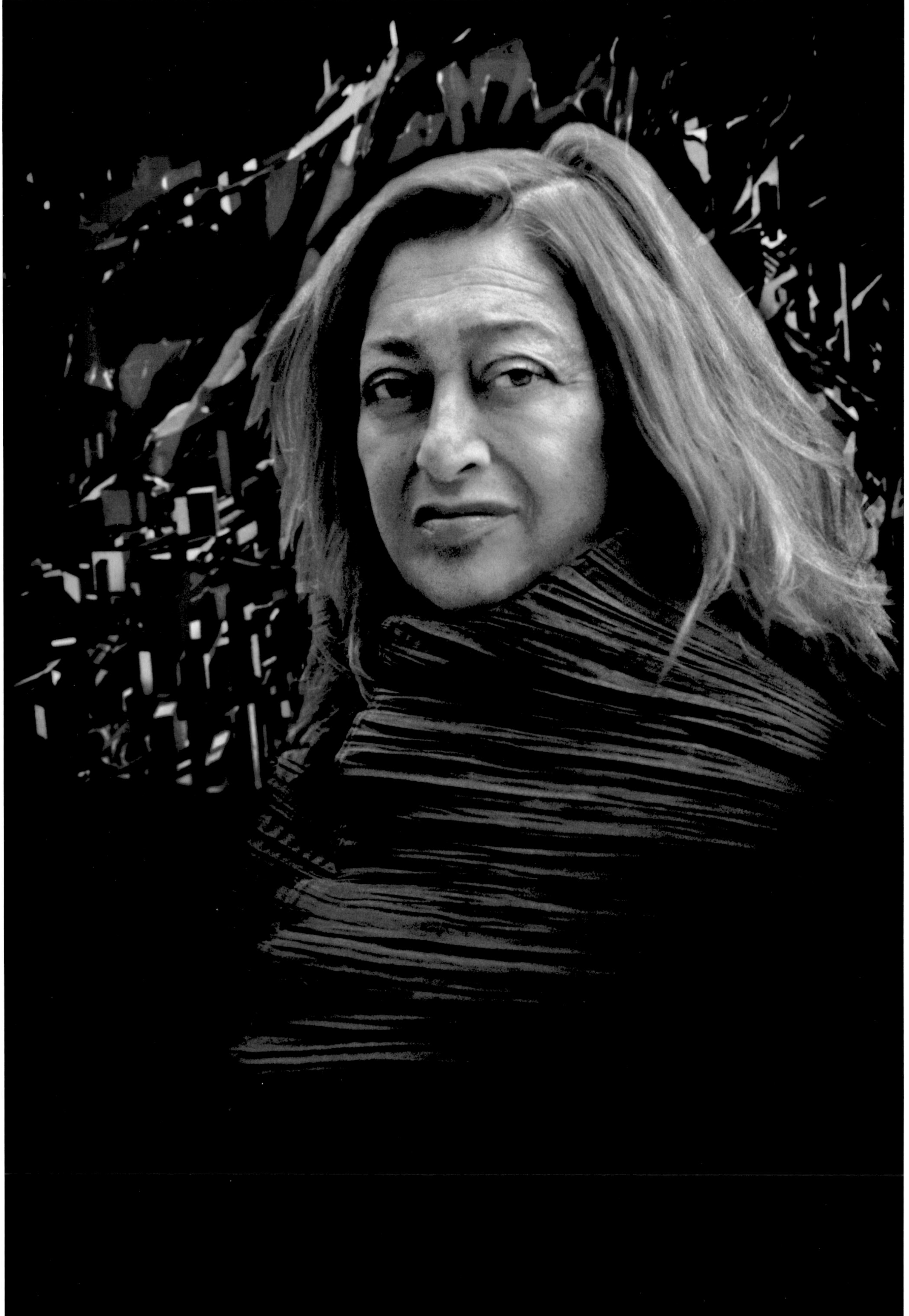

## SONNY ROLLINS

I'd been waiting outside his dressing room for hours, enjoying the music but getting nowhere. Sitting next to a woman who was happily knitting, it dawned on me that this was the musician's wife, Lucille. His exact contemporary, Ornette Coleman, preferred alto, while Sonny Rollins was happier on the tenor horn. Mrs Rollins could see my agitation, put down her knitting and tapped on the door, 'Let him in Sonny, he wants to take a photograph.' Music stopped. Door opened. There he was, cool in black beret, white beard and tenor sax. He nodded, turned to the mirror and played.

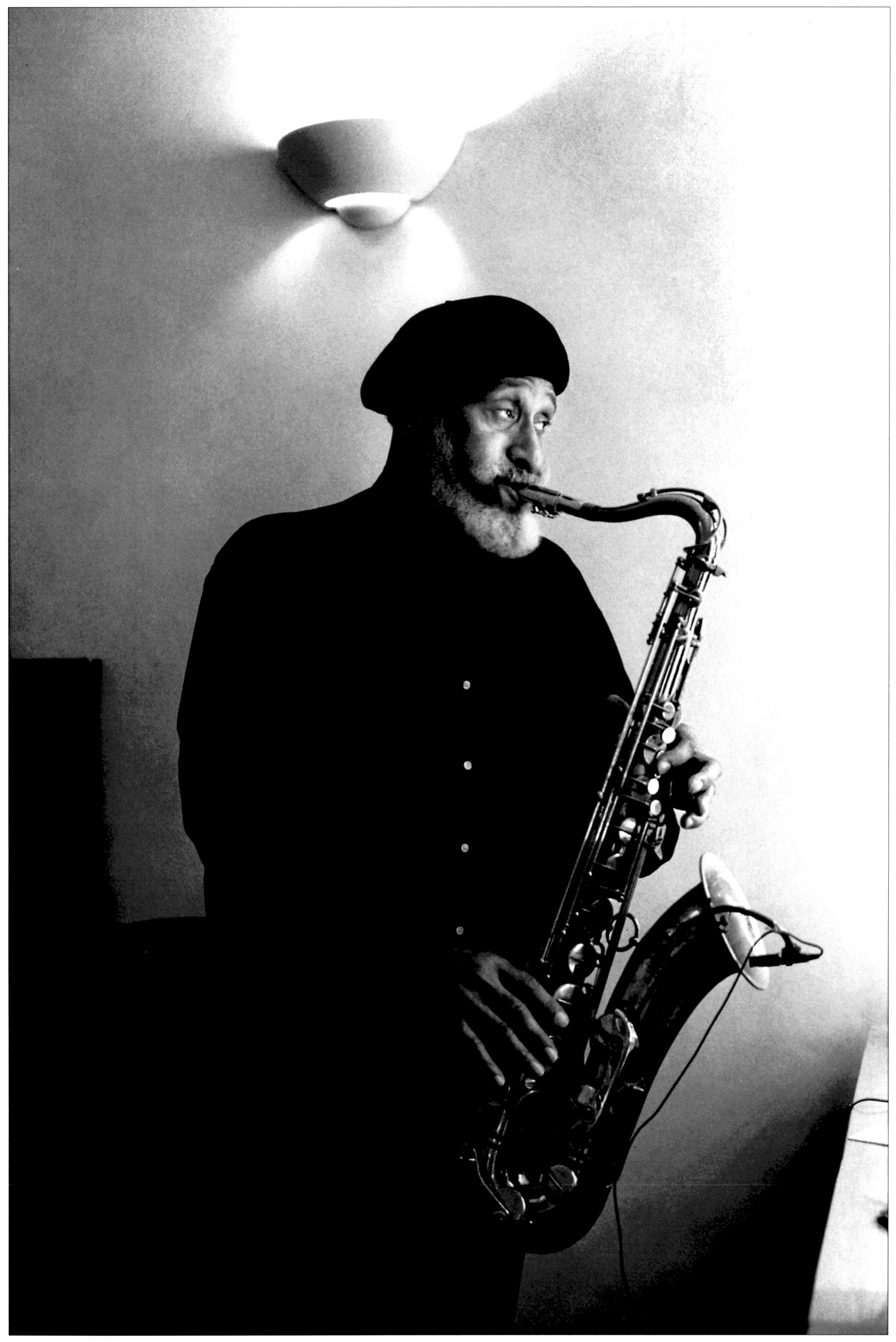

# SHIRLEY BASSEY

I saw Jacques Tati at the cinema and listened to Al Read on the radio with my father who loved observational humour. He took me to the Adelphi Theatre to see Read's *Such is Life* and Shirley Bassey, still a teenager, was on the same bill. Now, at the Royal Festival Hall, she shimmied through her repertoire, including the James Bond theme songs. I was hoping she'd sing her first hit, the 'Banana Boat Song' but Stan Freberg's wonderful parody had blown it out of the water ... 'Too loud man, too loud, like it's too piercing.'

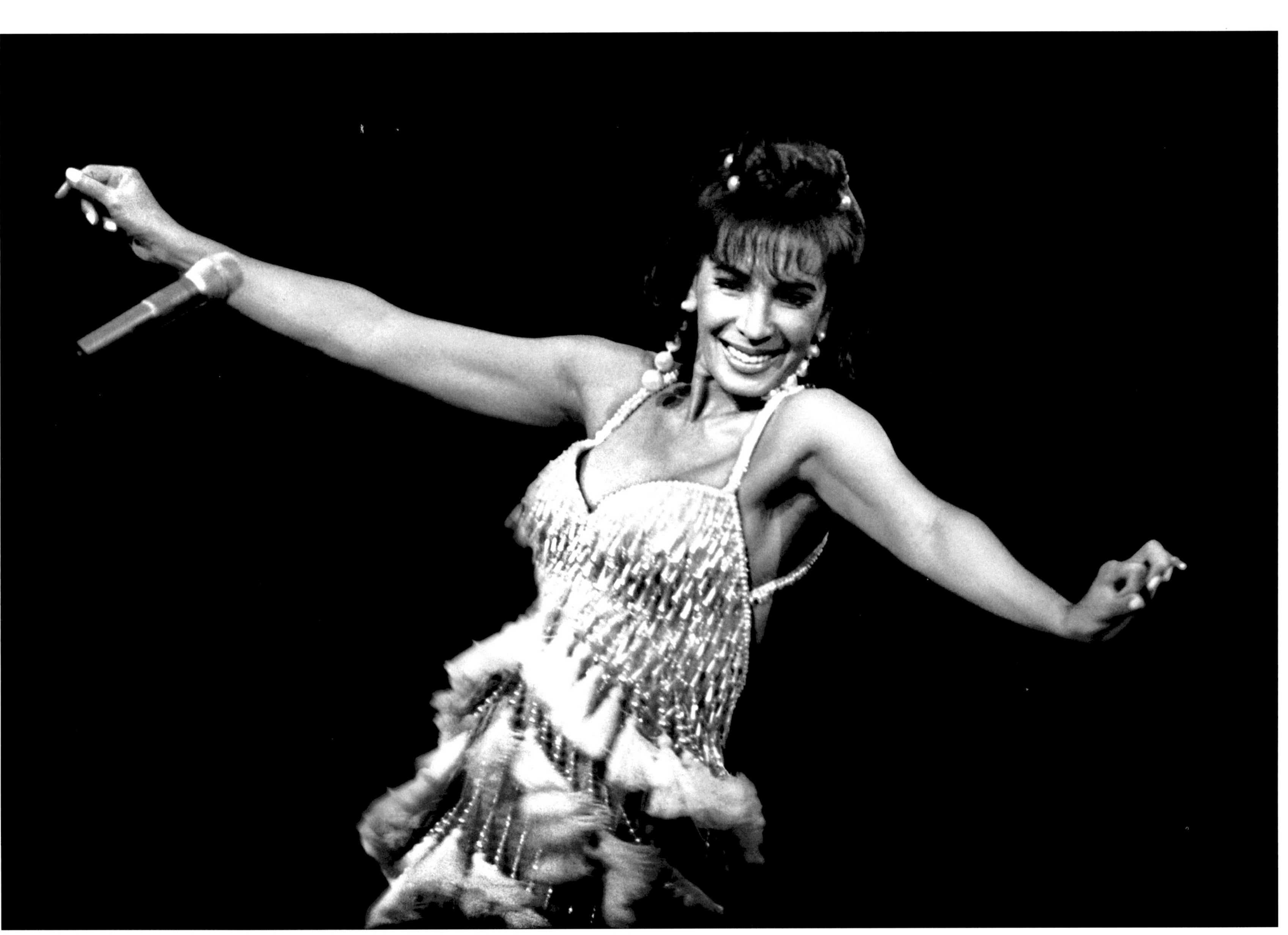

# PAUL SCHRADER

He was staying at the Soho Hotel, expecting to be photographed there, until another idea presented itself. The walls were lined with paintings chosen by interior decorators …

'Are you interested in art?' …

'I'm interested in people.'

'OK, let's leave the hotel and see what we find' …

The National Gallery had placed weather-proof reproductions of its better-known works around the area, in alleys, in the market, and spotting the master works, he took an instant shine to the Titian. The writer of *Raging Bull* and director of *Mishima* relaxed in front of *Bacchus & Ariadne*, getting a kick out of mixing with the characters in Berwick Street Market.

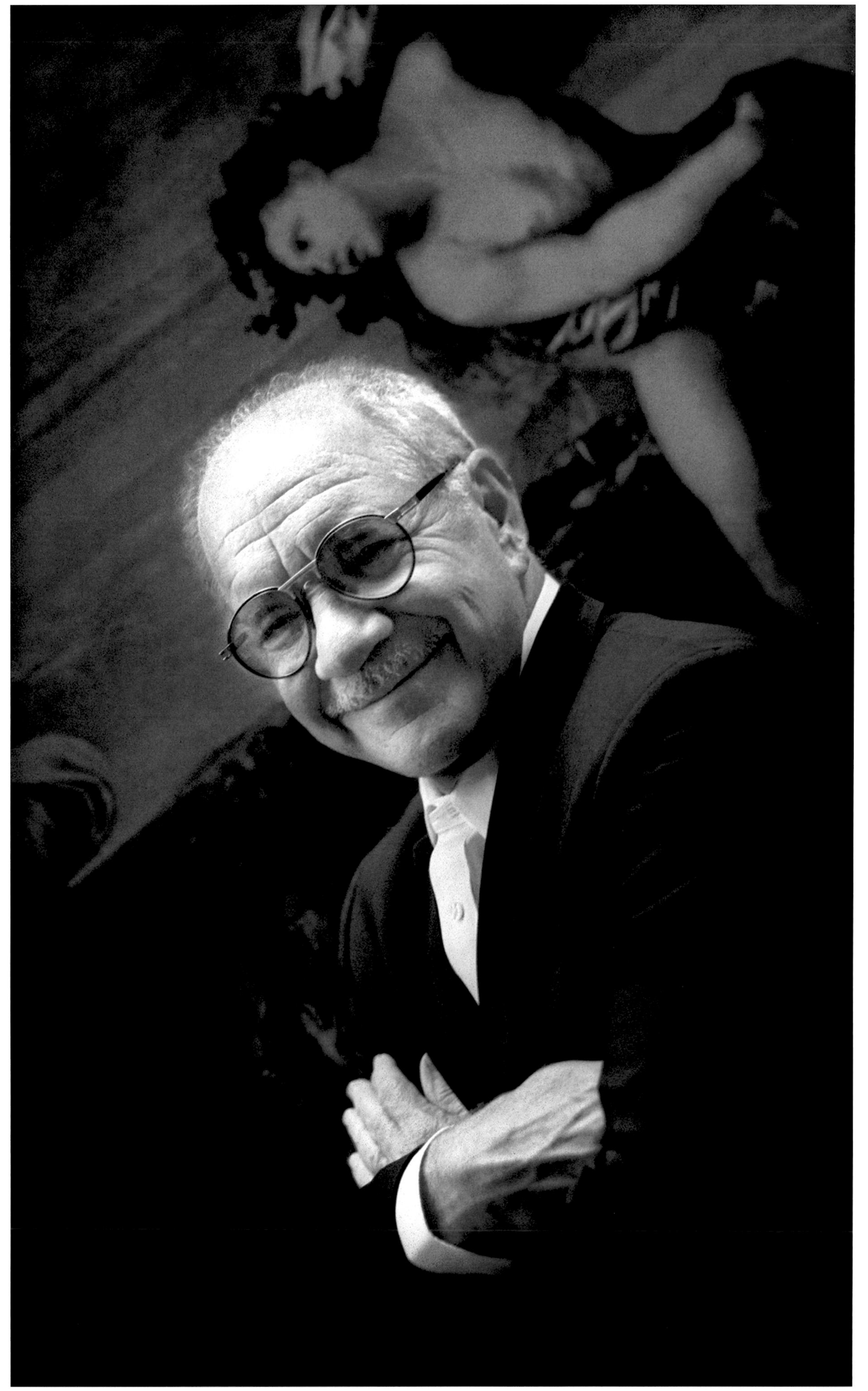

# JONI MITCHELL

She wasn't enthusiastic when I entered the room, I'd been stuck in a queue of journalists and photographers and now it was my turn. Just arrived from Canada, she was clearly jet-lagged. 'Do you have a hat and perhaps some jewellery?' I was thinking of Man Ray's portrait of Nancy Cunard covered in bracelets. The idea of dressing-up brought her to life, she began rummaging through luggage, tiredness gone, she tried on everything and even started singing. Suddenly it was over, time to go.

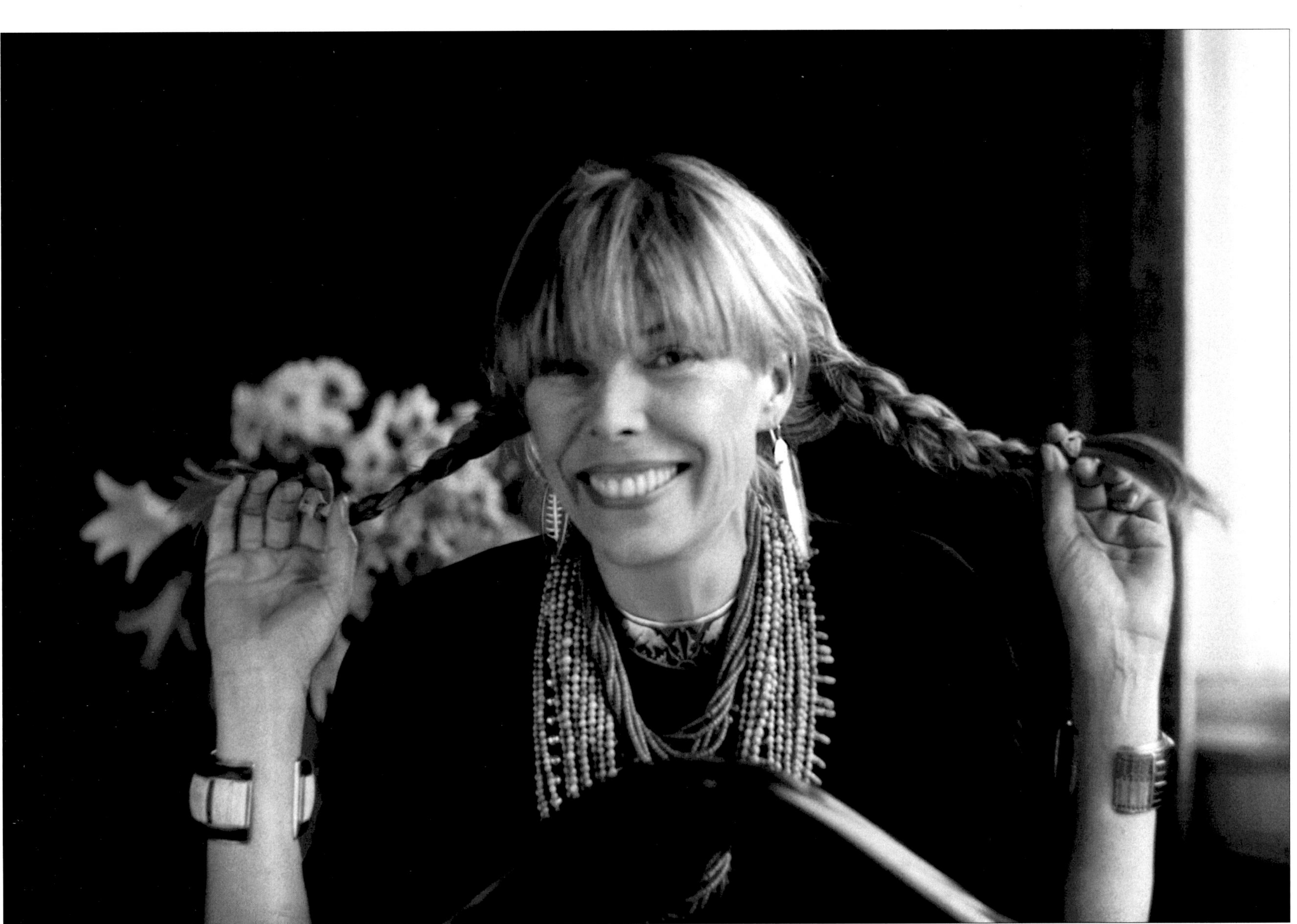

# HENRY MANCINI

A deep gravely voice from the New York office said ... 'We're re-releasing Hank's entire catalogue, ok, now here's the concept ... we want each album represented by Hank sitting in a different chair.'

'Is that it?'

'That's it.'

On the first day they wanted documentary pictures of him conducting an orchestra in the recording studio, the second with the chairs, and there was little time. A stylist was hired to find interesting chairs. He was charming and svelte in a dark suit and bow tie, if a little stiff ... it took some persuading to remove his jacket for a more relaxed look. Some chairs were bought, some borrowed and one in the shape of an elephant was hired, too expensive even for the record company. When he saw it, he was knocked out ... 'Gee fellas, you shouldn't have, that's just great!'

It was pure chance; we'd forgotten his composition 'Baby Elephant Walk'.

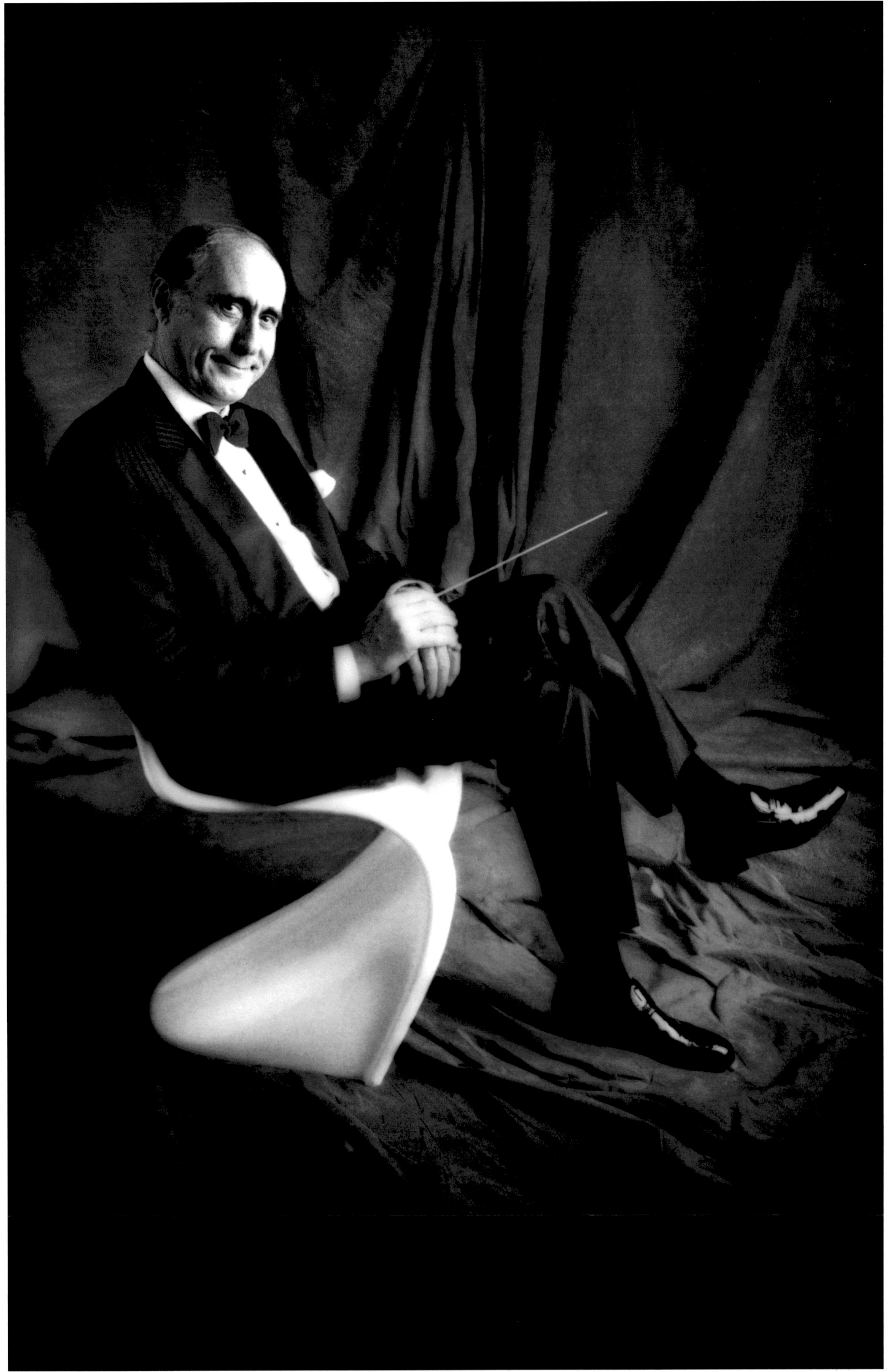

## JOHN SMITH & FAMILY

Known as the 'greatest Prime Minister we never had', John Smith succeeded Neil Kinnock as the Leader of the Opposition. The session was shot in his Edinburgh home with his wife Elizabeth and daughters Sarah, Jane and Catherine, posed with an almost Victorian formality, appropriate for the occasion, which belied the hilarity that preceded it.

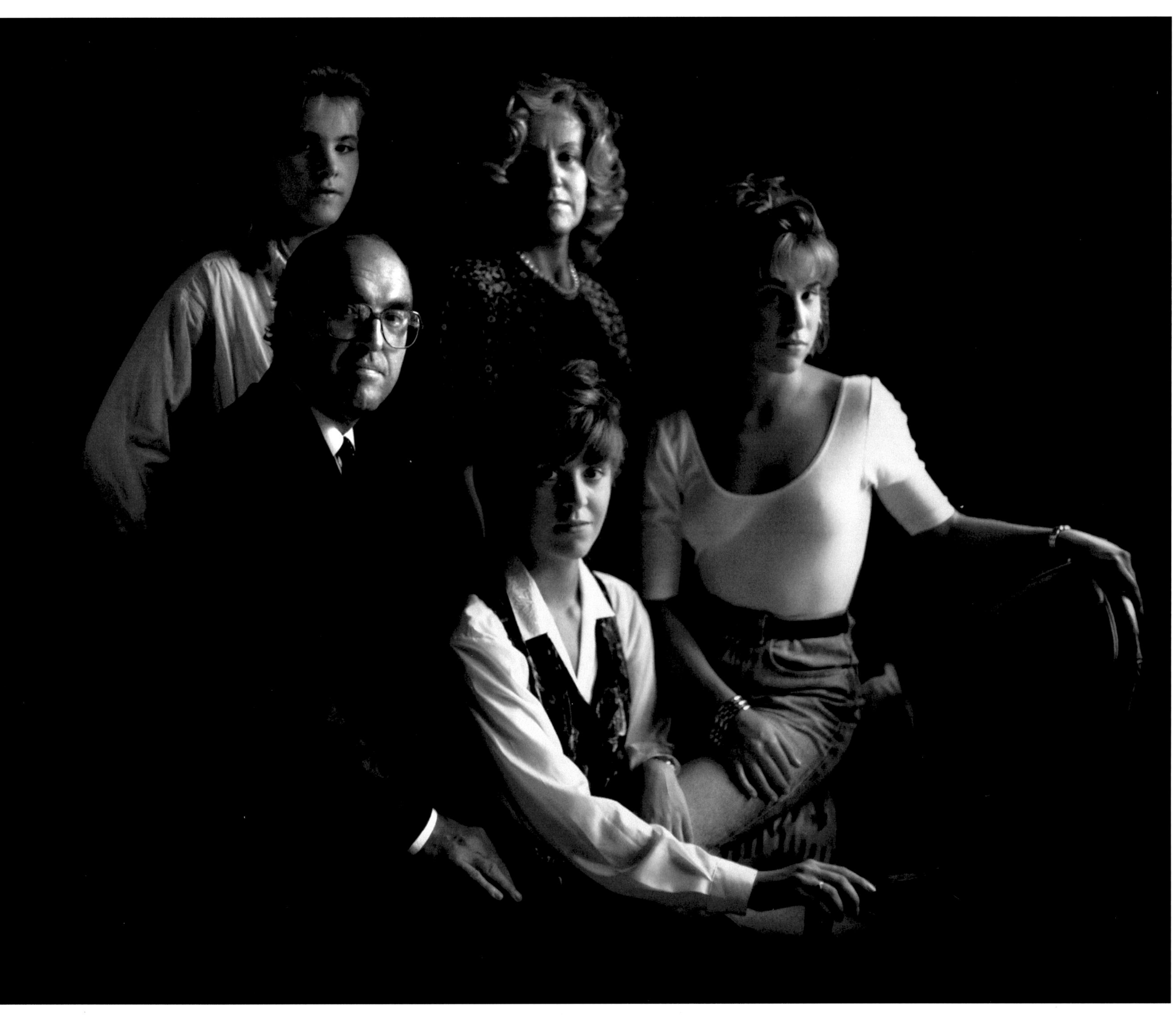

# JULIETTE BINOCHE

The Almeida in Islington came up with the novel idea of luring international stars with the opportunity of appearing on the London stage in a local theatre for a peppercorn salary ... and it worked. The play was *Naked* by Pirandello. Some time later our paths crossed again when she danced with Akram Khan at The National Theatre, raising a few eyebrows, though in the Hollywood heyday dancing actors were a commonplace.

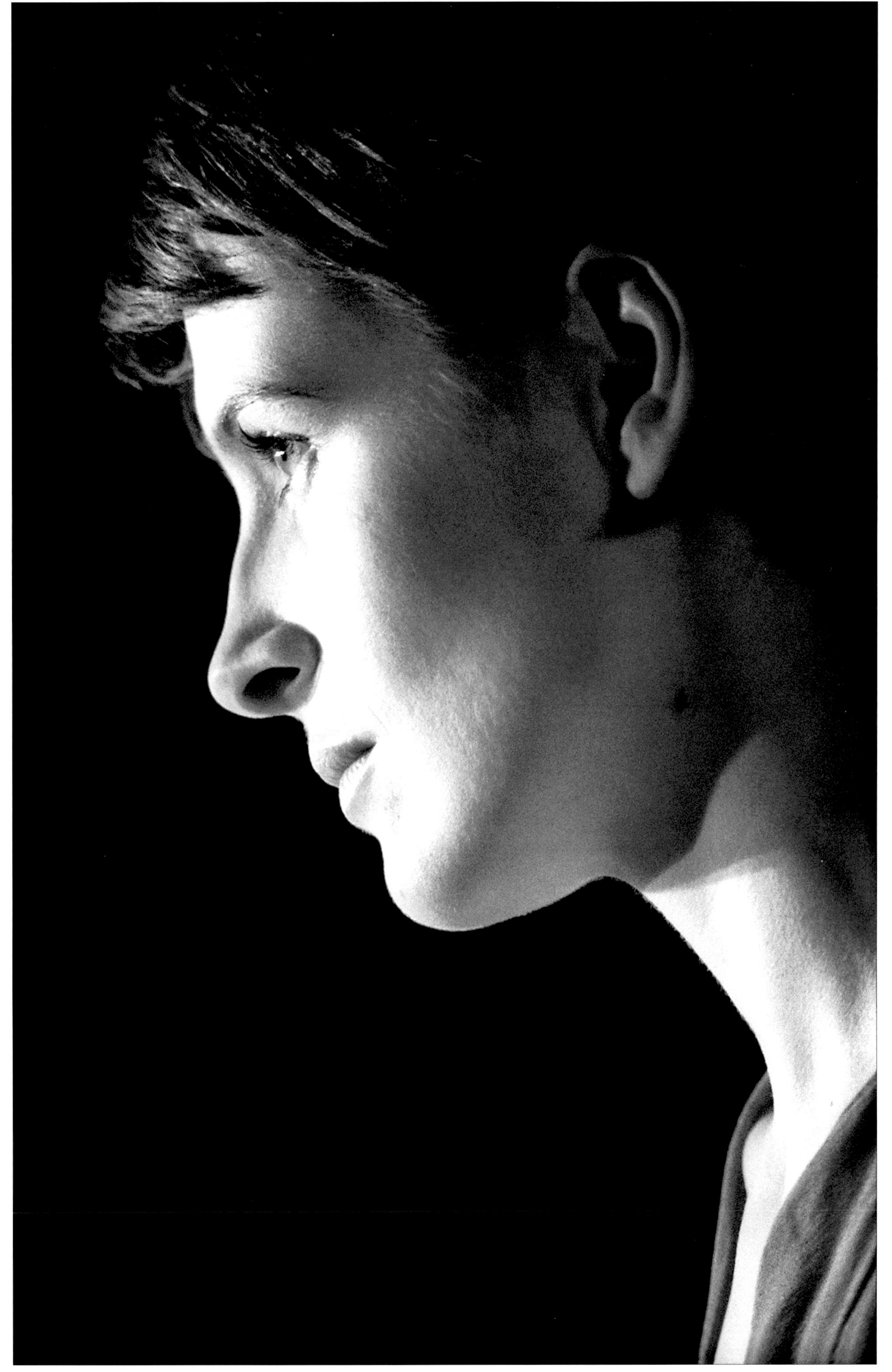

# ANTONIO PAPPANO

'He's not really a conductor, he's a storyteller' ... so said a cellist from the orchestra ... fair enough, but he's a pianist and also Music Director of the Royal Opera Covent Garden and Accademia Nazionale di Santa Cecilia in Rome, which is where we go for the portrait. The brief, in January, was to photograph the maestro in a series of Roman locations, including the new opera house, and to make it look like summer, all in a few hours. He gave a hilarious running commentary of the neo-realist films of Rossellini and the dream world of Fellini then straight into a rehearsal with the orchestra. A storyteller ? ... absolutely.

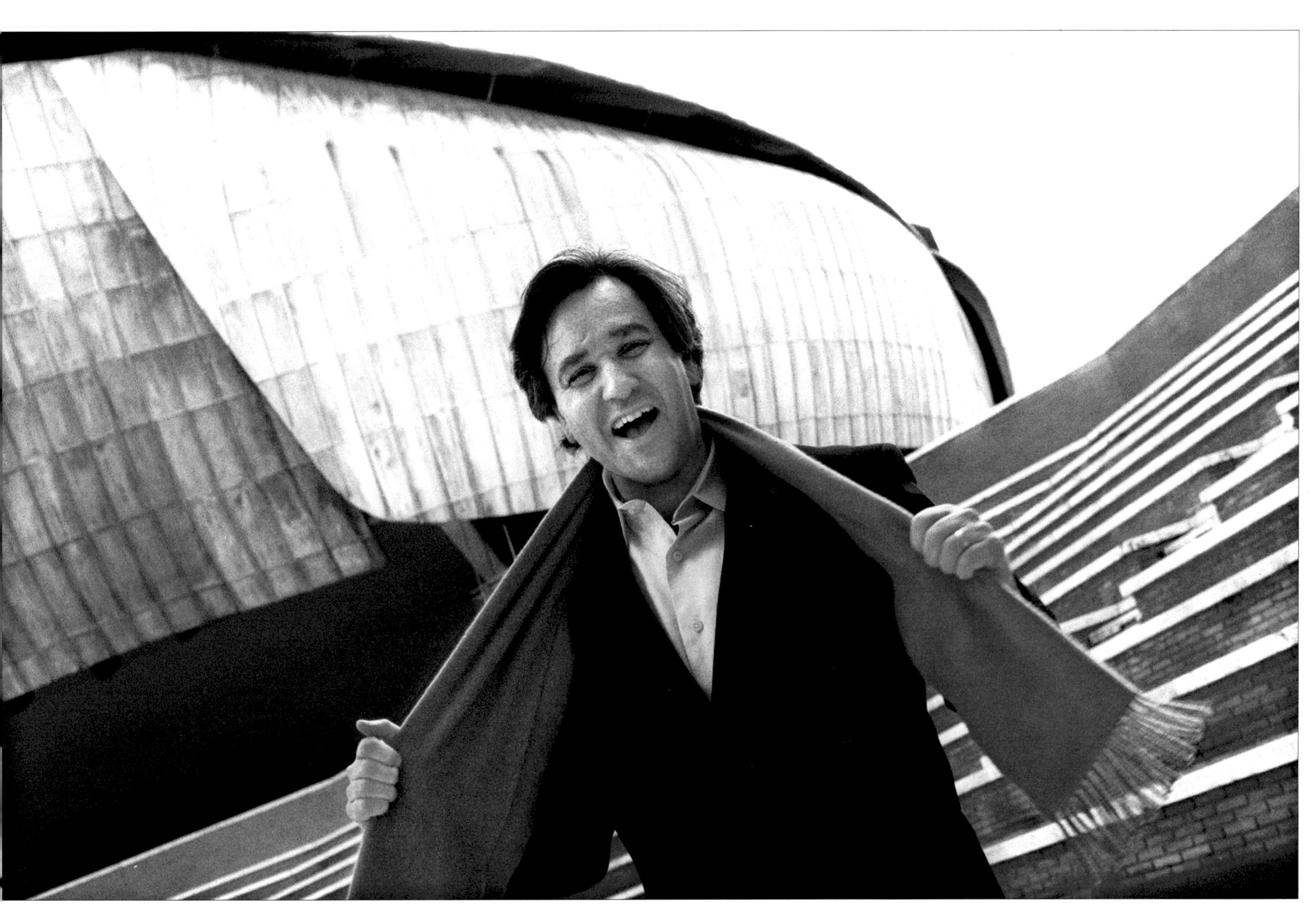

# TEARS FOR FEARS

We shot a few publicity sessions in various photography studios during the mid-1980s for posters and record sleeves, among them *Shout*, *Head Over Heels* and *Everybody Wants To Rule The World*. Then changing gear to cover them in situ recording, on the road, backstage and amidst the chaos of a live concert. After a lull in the 1990s, Roland Orzabal and Curt Smith are back in the recording studio and making new music.

*Footnote:* A classical record company requested we duplicate the composition with two eminent Russian musicians. Heads crammed together they were reminded of former Soviet leaders and laughed so much the idea was abandoned.

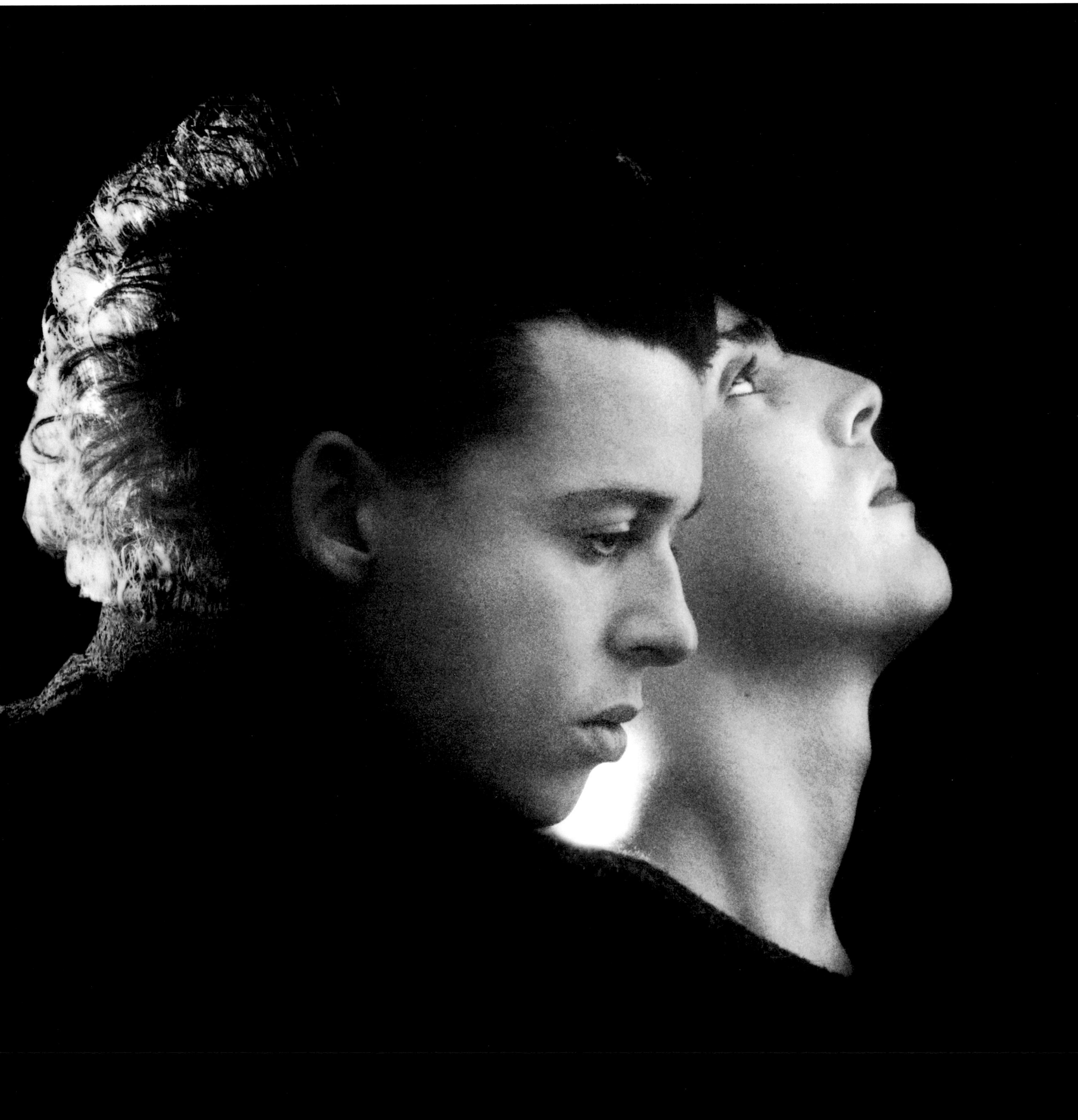

# JULIE CHRISTIE

Learning the part of Yelena Andreyevna for the play *Uncle Vanya* was the latest challenge for the actress more accustomed to working scene by scene or shot by shot and out of sequence for the cine camera. Mike Nichols was directing the Chekhov on Broadway, with Elizabeth Wilson, Lilian Gish, George C. Scott, and Nicol Williamson as Vanya. New York unions are very strict about access for photographers so pictures were made off-set in daylight.

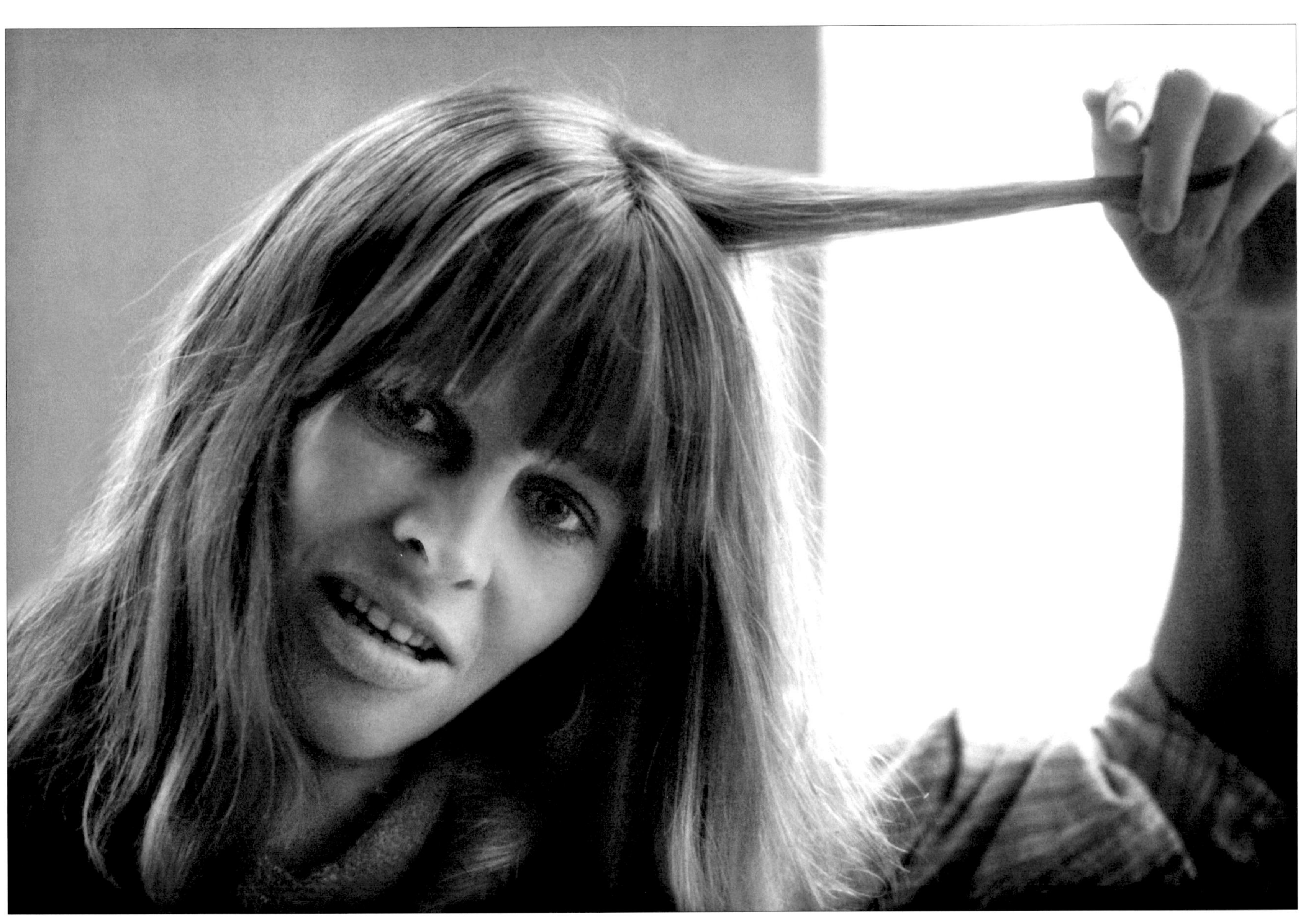

# VALERY GERGIEV

The invitation was to the Kirov Opera in Leningrad, now post-glasnost and perestroika the Mariinsky in St Petersburg. I was given carte blanche to work with both companies, the opera and the ballet. The chief administrator was also a baritone, the tour manager played the oboe, it seemed everybody had two jobs. The ancient building's doors were guarded by babooshkas, each impassive in their guarding duties, abstractly engaged in knitting. Gergiev had conscripted an unknown from the chorus to be groomed for the lead in *Eugene Onegin*, plunged into an intensive course to learn the part of Tatiana in record time. She had a different coach every day, dialogue, singing, movement and costume, for the opening in just one week.

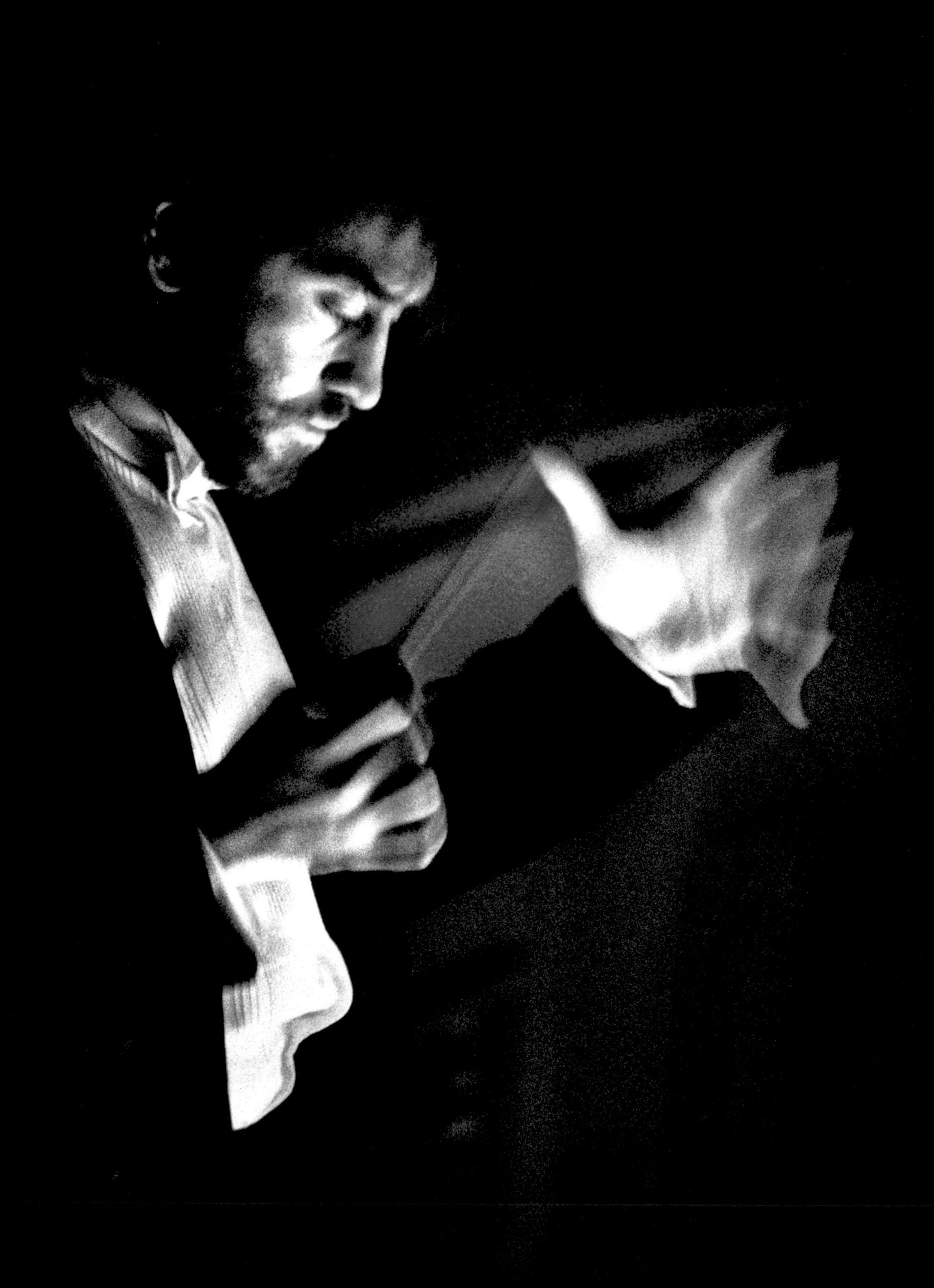

# IREK MUKHAMEDOV

When he left the Bolshoi to join the Royal Ballet, choreographer Kenneth MacMillan thought he had found the perfect partner for Darcey Bussell, but *en pointe* she was too tall for him. He was better suited to Viviana Durante and together they danced through the MacMillan repertoire. Here he's rehearsing at the Barons Court studios before the remodelling of the Opera House at Covent Garden. The Head of Marketing called ... 'We wanted to say thank you to Princess Margaret, framed your print of Irek and sent it over to Buckingham Palace, is that alright?' The following day ... 'It went to the wrong Princess, Diana won't give it up, may we have another?'

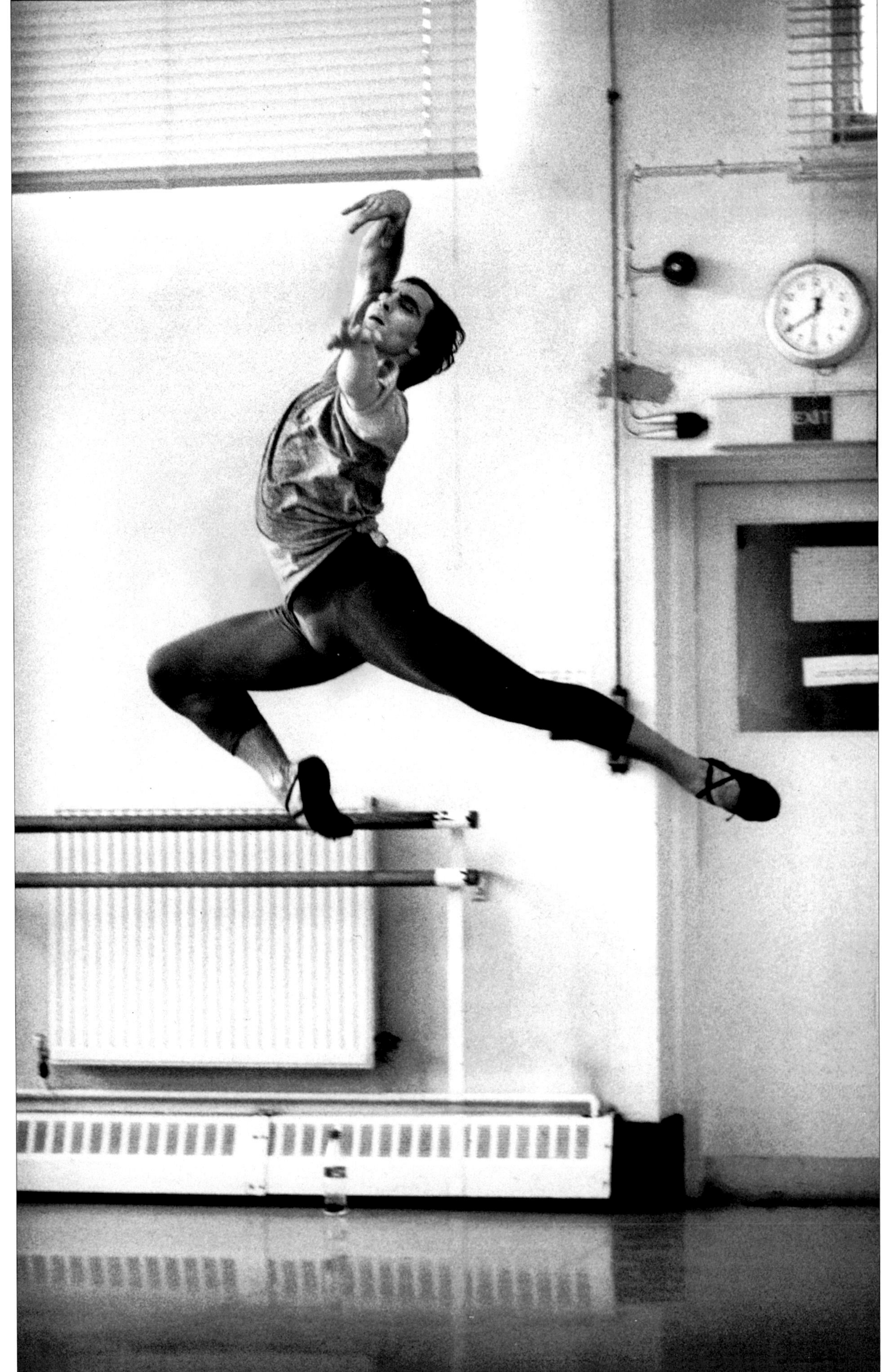
EXIT

# SALIF KEITA

Rob Partridge explained ... 'He's a Third World superstar and he doesn't speak English.' Salif is from Mali and we managed to communicate using my rusty schoolboy French. His singing is delivered in a high vibrato with a powerful attack, an unmistakeable voice and a remarkable appearance. An African albino with blonde dreadlocks and a hunting jacket threaded with human bones. We met several times for various record sleeves, *Amen*, *The Mansu of Mali*, *Metropolis*, but the most recent was at a bus-stop in Camden Town ... stopped the car, he looked up and mimed taking a picture, I smiled and took him over to Island Records, once again struggling with French small talk.

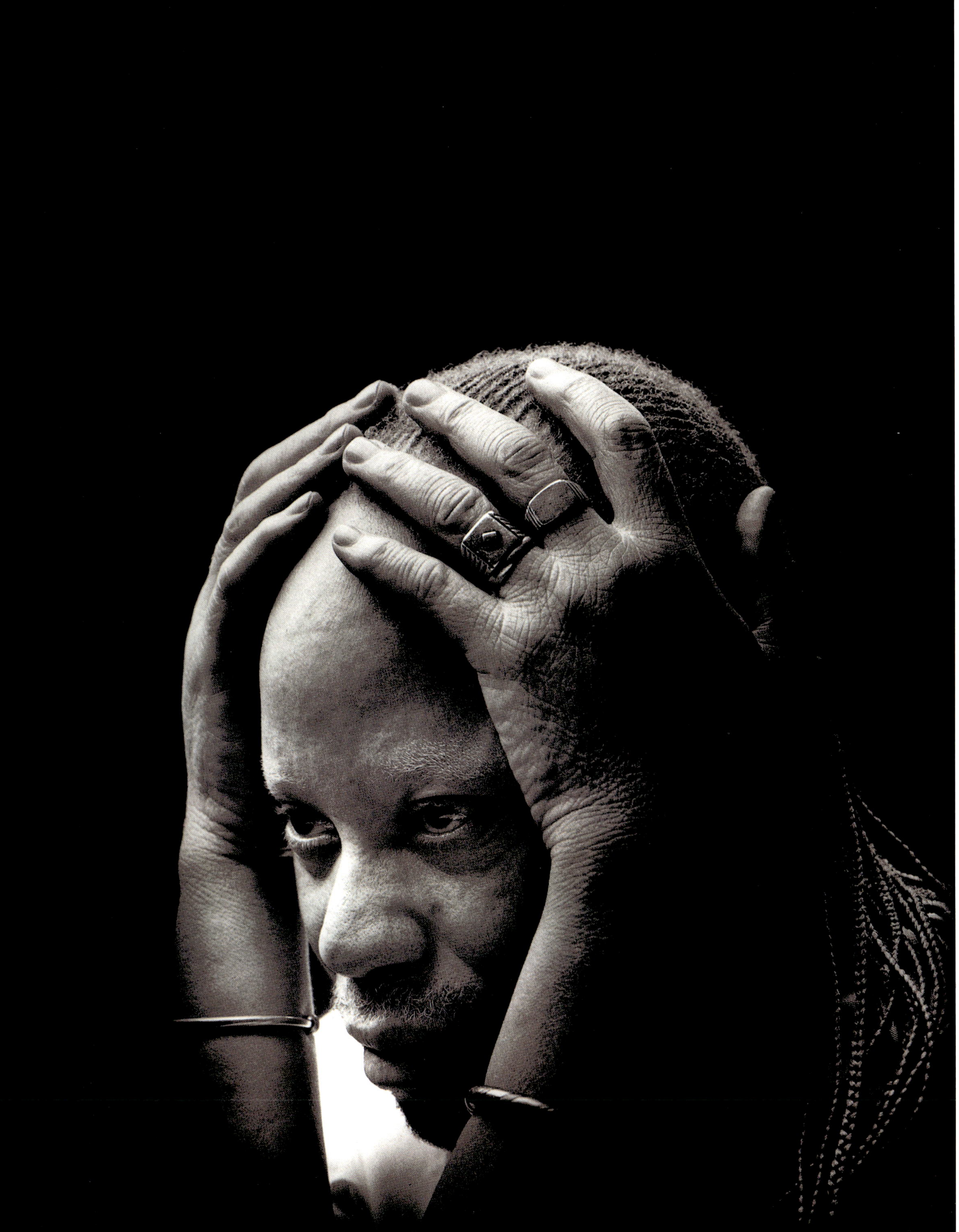

# DOLLY MIXTURE

The Raincoats, Mo-dettes, Slits, Leopards, Flatbackers, Girlschool, Table Twelve, Innocents, Bodysnatchers and The Klitz were among the girl bands proliferating on the music scene in the late 1970s. *The Sunday Times Magazine* thought it was a phenomenon worth recording. Rachel Bor, Debsey Wykes and Hester Smith are the trio that make Dolly Mixture, moments before they trod the boards at a favoured punk venue, The Hope & Anchor in Islington.

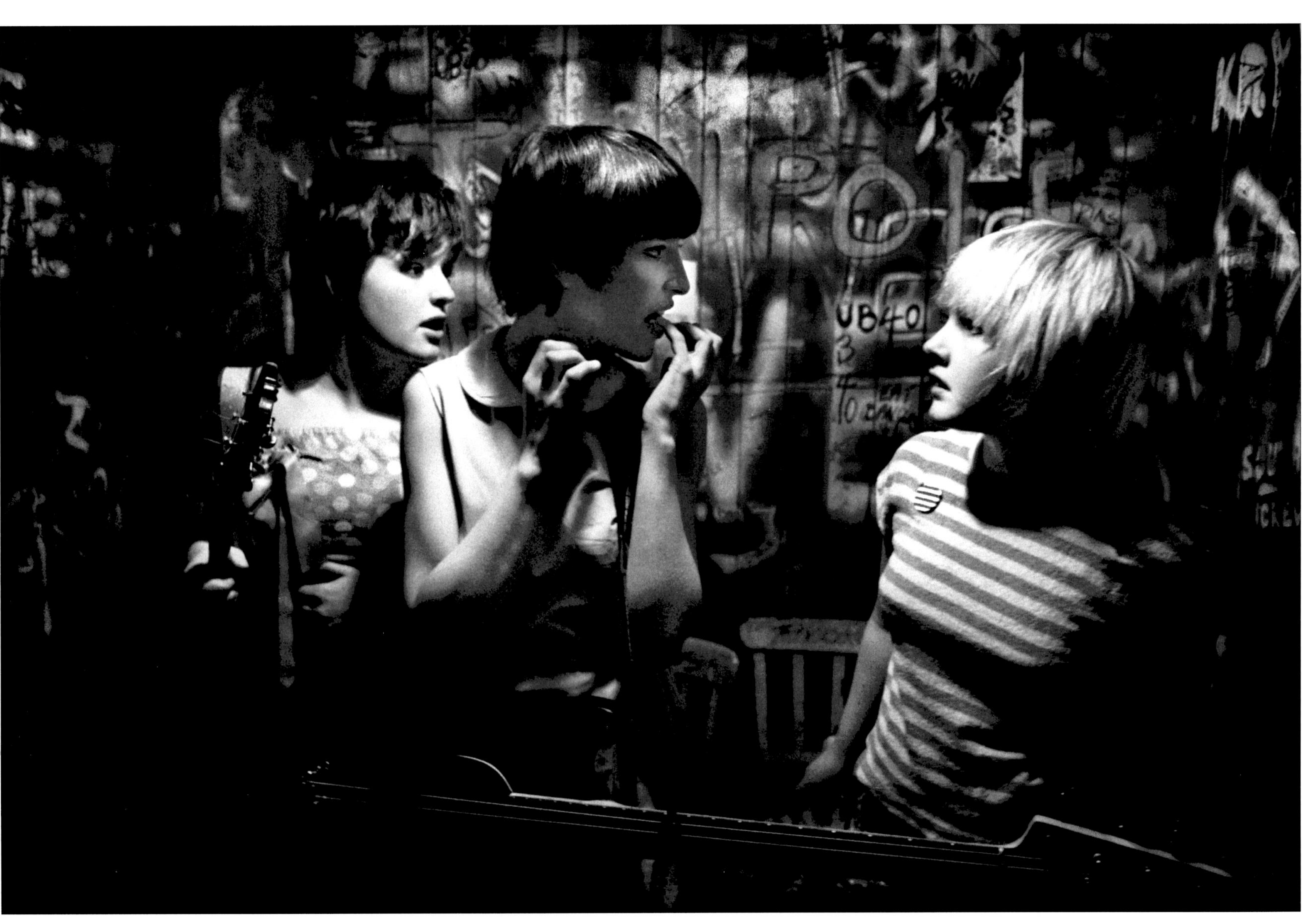
UB40

# ANTONY GORMLEY

The sculptor's studio in Camden was littered with dozens of the cast-iron man rusting and resting at all angles in the open air prior to being despatched to various rural and urban landscapes around the UK. They reminded me of the terracotta soldiers in Xian before they'd been properly excavated and cleaned, which were a fraction of the army ordered by Emperor Chin to escort him to the next life. No sign of rust on Molecule Man who was afforded shelter inside, out of the elements.

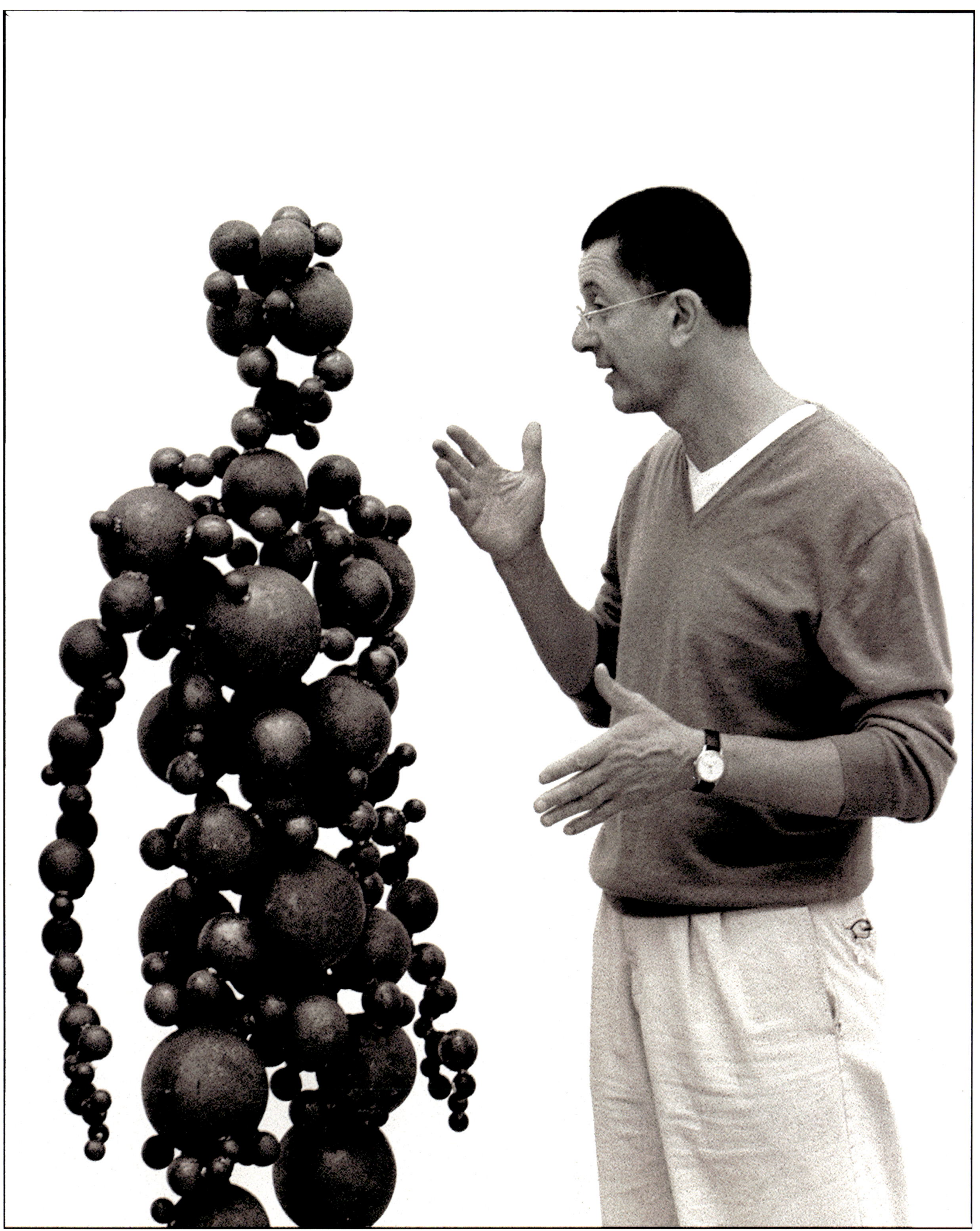

## DAVID HOCKNEY & JOHN COX

Sent to the Rector's office at the RCA, Robin Darwin noticed me gazing at the row of etchings all around the room ... '*The Rake's Progress*' he said, by David Hockney, and I mumbled that I'd studied printmaking at Walthamstow Art School. As we chatted about his favourite subject he forgot all about the misdemeanours that had brought me to his office. Years later I photographed the designs by Hockney for Glyndebourne Opera's *Rake* directed by John Cox. The pair collaborated again on *L'Enfant et Les Sortileges* and even later on *Die Frau Ohne Schatten* when this portrait was made at Covent Garden with them balancing on boxes to reach the light.

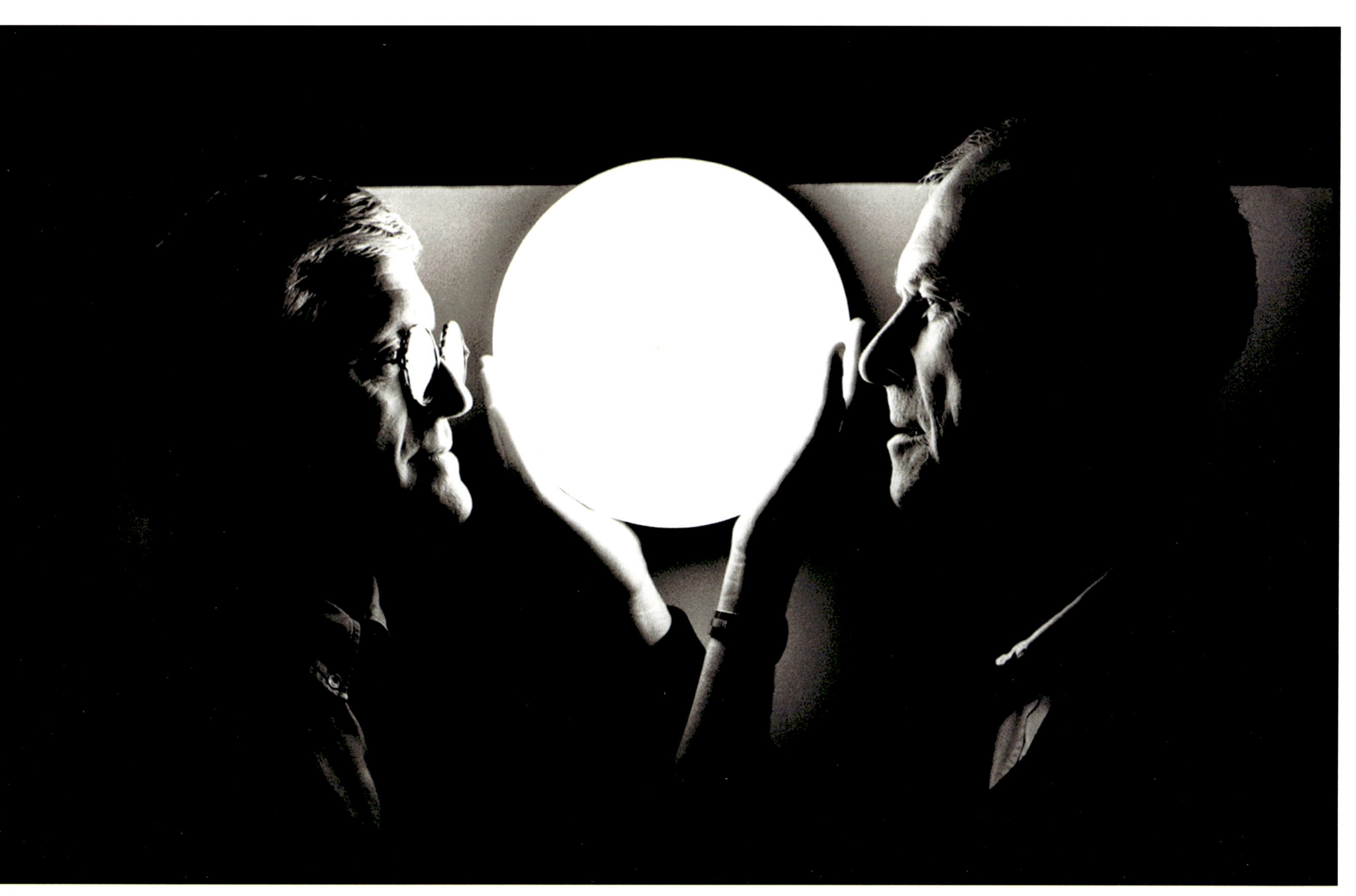

## PETER USTINOV

He was in London to direct an opera at the Coliseum, tired and certainly not in the mood to be photographed. I was about to be shown the door when I remembered the oranges ... 'There's a painting on my kitchen wall, of a woman in a black dress, sitting in front of a bowl with three oranges' ... I had his attention. He was in town for Prokofiev's opera *The Love of Three Oranges* ... 'and the woman in the painting is your grandmother' ... His eyes widened. I'd seen an exhibition of the Russian theatre designer Leon Bakst and recalled the details. The house phone kept ringing, each time he used a different female voice, adopting a variety of personas, a rehearsing soprano, a newly-wed, a hotel maid, which made my life much easier.

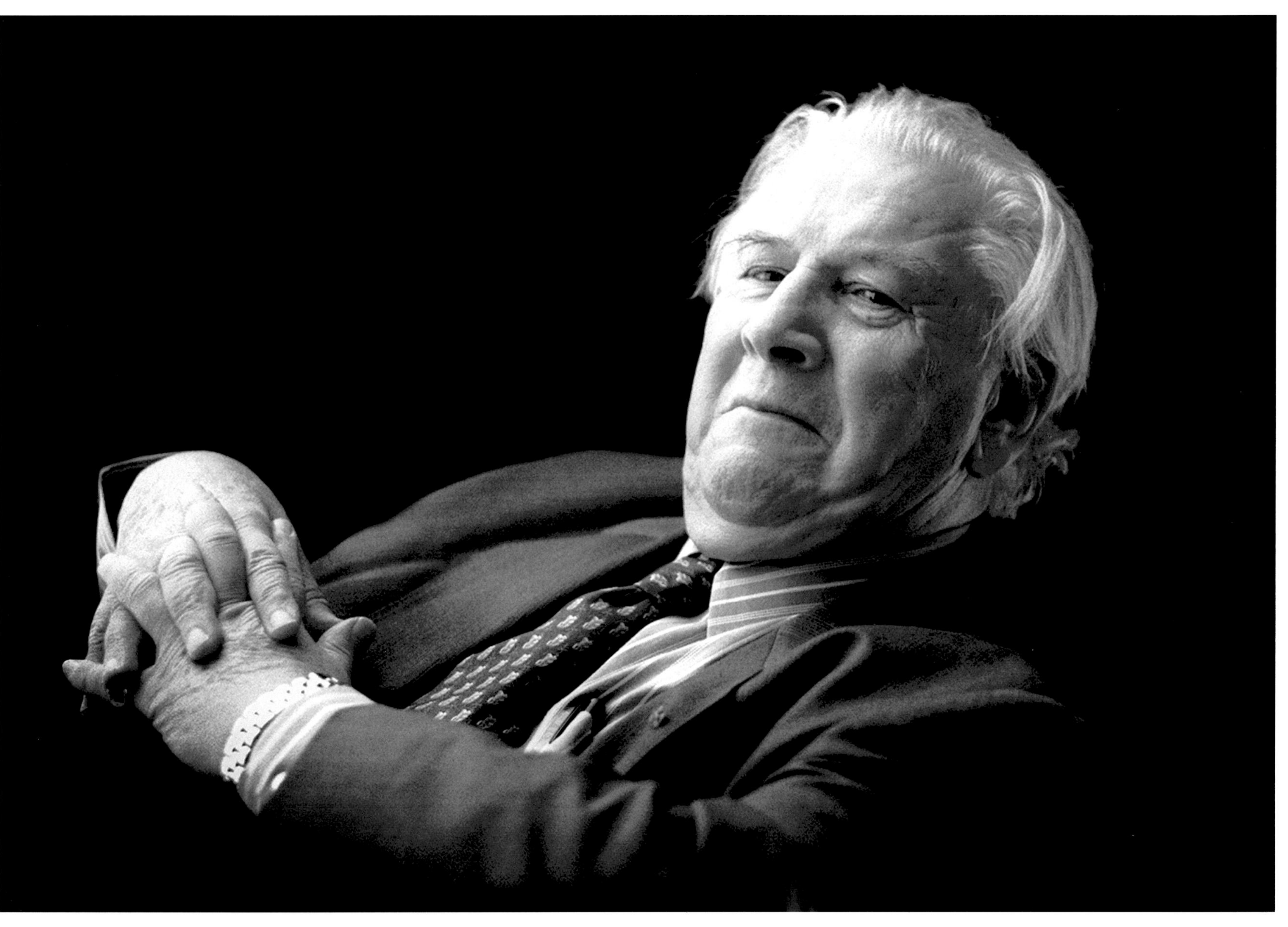

# KASHGAR MARKET

The young lady wears a western scarf with her hair plaited into a hundred and eight strands. I didn't count them but presume so, as it is common among Tibetan women. Kashgar is where China meets Pakistan, Afghanistan and Tajikistan on its Western border. Over the centuries, descendants from merchants travelling the Silk Road settled in this most cosmopolitan of market towns. As many as fifty-five nationalities make up the population that are ethnically distinct from the Han Chinese, Uighurs, Kazaks, Kirghiz, Tajiks, nomads, herdsmen and traders amongst them.

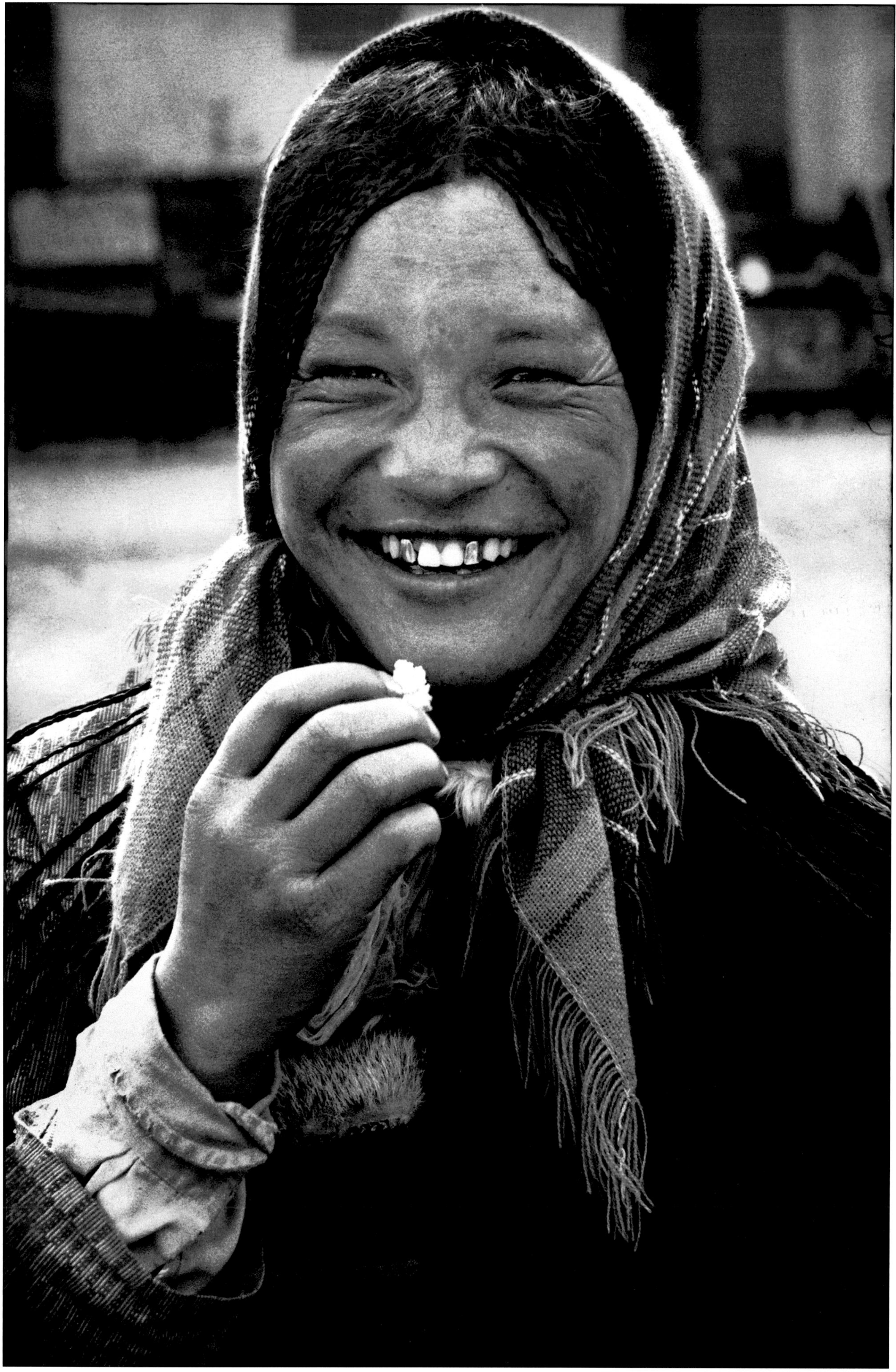

## MARK RYLANCE

Theatres in the City of London were banned in 1572, due to the plague, so they moved to Shoreditch outside the jurisdiction, where Shakespeare was hired as an actor and playwright. An archaeological dig in 2008 unearthed the remains of The Theatre, the treasures being removed to the Museum of London. The day before the site was to be bulldozed, Mark Rylance arrived in a summer shirt, shorts, straw hat and gave an impromptu speech from *Henry V*, watched by his wife and a handful of conservationists. He was shown a broken porcelain box, which originally held the theatre receipts, kept safely at night in an office, which became known as the Box Office, the name surviving to this day. The Bard and his friends dismantled the building, floating the timbers across the river to build The Globe, which over 400 years later saw Rylance as its Director.

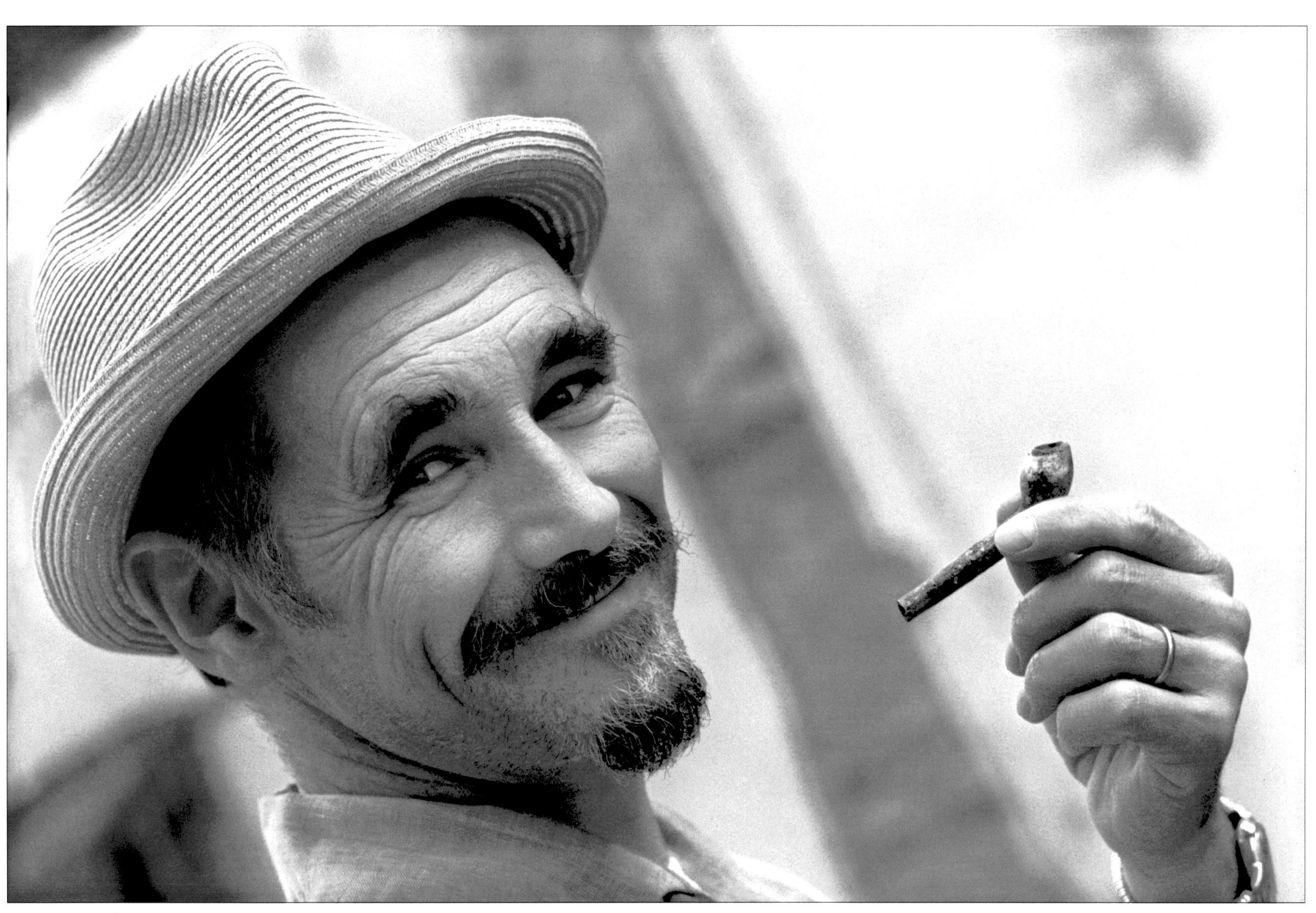

# JESSYE NORMAN

The restrictions on the shoot left me wondering what to do. The Barbican spokeswoman said … 'She won't be photographed singing, arriving on stage, leaving the stage, or backstage.'

'So what can I do?'

'Receiving the applause.'

Positioned at the very back of the auditorium, tripod, long lens and a doubler, waited through the concert without exposing a frame, then finally, as the applause erupted … click, click, click. During the performance my mind wandered to the apocryphal story of her becoming stuck in a revolving door and somebody helpfully suggesting … 'turn sideways' and the reply came …

'Honey I ain't got no sideways.'

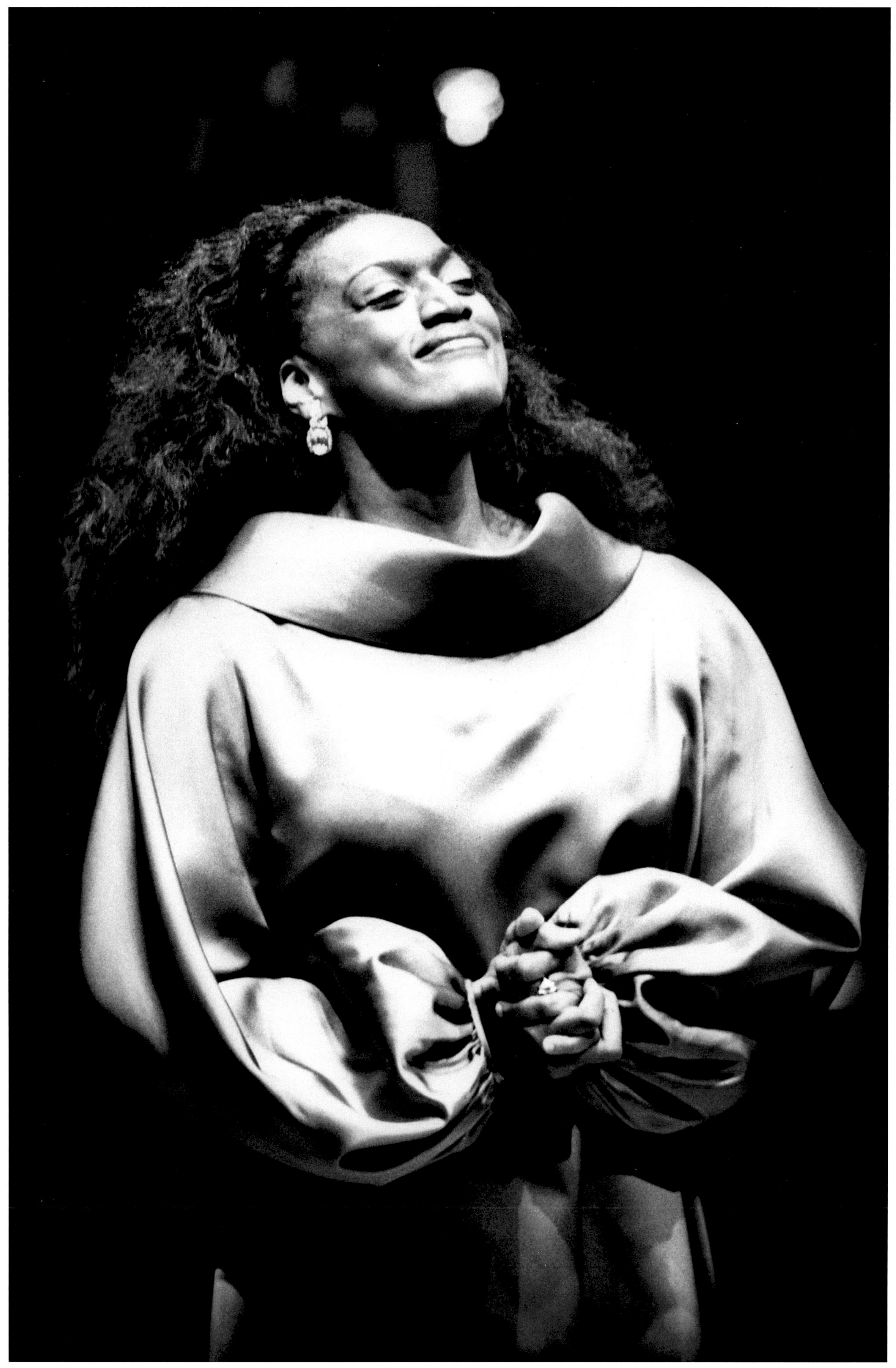

# ANTHONY NEWLEY

It is not often that a photographer is welcome behind the scenes, yet the invitation was to record the actor being made up for the Christmas musical *Scrooge*. I mentioned seeing him as the Artful Dodger in David Lean's film of *Oliver Twist* and he retorted with the chestnut ... 'Who the Dickens wrote Oliver Twist ?' ... then, in character turning from the mirror, he made a face.

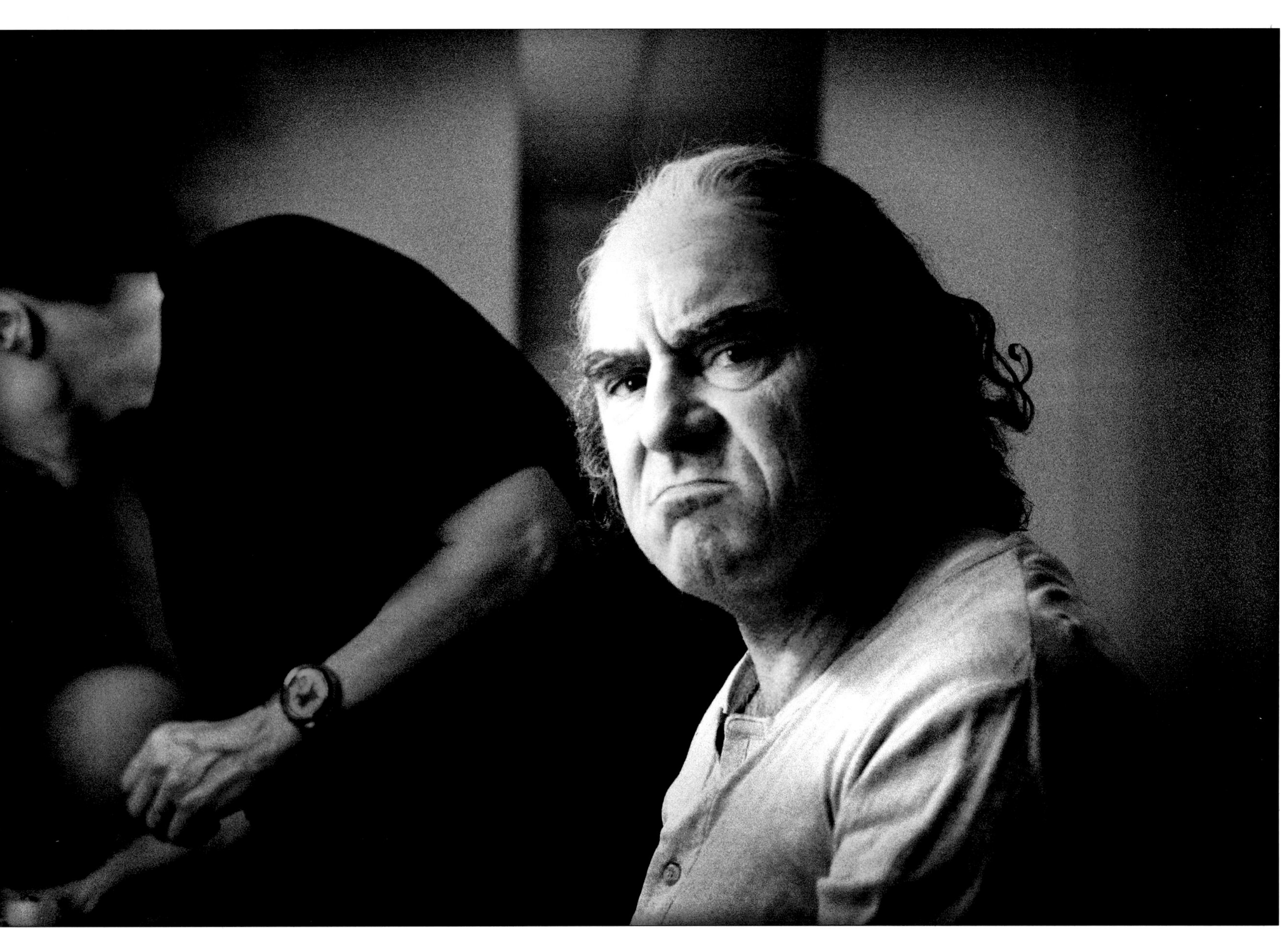

# DEBORAH BULL

... 'I'm sharing a flat with a ballerina, she never gets to dance the lead, I'd like you to shadow her for three days', the editor explained. Like all dancers, the day started with class, moving on to Notting Hill to see Andreas, the body toner. 'Originally I wanted to be a trapeze artist, don't really have the perfect body shape for ballet, so Andreas is reshaping me' ... She wasn't kidding, he bent, pulled and pushed her through a routine that would challenge a contortionist. Back to the Royal Ballet, the dressing room in the old building. A little blue daylight from the open window mixed with the yellow tungsten mirror lights making her glow as she applied stage make-up. The photograph appeared as a double-page spread in *Life Magazine* and Deborah went on to dance Odette/ Odile, the lead in *Swan Lake*.

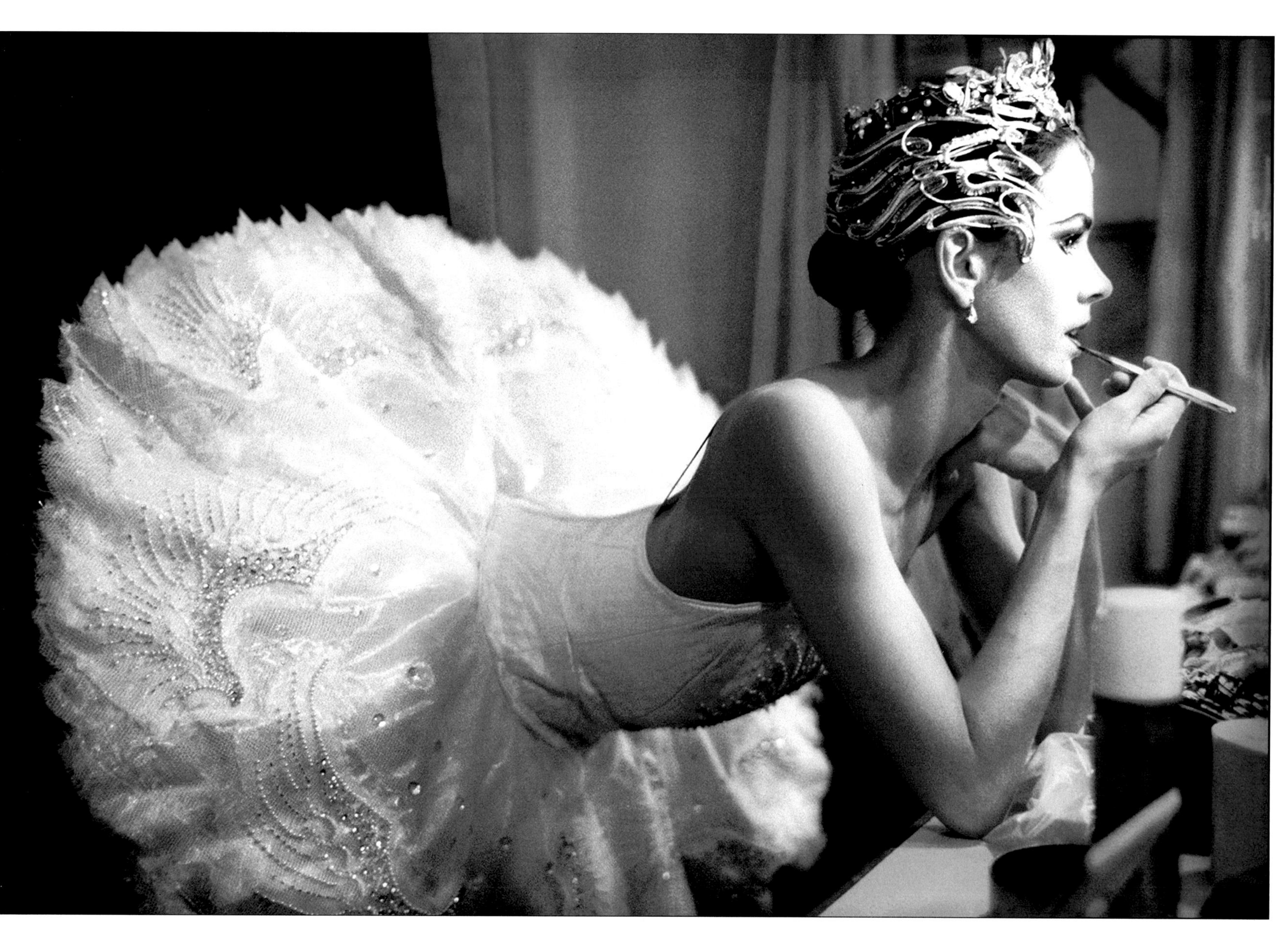

# IAN DURY

Dave Robinson from Stiff Records called ... 'I'm sending over a white label, listen to it and tell me which one's the single' ... An early pressing of Dury's second album *Do it Yourself* arrived and was listened to. The convention then was to promote an album with a track from it. I liked all of it but didn't think it contained a single. Robinson exploded over the phone ... 'That's what I've been saying !!' Dury was touring with The Blockheads in Europe, Robinson called him in Italy and demanded they go straight into the studio, which they did and came out with 'Reasons to Be Cheerful'.

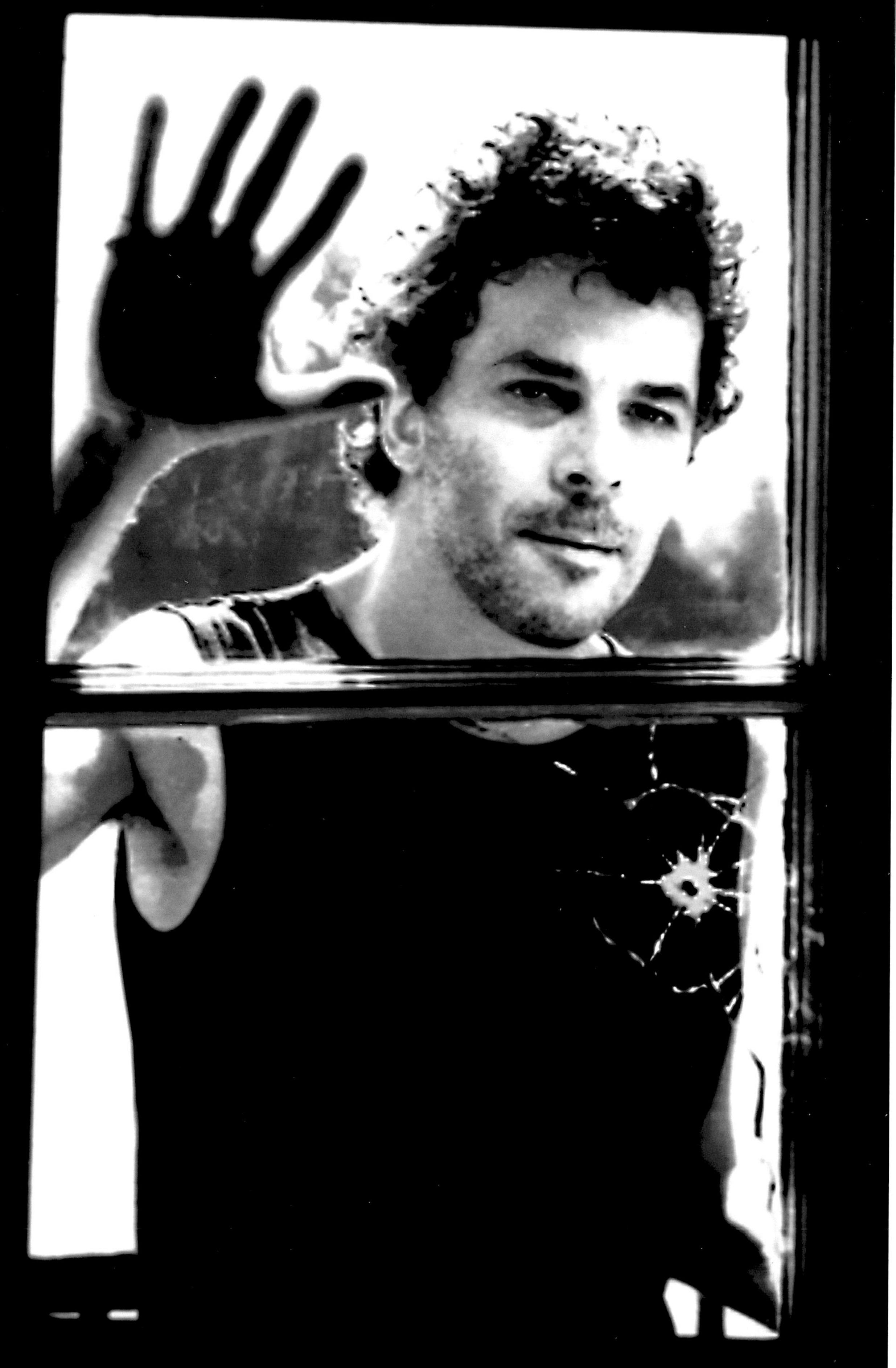

## LAURIE LEWIS

Laurie Lewis ARCA, MA, MFA attended art schools at Walthamstow and The Royal College in London, and the University of California, Motion Picture Division, UCLA. He made documentary films in the USA covering the Chicago Democratic Convention riots and on Gun Control for Warren Beatty. In the UK he made a feature on the camera-makers Gandolfi and concert films with Frank Zappa, The Rolling Stones and Ian Dury. As a photojournalist he has worked in disaster zones covering earthquakes in Kashmir, volcanic eruptions in Iceland, and has shot magazine features in Nicaragua, South Africa, Russia, China, Indonesia, the Himalayas, France and the USA. As arts correspondent his work has appeared in *The Sunday Times*, the *Sunday Telegraph*, the *Guardian*, the *Independent*, and *Rolling Stone*, *Time* and *Life* magazines, focussing on classical music, ballet, dance, rock'n'roll and jazz. The portraits, made in the studio and more often on location, appear in collections in the V&A and the National Portrait Gallery, London, and the Hôtel de Crillon, Paris. Exhibitions of Laurie's work have been held at the Royal Academy and the Photographers' Gallery in London, and at The Hankyu Gallery in Japan.

Print sales: www.laurielewis.co.uk

Acknowledgements:
Stuart Ray, Euan Duff, Gunn Brinson, Pamela Marke, Mike Spry, Sue Davis, Colin Ford, Duncan Campbell, Michael Church, Jonathan Christie